Bipolar 1

A Psychotic Experience

Kevin Rowan

iUniverse, Inc.
New York Bloomington

Bipolar 1

A Psychotic Experience

Copyright © 2008 by Kevin Rowan

All rights reserved. No part of this book may be used or reproduced by any means, graphic, electronic, or mechanical, including photocopying, recording, taping or by any information storage retrieval system without the written permission of the publisher except in the case of brief quotations embodied in critical articles and reviews.

iUniverse books may be ordered through booksellers or by contacting:

iUniverse
1663 Liberty Drive
Bloomington, IN 47403
www.iuniverse.com
1-800-Authors (1-800-288-4677)

Because of the dynamic nature of the Internet, any Web addresses or links contained in this book may have changed since publication and may no longer be valid. The views expressed in this work are solely those of the author and do not necessarily reflect the views of the publisher, and the publisher hereby disclaims any responsibility for them.

ISBN: 978-1-4401-1078-8 (pbk)
ISBN: 978-1-4401-1079-5 (ebk)

Printed in the United States of America

iUniverse rev. date: 12/10/2008

Foreword

KEVIN AND I acknowledge we have not always seen eye to eye about his care and treatment. That is not particularly unusual between psychiatrist and their patients with Bipolar Affective Disorder. I was therefore a little surprised when he asked me to write a foreword to this book. That is not to say Kevin and I have major differences of opinion, but he sees me as part of the body of "professional opinion" which necessarily views Bipolar Disorder differently from those who have had personal experience of it.

Kevin has been through a series of ups and downs in his life since I have known him and not just the mood swings of phases in his illness, but major social and life changes. It must have taken a great deal of effort and emotion to commit his experience to paper. There is no doubt it would have been distressing at times to recall the contents of his psychotic episodes.

Many sufferers from Bipolar Disorder have little memory of their thoughts or actions during acute episodes of their illness, either they are depressed or hypomanic. Kevin describes his thoughts and experiences with unusual clarity allowing us to follow, if not understand, the workings of a manic mind.

Following the adversities over the last few years Kevin now seems to have found a lifestyle which is much less stressful. He seems much happier with his lot and his Bipolar Disorder has been more stable. Perhaps he and I have reached a satisfactory compromise regarding treatment.

Dr Megan Munro
Consultant Psychiatrist
Birkenhead
2008

Introduction

THIS IS AN account of life experience. There will be people who believe and people who think it is the product of an inventive mind, simply because of the bizarre nature of events. Everybody is able to understand how we relate to our environment. The things we do, the things we say, the way we think, are all influenced by the input of stimuli, be it sound, vision, communication, smell and touch. We take it for granted, It's how we interact, in the main we do it without thinking its automatic and is honed through life experience and the confidence in expected results from a given situations.

Imagine if you can, the world stays the same, but you alone have a different experience, your cognitive process no longer works the same as other people, your mind malfunctions so that you experience involuntary thoughts that you believe are as real as a conversation you may have with another person. That's the difficult part to understand, because everybody can relate to their own personal experience and filtering rational from irrational is second nature to most. What if you can't filter the irrational? What if you believe it to be true?

This is not an attempt to relate my life story over the past sixteen years. There has been much misery and frustration dealing with the after affects of mania and the side effects of the treatment used to control the condition. The loss of a loving marriage and comfortable home; the disruption of a good career; to ever regressing financial instability and uncertainty. It is an account of involuntary thoughts of the mind that caused actions and reactions in everyday activities. Occasionally, I digress and talk about glimpses of my life that are important to understand the context. That's all they are, it's not an attempt to be comprehensive about any situation.

Side effects were the main reason why, in the early years of the illness, I refused to take medication on occasions. I was a young man, into sporting activity and into feeling good, in short the medication regime didn't allow the continuation of this lifestyle. So I stopped my medication and had a number of re-lapses. Later having realised the seriousness of my condition, after facing time in the cells and appearing before the County Court, I adhered to the medication regime. In trying to fine tune the medication by experimenting with the dose in order to get as close as I could to normal feelings, under supervision, I had a further two re-lapses.

That, I suppose, is all the relevant detail you need to know about my life. What interests me, and what I have never fully explained before, even to the psychiatrists who treated me, is the depth and consistency of involuntary thoughts.

Psychiatrists, in my experience, are not overly concerned with what's in your head. They take time to find out about what is happening in your life and how you are coping, but in my case, nobody ever really explored the way my thoughts had progressed. What I was thinking during each episode, how it had affected me. Whether I had any issues with the thoughts I had experienced or whether I had accepted that they were not real. In reality I was confused and still coping with aspects of mania both in terms of the experience and how I related to life in general given the context.

I had a short time when I was referred to counsellor who asked me how I related to my family and events but as I had little to say, other than I was self contained (the fact being I did not have meaningful contact with my family and was isolated). I answered her questions, but couldn't quite understand where she was coming from. She said she couldn't help as I wouldn't open up. If she had asked me about what was going through my mind in periods of psychosis maybe we would have progressed. I happened to forget an appointment with her one week, it entirely slipped my mind. (I was lying in bed sleeping, like I did most of the time when I was in a state of depression.) She seemed particularly aggrieved at me wasting her time. After this she decided there was no benefit in our meetings and cancelled them.

Eventually, I have come to an acceptance of the whys and wherefores of this experience, but it has been almost a solo journey of understanding and has not been without its difficulties. The overriding result has been my isolation from my original circle of contacts. There were never a great number of friends to start with; I kept in touch with a small number of people. I still have very valuable support group of adults which consists of Tommy my uncle and his wife Mandy. By support group I mean people who listen with interest to my conversation, not necessarily my health problems, and reciprocate with what's current in their life. Obviously my children and their love for me has been the greatest tonic through all this time. Presently my daughter is 11 and my son is 16 years old. I don't think I could have survived without their presence and support.

Social relationships do not exist at all; I have no circle of friends. There are reasons for this. With subsequent episodes I became more and more engrossed in the experiences and I had and sought to understand them. I would talk to friends and colleagues in work about them without being able to explain in full my experience of 'voices' and how it had affected me. Well, you can't admit to this kind of thing, who's going to believe a word you say? Most of the time my overall demeanor was dour and miserable dealing with depression, so it was hardly entertaining stuff. I have always been a resilient character and was absolutely devastated that when trying to explain my feelings to people I broke down in uncontrollable tears; I stopped trying in the end. This emotional lack of control happened at times in work, changing people's perception of me, in the company of friends and during appointments with my doctor and my consultant. My perceived hopelessness of my situation was not allowing me to communicate with people effectively. Particularly after the breakup of my marriage and in response to my behaviour, friends stopped contacting me and eventually I stopped contacting them understanding they had little interest in keeping in touch.

There was a huge section missing from the required information to make sense of my experience and even if I filled it in, nobody would believe it. This book is the missing section, I no longer feel the need to worry as to whether anybody believes it or not and I no longer need the support of a wider circle of contacts.

My experience of psychiatrists is that they look at the impact life is having on your circumstances and they treat physical symptoms, so if they diagnose that you are not relating to events in a normal context and are showing symptoms of mania, or depression etc, they use tried and tested drugs which act on parts of the brain to bring a balance of normality back. There is always a price in terms of side effects. My first two consultants explored my thoughts trying to determine what was wrong with me. At this point I was still very much defensive giving little away. My thoughts were "You don't talk about this kind of thing." They knew I was experiencing problems with my thought process. Since then, from about 1993 onwards, there has been no further exploration and when I have mentioned voluntarily that I was experiencing 'voices', little time has been given to the subject, I came to the opinion that even the experts in this field didn't understand or believe my experience.

I have had discussions with my consultant as to why 1mg of risperidone prevents me from experiencing the involuntary thoughts in my head. She believes 1mg is not a therapeutic dose and is irrelevant. In practice for me 1mg of risperidone is enough to stop the involuntary thoughts, unless I am in a stressful situation. The times when I worked at the level I was trained at, meant that the thoughts returned and I asked my consultant to double my risperidone to 2mg, which she did, never really believing it had any effect. In fact, the thoughts stopped and my mind became more stable if a little slower. I could perceive a loss of mental agility and a return of sluggishness even at this level and would ask to reduce the dose again after the thoughts had stopped for a significant time.

On the two occasions when I have stopped taking risperidone, I have had a relapse. The first time, I was visiting the lithium nurse and one of the chemists from Clatterbridge Hospital changing my medication from sodium valporate, risperidone and dutonin an anti-depressant. The dose of risperidone was higher than I am using now. The reason for being with the lithium nurse was that I had found over the years that my medication slowed me down too much, in my thoughts and in my physical response. From being an avid sports person before my illness, when medicated I could never be bothered. I slept more and lost interest in my hobbies and in reading. In fact I was depressed almost constantly. I had always been wary of lithium because you have to take regular blood tests to ensure you have safe levels in your blood stream. Too much and it becomes toxic, too little and it's not therapeutic. In retrospect, it's no big deal. Lithium feels a lot more comfortable to me than any of the other medication I have been on. I can't however take it in isolation or the involuntary thoughts return and I gradually head down the path of mania. The reason I know this is because along with the lithium nurse and the chemist, we discussed changing over to lithium, I was advised I should not need any other medication and we would work towards it.

The nursing team would keep in touch with the consultant and we would progress. To cut it short, I changed over to lithium and progressed to using it alone. I had a relapse and the nursing staff backtracked and said that's not we intended, the consultant needs to ok everything, backsides were covered and I was in the wrong. At the very least I must have misunderstood their instructions because I was not trying to take inadequate levels of medication.

On the second occasion, I was taking lithium and 1mg of risperidone. I was trying to run a franchise operation and I was very depressed. I know risperidone has a depressing nature, but yes, I agree 1mg is not as significant in this regard to higher doses I had been on. Anyway, my solution was to stop taking the risperidone to try and become more positive. After all my consultant was telling me it's not a therapeutic dose and is neither here nor there in your case. So the risperidone came out of my system and yes I brightened up and yes I felt more active, even started exercising again, but the cycle of thoughts came back. I began losing rationality; I stopped the lithium as well when I was already in a state of mania.

So this account is my recollection of events. Unfortunately it can't be word for word (think of how often you think and you will begin to understand the volume of thoughts) the reality was very much more expressive and intense. I have substituted fictional names for the actual names of people mentioned. It has been difficult placing all the events in sequence. My memory has been aided by recalling the physical events that were significant and remembering what I was thinking about at the time. I have managed to document nearly all my experience, but the sequence of some events may be a little out of sync with actual events. I believe, from memory, I had eight episodes of psychosis, it may have been more or less, you have to remember I did not have all my faculties at the time. I cannot remember either the number of times I have been sectioned; it was not every time, but at least half. Nor can I remember exactly how many times I have been arrested by the police. It does not really matter in this context. If required, events could be matched more precisely to my medical records. I do not think this would add to, nor detract from, this account. The experience is evident and the taboo world of "voices in the head" is described in detail.

You may make up your own mind. I am sure any research involving the people I have named in the book, will throw up a significant correlation between their memory of events and my narrative.

I hope you enjoy the sometimes comical situations, are shocked by some of the dangerous situations I put myself in and appreciate the concerns of the people who were dealing with events not knowing my interpretation of the world.

To describe the experience, I have chosen to use the following format:

Standard text is used for normal conversation and descriptive narrative.

Italics are used for involuntary thoughts in the form of conversation from an anonymous source.

Name: Italics are used for involuntary thoughts that are identifiable by the sound of their 'voice' as family, friends, acquaintances or other identified people.

B: Broadcasts of thoughts from myself to either another person or to all.

The Catylist

THE WEEK HAD been very difficult; I was at work feeling really unnerved. The feeling you get when you are nervous about something but you are hot and distracted at the same time. Paranoia had set in days before. The company had announced redundancies and all I could think about was the prospect of not having a job. It hadn't helped that my role was under scrutiny and I had realised the seriousness of it during a branch visit.

I had been providing sales support to the direct sales force in the form of a bureau mailing service. Taking data from a couple of sources from the Company database, I had sourced a company that ran the two Company data files of customer and salesman records together, to make a single database capable of interrogation and mailing extracts.

The database could effectively de-dupe customers by their financial advisers and to produce mailing prompts based on data such as policy anniversary, renewal dates, date of birth etc. This functionality was not readily available with the in-house database, in common with many other Companies at the time. Customer databases where made up of various operating systems built for administration that were not always compatible and often not flexible enough for direct mail activity. It was always a short term solution as there was a lot of investment activity in developing a corporate database which was meant to address the compatibility and flexibility issues.

I had probably been in this role for about 10 months and had sourced the bureau providing the data manipulation put together a proposal and presented it to my immediate manager. She was enthusiastic as her role included providing incentives for high sales achievers and she saw this as an opportunity to give them something more. I had given her the opportunity to re-allocate customers without an existing financial adviser to a new adviser for servicing purposes. A process that was impossible under the in house administration system without allocating existing renewal commissions to the adviser. Secondly; a direct mailing package that could be personalised from the financial adviser, to the customer; thirdly the packaging of mailing lists for top advisers and fourthly a quarterly, photographed, personalised magazine for top advisers. My manager was not really concerned too much about cost, as it was in budget, or about measuring results; she just wanted to give something away to the high achievers to increase her kudos with them. You have to remember this was the days before the full impact of the Financial Services Act had taken effect and top salesmen were sought after by financial services companies and paid very high commissions and given other financial incentives such as exclusive foreign holidays in the form of annual conventions.

Prior to the announcements for redundancies, my manager had asked me to prepare a 35mm slide presentation for the national sales manager and to sell-up the benefits of the promotional activity I was handling. I did this and concentrated on the sales promotion aspects and the data analysis that showed an increase in customer servicing. The increase in customer servicing however reflected more on the cleansing of the database and successful, de-duping of it, than on evidence of new sales. This was to play on my mind as I became less able to cope with the stress of work. My manager had in effect encouraged me to present to the national sales manager a sparkling view of the activity so she could distance herself from the decision making.

So the day came when I was really flattened in terms of my contribution to the company. A couple of times per month I used to give branch presentations of the promotional literature and database functions under my control. Usually the reception was good. Don't get me wrong, I was aware that direct sales forces are very hard to please, but I never got any real negative feedback and it was usually quite enjoyable. However, on visiting Chester branch, for some reason in conversation with an adviser we moved into the store room. I had never felt so deflated in all my life, the stock room must have contained 95% of the promotional support material I had been sending out for the past 10 months, it was not being used at all, just stock piled and I was absolutely floored. There were around forty branches.

My mind went into overdrive, if it wasn't being used here, what about the rest of the branches. I was concerned about the budget I had used and retrospectively the lack of adequate monitoring of usage and cost effectiveness. My mind turned to the previous role when I was asked to project a budget for printed promotional literature. I worked this out based on estimated usage by advisers and came up with a figure of about £460,000. My manager had said, based on experience, it was more like £1 million and I should work to that figure. So I went away and factored the increase in each item so that it totaled £1 million. Stocks of literature were too large in practice and there was huge wastage.

For the first time in my life self doubt took a hold of me and I began to mentally retrace my actions, over and over again. I was devastated by my inability to stick to guns on budgeting for printed materials and later for testing and measuring database activity and direct mail effectiveness. In addition there was an investigation going on about financial advisers who had been allocated customers for servicing purposes and were receiving renewal commission for policies sold by a previous adviser. I knew that my system was incapable of this as it was not linked to the administration systems, but even the head of administration was pointing a finger at me.

So now I was convinced I was to be made redundant, I was also thinking that there was a huge fraud investigation going on based on misappropriated company money. Auditors were working in the department on a daily basis and signature levels were being reviewed. I was thinking my manager was distancing herself from me and I was generally paranoid about people in the department and thought they were all talking about me. When visitors came onto the department to speak to my manager I immediately thought they were there to talk about me. The thoughts became cyclical, searching all the time for the reason why I did things. Searching for the reasons why my manager acted the way she did. I was sleeping less, not able to break the thought process, not able to rest.

At home Tricia had noticed how I had become pre-occupied. I was unable to focus on a conversation, not able to settle to watch TV, or to read a newspaper. I was drinking alcohol more than usual, not great amounts but a little more than usual. She was also six months pregnant with or first child.

This particular illness is often genetic and often has no obvious cause. Stress can be a factor for bringing the illness on, it may happen regardless, but here is the trigger in my case. Not so much the actual influence of events, but my perceived importance of the events. Retrospectively, I do not believe there was any particular conspiracy against me, my mental state had contributed to misplacing the intentions of my manager and I had a naive view of the business process. I obviously am not a person that can deal with stress too well. Until this point I don't think I ever really felt any and then, redundancy, fraud investigation, mismanagement, first child, paranoia and my mind crumbled.

Episode 1

Going into work, my mood was high but not very stable. I was in early and I headed off to see my manager's boss. On arriving at his desk there was only his secretary about. She said Phil would be about later but she said "You can have a read of the newspaper if you want to" as it was early. The newspaper had Gerry's name on it, the National Sales Manager. I was already starting to believe that thought transference was possible. It was significant that it was Gerry's paper. The Company had been listening to my thoughts on fraud and was delighted I had answered some questions; this could be my new position.

The reality of how your mind slips from rational to the irrational is gradual. You have thoughts and you get carried away with the thought. Subsequently, either five minutes or half an hour later you are back to what would be considered normal. You relate to people around you normally again. The major difference is that you don't think the short period when you were unstable was unusual. That is why it is so difficult for the individual to recognise that there is something wrong with them. As a manic episode progresses you get less rational periods and more irrational periods until you are in serious trouble.

Back at my desk I set about the usual tasks, watched the office start to fill and listened to the department chatting. They all seemed to be chatting about me, not directly, but the things they said all impacted on me. I was opening my mail; a direct marketing magazine caught my eye. All the articles where about my work, things I had done, the benefits of them, a text book operation (not in reality, in my interpretation). I started to laugh, a manic laugh, I spoke to Claire and pointed out the articles, I walked down the office to talk to Jayne my manager, she looked at me puzzled and laughed nervously. Her secretary said "What are you up to Kevin?" and she also laughed.

I needed to get away, get some fresh air. I walked out of the office and out of the side door leading down to the car park. As I walked about, I thought about the situation I was in, trying to make sense of my thoughts. More than anything I was identifying my mistakes.

That's a black mark.

I thought about my budgeting of printed literature, then I thought of mitigating circumstances and I smelt bad odour, like old perspiration and rotting eggs only blacker. I thought about the database and the output I'd produced, if only someone had told me.

That smell again.

You can't pretend you didn't know.
You're going to pay the price.

My pulse was raised at this point my mind going over and over the same thing. I walked from the car park down a raised walkway with offices to one side. A man was walking carrying a large table, the leading edge nestled in his right hand at full stretch and his left about head height, balancing and stabilizing the weight.

I'm at work, moving this furniture, I sleep at nights, what do you do?

It seemed a strange sight, somehow out of context, I thought of the police and the smell came again.

Making my way down to street level, I crossed the road towards St Nicholas's church. I hadn't set foot in a church for many years, except for the odd wedding or funeral. Overcome with nerves I was trying to make sense of things. I walked into the church and saw two or three doors on the right hand side. I was looking for a priest to confess my sins. Each time I thought of something, I thought people would doubt, the smell returned and I was going to hell. I needed a priest to make sense of it. I entered one of the rooms and tried to speak to somebody. I had no idea who he was or what his job was but my words failed and he looked at me and said "I'm very busy at the moment, I have appointments to go to" and he guided me out of the door.

I stepped backwards and turned to look at the church, walked through the double doors dividing the entrance hall and took a pew three quarters of the way from the back on the right hand side. I sat and listened to the silence and noticed the few faces breaking the solitude. Over my shoulder, one in particular caught my eye, a woman in her late fifties, early sixties. She was of solid build not overweight and full hair auburn in colour.

B: *It's Ivy, my dad's sister.*

I can't remember ever meeting her so I don't know what she looks like, but she knows it's me, she knows I'm here. I don't know my Dad's family at all. I have met his brothers less than half a dozen times in my life and his sister only when I was a baby.

I left the church without acknowledging the person I thought was Ivy, good job really she would have thought I was mad. I walked back to work still smelling my bad thoughts still thinking how to make things better. Back at my desk I was distracted and unable to work.

Jayne became concerned and asked me to go and see Phil who was by now at his desk. When I arrived he was reading his paper and there was an article about landing on the moon. I began thinking the Americans hadn't done this, the Russians had done it first and there had been a cover up. I said something I can't remember to Phil and he replied similar to this:

"Boo grob nah wee do fleet prop doo wah"

To this day I don't know if he spoke gobbledygook or I just heard that. We exchanged no other words, Jayne came to collect me. She called Tricia and told her I wasn't very well and she was bringing me home.

Tricia was concerned and spoke with Jayne, something along the lines of 'Kevin needs some rest and maybe a visit to the doctors', Jayne said her goodbyes and headed back off to the office.

I sat pre-occupied in the sitting room while Tricia asked if I wanted to make an appointment with the doctor. I didn't, I just wanted to think, to work it out to make sense of what was happening.

Police: You could be in trouble sonny.

B: I can trace it back, I now where it all went what's the problem.

Police: The Company wants to recover their losses. This is a fraud investigation

B: To commit fraud you have to deceive for financial benefit.

Police: We've seen your bank accounts, we're searching for hidden sources.

B: What you've seen is what there is, nothing more

Police: If you help piece it together you could save yourself a lot of heartache.

B: What you've seen is what there is.

Police: Then you're exposing waste with only your word.

B: Yes, what proof do you need?

This police investigation rumbled on in my head, becoming more and more real. At the same time I started to think about my life.

This is your first isn't it?

B: First what?

First wife, you need to move on, start a fresh, you're a stag, and you're not meant to be with one person for the rest of your life. You have to walk away from everything, all your possessions, all your family, and all your friends and start afresh, a new life in a new place. Start by retracing your steps in life, re-visit all of your mistakes and put them right on the exact spot. You need to travel to the destination and call the person you wronged with the power of your mind, if they answer you are forgiven, if they do not, they are dead to you and you can disregard them forever.

Your travels will lead you to a place where you will be welcomed by a female into her home, but she has to accept you with nothing at all. You will grow younger and your life will start again. You have fulfilled your destiny with your first wife; a son is on the way you have to move on. You will always be there for Tricia and your child but only in spirit, always close, never far, but she will only meet you in exceptional circumstances and she will age as you grow young.

I struggled with the thoughts in my head, I was by now feeling the need to keep moving, walking a lot, striding along while thinking and answering my own thoughts. Tricia and I went for a drive. We took a short trip to West Kirby promenade. This was a favorite place for Tricia and I in the early years, a short drive from our home in Upton. We parked up and leant against the prom facing the marine lake. The words started to flow, mimicking earlier thoughts.

"I'll always be around for you and the baby, but I have to leave. I'll be here for a little while longer, but then I will have to go"

"Kevin, what are you talking about, what do you mean you have to leave?"

"I have to go, I don't know where I am going but I just have to go."

"You're not making any sense, where are you going to go?"

"I'll be around I have to go."

The conversation continued heated at times, despairing at times, we drove on to Royden Park and parked up, the conversation continued in the same vein, but when I said I have to leave, I felt pain in my chest, physical unbearable pain. I remember thinking this is what love does to you, separating is painful. I was learning the truth about love and life, the longer you stay the harder it gets to leave. Now I understood the term your love is killing me.

That's why you have to leave now; this is your first isn't it?

Tricia was obviously very upset, I was no help to her, it wasn't a normal this is the end conversation, there was little emotion from me, I was driven by thoughts of moving on and an underlying feeling I was doing the right thing , detached and brutal. Inside thinking, where to now, Middlesbrough? (Where I studied) Pendle (mystic connotations), just walk and see, drive until the car runs out of petrol and walk.

You have to meet your new wife naked and alone and she has to invite you in of her own free will. You cannot ask.

Females from my past started chatting to me in my head.

Sarah: Hi Kev how's it going?

B: alright Sarah, what are you doing?

Sarah: I'm here Kevin, the house is empty, just me waiting.

Back home I'd become engrossed in the television. I started to recognise people from work disguised in news bulletins. There was Andy a senior manager from work, the guy pointing the finger at me for allocating renewal commission. He was under scrutiny according to what the police told me. He was smiling.

Andy: You won't get away with it Rowan

Saturday night and Noel Edmunds was doing his live TV bit in somebody's home. Coincidence mixed with involuntary thoughts not for the last time. I was drinking beer and he looked straight at me and said

"Better make that your last" he was about to put some unsuspecting member of the public live on TV, but he was talking to me.

The TV was communicating directly with me and I became engrossed in everything and anything that was on. Often imagining commentary was aimed directly at me, and more and more often communicating by telepathy with the people on screen. It wasn't only the TV; the radio became another source of messages beamed directly for my attention.

The thoughts are often cyclical in their nature and over a period of two or three days I re-visited the fraud investigations over and over again, searching for answers, searching for the solution. I began to gain acceptance from the investigative team - the police, company management, it was going in my favour, I was to return to work with a promotion to run the place the way it should be, but when. I would be notified in due time.

It was not the last of retracing events at work in my head. New evidence would emerge and I would be notified by the police and asked to explain events again, then back to the beginning, I would run through a question and answer routine. All this time I would be carrying on everyday life, as I thought, as normal.

My favourite relaxation was to walk up and down the borders of the garden looking at the progress of the plants and shrubs, and then I'd stand and peer into the garden goldfish pond watching but not seeing, thinking, thinking, and thinking. Inside the house I would stare blankly at the TV screen if there wasn't a message for me in the program, sometimes smiling to myself at the thoughts going on in my head. Tricia would ask, "What are you smiling at?" and I'd say "Nothing, something funny was on the TV? "Was a stock answer or any other explanation I could think of, but I couldn't tell her the truth.

We don't talk, everybody knows, but you can't say. If you say you know, you'll be locked away, nobody will believe you.

This thought prevented me from discussing my thoughts with the doctors for many years.

You have been deaf, but everyone has been able to hear your thoughts all along. Why do you think you have got this far, everybody thought you were blanking them, they would say things to you to find your weaknesses, to gauge your reaction and your reply was always something like, Fuck you fuckface, nobody could get near you, nobody understood, but now we know, you're not hiding your mind, you were deaf.

Tricia was the closest person to me and she knew I wasn't right but she couldn't convince anybody else because if I met somebody I would revert to normality and respond accordingly.

This was now getting frightening, I was communicating with people I knew and some that I didn't, but wasn't sure who could hear me, just the person I was talking to, or everybody. The art was to be able to communicate with your mind but not give any physical indication that this actually happened. The voices advised me that if questioned face to face, all knowledge would be denied. All subsequent communication in real time had to be based on trust and understanding and that was the test for all.

It's Tricia, you have to get away, she's re-born she's your first but you are not her first. She is old and needs your life to keep her youthful. Its ancient practice of parentage and offspring, you need to get away. Keep all the windows open and drink plenty of water, you can't let her control your mind. She knows you're waking up and are no longer deaf; she will try to keep you to extend her life. She is already over 150 years old but a succession of purity through the ages has bought her youth and time.

What does Kevin mean? 'Pure at birth', your parents tried to protect you by keeping you deaf, not allowing you to speak, so you would not be caught in the ancient ways of the sisterhood. Look around you, what do you see, it still persists.

I was out walking through the shopping centre in Birkenhead, I looked around and every female face reminded me of a female I knew.

We are watching you Mr Stag hahaha, do you have your dog with you hahaha.

Walking down the main shopping street, my heart was pumping my stomach churning butterflies, half way between queasy and a full adrenalin rush, I had to get out, I had to find space. A man walked past trailing an empty dog lead behind him, his dog two paces in front of him. This is how you walk the dog.

B: *What's a dog?*

Someone who hasn't mastered the art of talking and listening, someone who can't distinguish between right and wrong, someone who speaks but doesn't hear, someone who hears only the head beside their pillow, but their mothers know and tell them so.

In the car on the way home the DJ scoffed at new listeners and asked "Can you can really believe they have not heard it all before?" I interpreted every song as though it has a message for me and I wanted to reply. Getting home, the house was empty and I turned on my amp and turntable. Selecting Setting Sons by the Jam I started to broadcast back a selection of tracks. After the third song I tried to play Burning Sky, it's the first track on side two. The first few bars blasted out then nothing. Turning to look at the turntable, the arm had returned to rest. My head was spinning, 'they will not let me play my response, not only can they control thoughts and minds but also the physical.' In reality it was just one of life's coincidences, the turntable never worked properly again. If you put a record on the first couple of bars would play and then the arm would lift and return to the rest. To make it work you had to spin the disk backwards a couple of times then place the needle on the desired track. At that moment however, I thought shit, they know what I am thinking, they can speak to me and they can even make appliances and maybe more respond to their control. I flicked to the tuner wanting some feedback from the radio, the indicator lights for the station flickered went out and came on again, and I was out of the door, running. Out of the close where I lived and jumping the wooden fence separating the housing estate from the Upton By-Pass. Crossing the road and into the adjacent field. There are two small wooded areas on the land, one containing a pond in the centre. Passing the nearest group of trees and heading for the footpath at the other side of the field. The path leads to Arrowe Park and it's quite popular with dog walkers.

Lady in a blue Anorak: I'm walking my dog, where's yours.
Couple with Boxer: You need your dog to enjoy the park here
We know who you are and where you're going.

Every person I passed had something to say and I jogged along until I reached the park.

The woman was walking straight towards me and I couldn't hear a word from her. We met not far from where the open grassland turns into trees not far from the back of the golf course. She drew level, smiled at me and said "Afternoon" I repeated the greeting and stopped in my tracks.

Why am I running? If everybody knows, why am I running?

"Is this your first, you have to move on" It was the woman who had greeted me. Maybe she understood.

I walked back home at a more leisurely pace, thinking about how to leave.

Sarah: I'm here Kevin

Susan: And so am I

B: I have to find someone who is my destiny, I have to walk to the door of the house I will arrive at by following my instincts, leaving all my possessions behind including my clothes and she will welcome me in.

Sarah: You know where I live Kevin

Susan: You will find me Kevin, just follow your instincts.

B: I don't think it's meant to be someone I know, you will ensnare me like Tricia and use my regression to keep you young, I have to find somebody pure to fulfill my destiny.

Susan: You don't believe that folklore do you? We can be together.

Sarah: My door is always open.

I set off in the car without thinking to take anything other than the clothes I was wearing. I started heading for Middlesbrough, to retrace my steps. I planned to follow the exact route I took when driving to Polytechnic from Kirkby. As well as Middlesbrough I had to visit Marsk, Redcar, Saltburn, Whitby, Hartlepool, Seaton Carew (New Brighton without the lights, sod this European junket malarkey, they should be twinned.), all the places I had spent considerable time in while at Teesside Poly. They were my kind of people too; I had to redress my mistakes. I am sure from my limited experience that people are the same the country over. It is about motivation and a desire to change things, not just for the individual, but for the common good. People are by their nature interested in individual welfare, the crime is the individual welfare of the few is paramount and the majority is content with their relatively comfortable existence, they have homes, food, and a social existence. They meet Maslow's hierarchy of needs, which in reality does not register on the scale of acceptability with the affluent society. In my mind, it's a crime and needs addressing, but hey, I'm a subject of care in the community so what do I know.

Susan: You're so close; retrace your steps with me. Find me; I'm not far from where you last saw me.

B: I have to get forgiveness for my wrongdoings, do you forgive me?

Susan: Come find me, we can be together.

B: I'm not too far, we can put things right.

Sarah: Everything is in place Kev, you have to come straight here, don't believe all the folklore, it's our destiny to be together, you need to come straight here.

B: I'm searching Westvale but I don't know where I'm going.

Susan: Just a little further Kevin, keep going, you will know.

Sarah: Your car will run out of petrol Kev, I know you will find me. Do you know we have our own Folklore? Do you know we are meant to be together?

I'd gone past Kirkby Station and turned towards Mill Farm, at the lights turned left into County Road and headed past my parent's house to the M58, I was on my way to Skelmersdale.

B: I'm coming Sarah, won't be long

Tracy: Kevin, it's your sister, what you are doing I've been listening to you.

B: Hi Trace, I'm heading for Skelmersdale to see Sarah, I am starting to regress and I need to be with my new woman so we both benefit.

Tracy: Don't talk stupid, that folklore stuff is dangerous. You need to get to the seat of the problem, you've been cursed by somebody whose path you have crossed and you need to reverse the energy. You need to go somewhere where the psychic energy is strong and reverse the incantation. Go to Pendle Hill and I will meet you there.

I was now by passing Skelmersdale and heading for the M6.

Remember to retrace your steps, you need to start from home and you need to do it on foot.

Sarah; Kevin your fading from me you need to come soon.
B: I have to go home, I have to start again.

I didn't join the M6 instead I turned back at the roundabout at the end of the M58 and headed home.

The windows in my road were all open, or at least every house had one or more windows open.

Leave them open it's the only way, drink water, don't let the house get too warm, you will sleep and you will fall forever.

Three days had passed and I had hardly slept at all, lying awake, thoughts repeating over and over, thinking this time the answer will become clear, but it was always the same, but I couldn't let go. Work, the politics of it, the need to conform, the inability to fathom what went wrong the questioning, the answers coming thick and fast but only loaded with more questions. I walked and walked around the neighbourhood. There were voices as I passed each door.

We don't talk in Upton.
My windows are open, make sure yours are too.
Look at my curtains, they are closed, we are not looking
We don't talk in Greasby
Police: Keep quiet Rowan, we are in control we watch we listen we keep order.
Police: You are a throwback, you should have been one of us, but it's too late
B: How can this be?
Police: You are a sentinel, a silent peacekeeper, you are programmed to re-act to events, you are the balance you are the extinguisher and there were many like you throughout history. Your purpose is to take down evil, but you will not know when or where and you may cease to exist in the process. You have hidden strengths and abilities and all will be good for you when you face ill prepared sloth and greed, but there is every chance you will meet one of your own, neither will back down, neither will survive. You are programmed to know when to act and when to step down, but if you make the wrong decision you obliterate two of the lessening number of sentinels. These are the

old ways of peace and life. If you don't move on in your life in time, take another wife, you will forever be trapped in a decaying body, the sentinel will be lost, like your father who gave his destiny for the love of a woman. These are the real men if you move and procreate you make the problem worse one day it will become clear, we are meant to regress to oblivion, not exhaust our existence. If you stay in contact with your son, he will not be able to talk and will grow deaf as you have exposing his frailties and opening him to many trials, but then you are beginning to understand.

Your days are numbered, we are the conformed sentinels, and we live much the same as everybody else, our powers diminishing over time. But watch for the piercing blue eyes and lean fit body, tall and untouchable. They diffuse trouble by staring into people's eyes; the brilliance of their hue is all engulfing and dispels hate, anger and discomfort. Those souls that have passed the point of no return along their evil path, react and try to fight back. They are lost in an instant. When draining evil, their eyes become tainted and they have to retreat to a place of safety with one of their own and gaze into each other's eyes to replenish the piercing blue. We have a few, they re-invent themselves in different locations every 20 years or so, it's frightening and awesome the world is not yet explained and may never be Rowan, you have time but it won't last.

B: *Fuck off plod*

I had been away from work for three days now, catching little sleep, walking through the night, listening to messages of support:

Keep those windows open.
We are not watching.
Our curtains are drawn.
Seek her out.
Start anew.
Grow ever youthful.

It was Thursday; I played football on a Thursday at the Prescot Leisure Centre. We played 11 a side on the Astroturf. The booking was for an hour at 6.00pm every week. I had been doing this for some time now as well as playing regular 5-a-side in work. It was 5.20pm, no chance of getting there on time but I'd just remembered the game, so I had to go.

Tricia wasn't happy, "You're distracted, you're not yourself, and you haven't slept for three days"

"I'm ok, I need to take my mind off things and this will help; besides I enjoy it so I'm going"

"Well I'm coming along; you can drop me off at my mums." Tricia mum lived in Kirkby, in fact both our families did, and we grew up there, went to the same junior school and met when I was 17, a year older than Tricia at a six form dance when the girl's comprehensive and the boy's comprehensive organised dances in the Kirkby Suite or the Kirkby Stadium. She was beautiful, very self conscious at the time because she had had psoriasis from very young. In the main it was getting a lot better for her but stress could bring it out again. I remembered she was fairly clear of it the night we met, and within a couple of days the next time we met it had broken out all down her neck. She was very uncomfortable speaking to me and I just looked at the beautiful young woman, sensed her vulnerability and fell in love.

As for me, I needed nobody, nobody needed me. Didn't build bridges, walked away from complications, ignored peoples frustrations and bounced from one situation to the next, never really feeling down, never really considering others, except Trish. Well, she might not remember it like that, but in the not too distant future I was to remember the times when it was me and Trish against the world, nothing could touch us, we were meant to be. In comparison to everybody else, she was the constant. I have very few contacts, some frightened off by my experience, and some left behind, a small number of supportive family members. For many years Trish was the only one who really believed the things that I have experienced because she too experienced it firsthand.

But my what a tough cookie this woman turned out to be, not straight away, in the early years she looked to me for support and I gave it as best I could, not every day in everything, nothing stupid like that, just when we had what we thought were major decisions, she valued my input we talked things through we made things work. Then, here at 29, in one fell swoop my credibility collapsed and this often arguable woman (we had our heated moments but it never lasted) who in over 90% of times took my logic as the best way to go forward suddenly, and it felt just like that, suddenly stood on her own two feet and said I'm taking charge of this situation. Even though I disagreed with her interpretation of events and her solutions, I have no doubt it helped her through the difficult times caused by my illness.

It was already dark by the time we passed through the Mersey Tunnel, heading for the East Lancs Road, that's one of the things I do, even when my mind is not disturbed, if I have a number of parameters, I home in on one that's familiar and work everything out from there. So I was heading for the East Lancs because Tricia was going to Kirkby, but Prescot would be quicker going down West Derby Road from the Tunnel because I was going there first. There's madness in it somewhere, but my mind was not on directions, I was thinking sentinels and their development over time.

Have you ever noticed the way your Father rises at 5.30 in the morning, even when he has been out late the night before, he needs little sleep.

My father worked shifts for most of my childhood. In addition my mother was a singer on the northern club circuit. My father would work his shifts and drive my mother to her venues which could be anywhere from ten miles away to working in Barrow-in-Furness, Morecambe, Blackpool, places like that. They didn't leave the club until after closing so it was early hours of the morning before they got home regardless of where they were working. It was not unusual some weeks for my parents to be out Wednesday, Friday, Saturday and Sunday night. So this man worked shifts of 2pm-10pm and 6am-2pm. Alternate weeks and fitted in the driving to and from clubs four nights a week. When the shift pattern didn't suit the club work, he would arrange to swap his shift with somebody else so they never missed a booking. I used to think how can he possibly do that and yet at weekends he was first up, walking the dog on the local school fields, sometimes picking wild mushrooms for breakfast and frying them when he got back. You jest, I'm not kidding, my dad was an evacuee during the war and spent his childhood on a farm, and you never forget do you. He used to go mad when the local kids had kicked the mushrooms over in their ignorance.

He doesn't have many close friends, none you can even name, but he is on nodding terms with many. You know this, you have seen his ways. This is not his first life; you are not his first born son. You know this is true you are the runt, not a true sentinel; it shows in your eyes, your shape, you were deaf and now you hear.

Sentinels have evolved, they no longer take out the bad for good, they move in and out of life keeping the calm, keeping the status quo. Your home town is an experiment, not only in the movement of people but in the management and equilibrium of the old ways. Why does your father walk the fields and paths of your neighbourhood, he is listening and watching. You know his acquaintances, you've seen them when they met, and played football, on the fields in Northwood, at the away games your father took you to, at the home ground in Speke.

They nod, they acknowledge, but they never chat. Each surveying their own area, each responsible to no-one, each calming and breathing hope into communities. Some are on their first, some their second and some are ancient but all are Gents.

And all they do is look trouble in the eye; piercing blue eyes stare deep into minds and deflate anger, aggression, derision and malcontent.

And if it escalates, well it's just blackness.

Roaring laughter in my head - *we don't remember!*

It was 6.20pm by the time I arrived at the sports centre. Tricia was asking about the arrangements for getting home. I told her to take the car and I would get a lift back to her mum's house.

She said it wasn't a good idea for me to play in my state of mind but I just said I would be ok and got out of the car.

I could see the game taking place from the car park and rushed into the changing room to get ready, Heroic deeds of men who played their code in the sporting world filled my head. They played fair and hard, their game being a place to relax and enjoy a fit and healthy body, exerting it to its limit. Some of these lads had been through it, they'd served in the war, they'd been up against their own on the German lines and sentinels had fallen with great consequence, obliterating each other, driven by national pride and the invincibility bred within. Only sentinels can take each other down and during the war they fell repeatedly through misguided honour.

The game beckoned. You need to know a little about my game. I enjoyed football and had played a little while at school and while at polytechnic but I was always slow, I was never blessed with any amount of pace so in truth the 11 a side game was a little beyond me. My distribution was poor, but I could put in a winning tackle if I ever caught the attacker. So while I had pretensions about playing in midfield, on selection I was usually right back because I was right footed. Occasionally left back; but seldom in other positions. For those that know the game, this is the least attractive position apart from goalkeeper, unless you're one of those mad bastards to start with. The modern game has seen this change somewhat with attacking full backs marauding down the wings and getting back to cover. Hey but that needs pace. So week in, week out I played right back, never saying much, never contributing an awful lot, running my heart out, loving the buzz of exercise and competitive sport.

I took to the pitch, they had a full complement of players, Patrick shouted over, you alright Kev, you can play for the opposition. We played the same team every week but I'd never played with them before and never socialised with them.

I walked into their half of the pitch and took up position as a centre half.

B: Just a nod lads!

I started barking out orders, "keep it tight lads" "half way line when we can" "who's left? Cover that"

The usual sweeper wasn't too pleased and said "Ignore him he doesn't know what he's talking about."

But I persisted, loud and strong, driving them forward when needed "Out, out, out."

Calling for cover "who's got the runner?" "Hold the line."

Your skills become evident, passed down from generations, you are learning and using your instincts.

My memory says I played well that night for about 30 minutes, afterwards Patrick had said to me in the changing room "how come you never play like that for us" and there was no hint of irony in his voice.

I left the pitch with 10minutes remaining on the clock my heart filled with sadness, I had experienced the ageing of sentinels that chose to grow old, I had shared their thoughts as I played of heroic exploits past and I had been invigorated by the passing of skills and the sharing of knowledge, the 40 yard pass, the whole team focus on the game, the minds are as one, it's a communal will for the completion of the pass and the game is balanced by the oppositions will to make it fail. Whether the pass fails, or is a success depend on the tactics of the whole team pitting their communal whits against those of the opposition.

You have experienced the passing of skills and knowledge for the first time, the more individuals in your network group the more successful it is.

Networking, I've never networked, I used to hate the thought in work, but this is the true meaning, networking your mind for a purpose, the more minds the greater the purpose. So sport demonstrates this 11 minds working in unison by a set of rules; pitched equally against the opposition. Just think of the professional game, a stadium full of supporters all willing their team to win all trying to break the network of the 11 on the pitch, strong minds, strong bonds, and the best can take on the away crowd and sustain the power of their network. The beautiful game, endeavour, honour, fortitude and a steely will to win, how many in the side have blue eyes?

I walked into the changing area, there were two people getting changed, I looked in my bag and realised I hadn't packed it properly. There was no towel, no shampoo, I needed a shower badly, you could always wring sweat from my shirt after I had finished playing, and I suppose I'm just made that way. I stripped off my kit and approached the two lads changing, "can I borrow your soap? "There was no politeness from me just matter of fact, the soap was in a dish and I entered the shower and lashed the container to the floor. When I finished I didn't acknowledge the bloke I'd borrowed the soap from just left it lying on the shower floor with the soap box. I took my T-Shirt from my bag and used it as a towel; I had a jumper so it wasn't going be important. I sat on the bench and drifted into a deep sleep my last thought was that I was ready to die. The days and hours of activity had caught up with me and for the first time in days my mind was at peace.

The lads came into the changing room after the game and Patrick and Paul were concerned, I woke in a state of confusion, couldn't work out how long I'd been asleep, wasn't sure what I was doing, wasn't really making sense in conversation. Paul arranged for Terry to give me a lift to Kirkby, he had a small van, a two door Peugeot, something like that and I think there were three of them already getting a lift. Outside we squeezed into the van; I was in the front with two of them in the back. Terry was chatting about things but my mind was working again. We were together in the van and it was going to end tonight. We would all be naked and would die at Tricia's mum's home. There would be other people there but we would be starting the regression. Man was meant to only have one offspring in his life. That would be pure and good as life intended, the more offspring produced, the more we varied from the good. The secret was every first born had the potential to be a sentinel. When the first child was on the way, the man headed off to meet his new woman and together they regressed to birth and solve the problem of life. That is how it was and how it should be, so progressively no first born children would grow old and die and sentinels and their women would regress through a beautiful youth back to non existence. If the rules of only one child where adhered to; the human population would itself regress and start the universe into a backward spiral. Righting the wrongs of history and putting the pieces of existence back together. I then understood it was population growth that was causing all the problems of the world, moving away from the pure and generating a future existence of misery. The struggle between good and evil was about ancient rights and ancient codes, we should be living pure lives, seeking pure solutions instead of populating the world with progressively more unruly people, so the third son of a fourth son would be less than pure and so on. And here was I, the second child runt, not a sentinel, less predictable and volatile, an accident of birth, no one quite knew. My team mates were as one, we were going back to Vera's to die together, to start the regression, others would follow and the balance of good and evil would be addressed.

I don't remember anything about Vera's house, it was not unusual for me to just knock there, collect Tricia and leave. I did chat to Tricia and at least say hello because Tricia was concerned and wanted my parents to see what was happening. Trish drove the car the short journey to my parent's house and we went in.

Whenever we visited my mum, there was always tea and biscuits or cake (well I suppose that's true of most people I grew up with, you're always fed and watered when visiting). So over tea and biscuits we chatted, Tricia told them all was not well and I wasn't quite right. My mum and dad were always the type to say get on with it you'll be alright and there wasn't any change today. "He'll be alright after a good sleep" I was a bit detached, feeling conscious of having no T-Shirt on and generally non conversational. There was too much going on in my head. We didn't stay long and Tricia wasn't impressed, she couldn't understand why people couldn't see what she could and off we went home.

It was still only about 9.00pm by the time we got home, Tricia left me watching the telly and went off to have a bath, I was mulling over the events of the day trying to make sense of things when I had a eureka moment. Its god, god exists and as the thought rushed around my brain I felt a spine tingling presence which lasted for a couple of seconds, it wasn't the first time. I'd felt this sensation, usually when something spooky was happening, I'd seen a vision in my youth, on discussing spiritual events. My sister loves that kind of stuff and experiments with it, she doesn't talk openly to me at any rate but I know it is one of her interests, or memorably when a neighbour said he was going to read my mind a few years back, but it seemed to make sense now. The fact that I had had these sensations previously always led me to believe that I had some sort of psychic ability. I always shunned it and never dabbled. I believe that the spirit world is best left to its own devices and if you don't mess with it, then you will come to little harm. But just now God existed and every time I thought the words the sensation came in floods. It is indeed a spiritual feeling and I still experience it, trusting it for guidance and for truth. I rushed up the stairs, kicked off my shoes and undressed walking into the bathroom I said to Tricia, "I know what it is". I stepped into the bath with her (we never shared a bath, don't suppose it was because we didn't want to, but the bath was far too small), "God exists Tricia, I know it's true". Tricia looked at me aghast, Kevin you're not well, and there is something wrong with you. Looking back now she was quite restrained, she stood up and stepped out of the bath, wrapped a towel around her, gathered her clothes and left the bathroom. I was left sitting in the bath thinking about God.

I can't remember how I got through the night. The next day I woke with the fraud investigation on my mind. I had to sort this out once and for all. I had to confront Jayne; I had to face her down. I had no thoughts of what I would do when I got there, I probably wouldn't remember but I had to work out how to get there.

I walked to Mary and Keith's house. We had been friends for about five years but had in the last year or so fallen out, probably due to my indifference and manner which rubs people up the wrong way sometimes. Keith was a helpful bloke, he owned his own business, so when Trish and I were in particular situations, he would offer to help. I didn't always feel comfortable accepting his help because I believe you have to sort things yourself, and then you're in debt to no-one, financially or otherwise. But Keith was persistent and usually wouldn't take no for an answer. Yes he was a good friend, but my impulsiveness and inability to be flexible ruined our friendship.

For example, one evening Terry, who lived opposite came home and parked on his path forgetting to put the hand-break on his car. I was away doing a branch visit using a company pool car so our Fiesta was parked in front of the house on the road. Terry's car rolled backwards and into the off side front wing of the Fiesta. Keith said "no problem, I'll get the car into the body shop in work and sort it out for a decent price."

Terry was quite eager to settle without going through his insurance and agreed to pay cash. I asked Keith for a quote which he duly obliged. I told Terry the price and left it at that. The car came back looking good and I received the cash from Terry. Keith said the cost was more than expected and there was some to add. My reply was "I've already agreed a price with Terry, how can I go back to him and ask for more".

In hindsight, Terry meant very little to me and had caused me bother by banging the car. I should have just gone and explained the situation to him. But hey, that's the way my mind works so I stuck to my guns. That however was not the breaking point.

Sometime later the brakes were playing up on the car. Keith again volunteered the workshop and they took the car in. It was there for about a week and I was my usual impatient self because I needed the car for work. I badgered Keith to get it back and he said they were nearly finished. I eventually got the car back the following weekend and Tricia and I were going off camping to Buxton. The brakes seemed stiff and when I pressed them hard they grated. Anyway, we went to Buxton, spent the weekend and came home. I had the brakes checked out on the Monday. I was absolutely astonished. The mechanic in the brake and tyre centre called me across to look at the brakes. The front discs had been ground down. The calipers were working but there were no pads in the calipers. I'd just made a round trip to Buxton with Tricia on board and could have been killed at any point. Obviously I wasn't about to pay for the work not done. So for me, the friendship had ended there, Keith would probably have said it was before then as I was slow to repay him and I was, but my funds were limited and I was having difficulty and I wished he hadn't volunteered because I knew it causes problems. I don't think Keith knew the condition of the car, maybe the workshop saw the car they'd been underpaid on previously and decided not to do the job properly, who knows. At any rate Keith and Mary were no longer good friends.

I walked to Keith and Mary's house, on the way I was talking with Mary.

Mary: He's not in he's at work.
B: Is it ok if I pop around to ask a favour.
Mary: Yeah it's ok.
Keith: Hello Kev, how are you doing, long time no see
Yeah, I'm just looking to get a little help to get to Manchester Airport, Tricia's got the car and I need a lift.
Keith: Mary's at home see what she says.
B: Ok. I'm coming to get you Jayne.
Jayne: I won't be here I've been taken away to prison, it'll be a wasted journey.
B: I don't think so; I think you'll be there.

It's about a 20 minute walk from where we lived to Keith's house and the thoughts re-cycled in various format, but I was off to ask for a lift to Manchester Airport and I was telling Jayne I was on the way.

Jayne lived in a place called Appleton (I think) at the time, in walking distance for me from the airport (given the way I'd been walking over the past few days) or was it more, I wasn't sure, but I had it in my head if I could get to the airport I could find my way to Jayne's.

I knocked on the door; Mary was obviously surprised to see me.

"Can I come in; I have a favour to ask"

"Yeah sure, do you want a cup of tea?"

"Thanks Mary, hasn't your lad grown?"

"Mary, can you give me a lift to Manchester Airport, I need to get there this morning and Trish has the car."

"I can't just now, if you wait until Keith gets home we should be able to sort something out then, is that ok?"

"Thanks it might have to do, I could do with getting there this morning but if I can't find another way can I come back to you?"

"Yeah, that's no problem"

We passed the time of day while I drank my cuppa, talked about her son and what Keith was up to. I finished my drink and said thanks and started walking back home. Mary and Tricia spoke of this meeting later, for some reason there was a visit to the police station involved, I think it was one of the occasions I had walked home from Clatterbridge and Tricia was getting help from the police. Anyway, their conclusion was that I had run up lots of debt and was fleeing the country, leaving Tricia to face the consequences, or at least that was my plan. Little did they know it was a revenge meeting?

In the afternoon Tricia called the doctor for a home visit. Dr Coolridge came, peering over his glasses and wearing his black leather driving gloves. I remember him questioning me about my thoughts and how I was feeling and I just answered fairly normally, not mentioning any of the involuntary thoughts at all.

Dr Coolridge: You never talk of these, if people know you will be locked away, you have to learn to carry on as normal, only answer the mind with the mind and use your mouth when spoken to.

Dr Coolridge was satisfied I was just a little stressed and prescribed a mild sedative and told me to take it easy for a while. Tricia was dumbstruck, she didn't really question him too much, he was a brusque personality anyway and Tricia had never really got along with his manner. He left and we were alone.

Then I came very close to talking about what had been going on in my head.

"Why didn't you tell me Tricia?"

I was thinking about being 'deaf and everybody else did this normally.

"What are you talking about?"

"You know, how thoughts work"

"Kevin you're scaring me, I haven't got a clue what you are talking about"

"You kept it from me, how was I to know"

"You're not right Kevin, you need help"

Tricia was on the phone to the surgery again, she wasn't happy with Dr Coolridge and she wanted a second opinion.

Dr Morson arrived about an hour later. She listened closely to what Tricia had to say and asked me a few questions. I think I was pretty much spaced out.

Dr Morson: I've come to put Tricia's mind at rest, you're fine you know you are. Tricia is worried you have to relax and calm down.

The Doctor didn't ask me much at all, but she arranged for a psychiatric consultant to visit. He arrived with a colleague; I think and asked for a glass of water.

Dr D'ajo: Are the windows open, you need plenty of fresh air, drink water she won't get you. I'm going to arrange for you to get some rest away from this environment, it's hard to fight witchcraft when you are feeling low.

Dr D'ajo: "You need some time to recover I'm going to admit you to Clatterbridge Hospital so that you can get well, are you happy to go there voluntarily."

Another of those coincidences in life had kicked in. D'ajo was the name of one of my tutors at Polytechnic. He was African and had a thick accent, the majority of the class complained that he was difficult to understand but for some reason, I always picked up his meaning, not always as straight forward as it would seem, understanding multi co linearity and its proof in algebraic format and his accent, was at times mind blowing. I have long forgotten what it was all about, but at the time I did very well in his classes, when all around I was failing miserably in most other subjects. I achieved high marks in his exams and didn't know how I was doing it. Of course, networking, we were mind sharing, I was understood when others did not. Suddenly my studies were explained, my BABS colleagues were networking, sharing thoughts, progressing together whilst I was doing my usual, self sufficiency, a barrier surrounding me and my thoughts, it was comfortable and I was in control. This man though had helped me to progress in spite of my seclusion and I trusted him and his name.

At Clatterbridge we walked down the corridor towards Kensington Ward. The male nurse accompanying us was a large man, barrel chested, late 50s with a hint of ginger in his hair. He was humming to himself, I followed with Tricia and there may have been other people but I can't remember.

Male nurse: I'm your dad, you know how it works, I know him, he knows me, and I'll look after you I'm your dad.

We approached the ward through two sets of swinging double doors. There was a small room on the left with a PC on a desk. It was the general office. I was asked to sit in the chairs facing the office and wait. I looked at the PC, I worked with one daily so all I needed to do was work out how to get me out of here.

Sean approached. His particular response to his world on that day was to greet everybody with a handshake and introduce himself. He did the same to me, more than once and so to everybody else. He seemed to shake hands all day.

Sean: I'm your grandfather. See the resemblance?

So the nurse that checked me in was my dad and Sean was my grandfather in regression. The next person I saw was a female nurse, she was very shapely with a pleasant face sporting a mole but she wasn't what you would call pretty. Attractive yes but that's just a man's point of view. I can't remember her name so I'll call her Karen.

Karen: I'm Linda Lusardi

The names continued to flow, everybody was somebody, every person was somebody famous and their voice was in my head.

I sat in the reception area for hours.

B: I'm waiting to go home

Then I was called into the room next door to the office. There were two Doctors in there they said they were doing a medical. I think a routine medical examination was carried out and the doctor or nurse whoever it was then said its all held together by your skin, pulled down to your belly button in case you go btheeeeeeew, and I was dismissed back to the ward.

There was a small common room on the ward and when I walked in I was immediately struck by the music system, it was almost identical to the one I had at home that I had recently purchased only it had been abused and was broken. My music system was my pride and joy and here was a close copy.

We are making you feel at home

I walked around the ward; the large common room was painted in the same apple white as our sitting room at home.

You'll be comfortable here.

The ward had a few disturbing characters. I had never experienced anything like it at all in my life. There was one woman in her 40s who was overweight and she would drool down the side of her mouth at times and she would also shout out, things like "Oh no not again" "I need to go, I want to go home" the male nurse would sit with her in her chair behind one of the stations on the ward. He would hold her and say, "your all right now" and other calming words, although the force of holding her in place was adequate for purpose if you follow, not exactly pleasant.

There was a chap who sat in the main common room most of the time who would continually cross and uncross his legs. He would also twist his hair on the top of his head. There was a boy in my primary school that used to do exactly the same thing, his nickname was Topper and so then was this person.

Topper: I'm going to get you Rowan, I know you from old. You're going to end up like me.

He constantly crossed and uncrossed his legs. I was aware he was doing it even when not in vision and the power of suggestion became increasingly difficult to control.

B: You're not going to get to me.

My legs were twitching; I wanted to cross my legs, every time he moved I felt like moving too. It became a struggle of wills and everybody was trying to survive. The staff used to organise quizzes occasionally using board games that had been donated. Topper was highly intelligent answering a wide variety of general knowledge questions.

Keith used to run the messages down to the garage. He was engrossed in religion and when stressed spoke as two different people, or at least answered himself.

Karl was a mentor, walking around giving advice; he was into martial arts, a common thing with mental health patients. When I say he was into martial arts I mean he talked of it, made the moves and posed. I don't think he was properly trained but you never know. On a later visit I met a bloke who said he was in to martial arts and he gave me a playful kick. I back kicked him in response. He responded with a flurry of kicks and punches that stopped just short of hitting me close enough for me to feel the wind from his limbs. I think he could do it.

Everybody had their story and as I returned to the Hospital several times over the next 14 years I began to understand the difficulties facing mental health patients, made transient friendships for the periods of my stay, and developed a great empathy for people caught in this way of life. I always felt thankful that as far as I was concerned, after treatment, I would return to near normality, or the normality I knew before I was ever ill. Some of these people never had that respite, some of these people dealt with what I considered my hell continually. Ok they may not be experiencing the things I experienced, but the mind is such a powerful organ, when it goes wrong the medics don't know what's going through your head, they treat physical symptoms and they now that certain drugs have certain effects. There is no great concern of the side effects as long as an individual functions in a way society can accept, and then they are healthy. I am purposely not lingering on the drugs regime, the side effects, the difficulties that come with living on medication, as it's a story of dreary living and dreary thoughts; it's not a happy existence.

Wolf arrived on the ward. He was white haired, in his sixties, about six feet tall. He was annoyed, grumpy and generally disruptive.

Wolf: Where is he, where's this stag I'll crush the life out of him. I'll take his heart and squeeze the life out of him.

I was sitting in the common room and as his words entered my head I had an intense pain in my chest.

B: I have to ensure he doesn't know who I am

Wolf: I don't need to know who you are I can feel your pain, your days are numbered.

B: Have you seen the breathing light?

Wolf: What?

B: the breathing light, it's here to shine on your darkest thoughts.

Wolf: You know my thoughts? Who are you?

The pain was easing, I had to keep the wolf's mind occupied or I'd be a goner.

Wolf: I'm losing my bearings on you, who are you stag? There's only one wolf.

B: I'm over the hill but under your skin, squeeze my heart the challenge has a start

Wolf: Piercing blue, what of you

B: Many colours changing hue, what light do you want to view my delight?

Wolf: hahahahahaha you're a runt, although the story says you'll dance the jig its just folklore you're just a pig.

B: I won't need the jig for you, your eyes have changed they're just blue. The piercing has gone with age and time and I shall relieve you of your crime. You hold a heart and squeeze and bleed but this wolf's day is not for you.

Wolf: Who are you, your rhymes don't wash with me, I need to know your clan, I need to sift your past.

B: the breathing light will dim your eyes and you will face the merest child and fear their stare because you see, the beauty of what life can be.

The wolf looked uncomfortable in his chair and he was moved off into one of the private rooms on the ward. For the next few days the wolf was not present on the ward, just a voice in my head.

I was in the next room to the Wolf. His thoughts were in my head but I knew I had to keep him occupied, I knew I had to distract him until he was weak and I was strong. I lay on the bed staring at the ceiling. I had taken my glasses off and just gazed at the light fitting. This was the breathing light. It was fluorescent tubes contained in a flat box with a plastic opaque cover. The lights could be dimmed so that they just glowed like a night light, it was that kind of effect, and I just remember that it was not a bright light you use to light a room, just an ambience of security.

As the previous night, as I stared the light moved in a breathing motion.

B: Do you see the breathing light Wolf

Wolf: Go away, you sound near to me, I'll find your name then crush your heart.

B: the light breathes your air, breathes your mind, look up at the ceiling and see the light.

Wolf: Where are you?

B: I'm in the hall below, we're playing cards the three of us, drawing lots to look into your eyes, when your spent and crush your soul.

Wolf: Who's playing cards, this is a hospital, I'll call for help

B: There are three madmen in the hall playing cards, what are their names you need to know.

Wolf: I need your name that is all, I nearly had you Stag, but then I didn't know you were a runt, what's your name runt.

B: One from three that's all you know, playing cards through the night, making wolf watch the breathing light.

Wolf: Who are you, how do you do that to the light, where are the cards?

B: the cards are on the table, the light is in your head, the names are just a card game, by the morning you will be dead.

Wolf: Whaaaaaaaaaa, help me somebody, the runt is going to get me.

When you destroy the power of a Wolf, a beast of evil intent, by taking his confidence away, you become a White Fang, stronger than a Wolf but the same breed.

Mentally, the ward is about survival, not physical, in perception, in an uncomfortable environment of other people's problems, each finding a comfort zone to survive in. A powder keg of suggestion and influence of rising stability and despairing despondency and people suffer and contend, improve and regress in waves.

When the treatment started I wanted to walk, the corridor was about 25 metres long and I spent much of the time walking from one end of the corridor to the other. Sometimes I would break into a sprint, kick off the back wall and return. I'd think of being spatially aware, fuelled by the thoughts of other patients keeping me aware of their positions I'd do the corridor backwards. I had blisters on my feet from constant walking. Tricia had come to visit and the nurses had told her they had given me enough medication to knock over a horse and still I was walking and running up and down the ward. I started talking to famous people.

Linford Christie spoke to me.

Linford: You need to get away; those drugs are bringing you down. You want to borrow my legs.

B: Yeah

I blasted through the two sets of double doors on the ward, down the corridor, down the stairs and onto the hospital service road. I sprinted like I've never sprinted before. I could feel the power in my legs surging through my body. I sprinted the length of the service road from the psychiatric ward to the end of the children's special needs school.

Obviously there was a lot going on in my head but I've never felt anything like it, the power, the speed, it was just unimaginable. I stopped and took a breath, the nurses were on their way shepherding me back to the ward.

One of the amusing things about being in hospital was the nature of the nursing staff. They are so used to dealing with the oddities of mental health they become accustomed to it and pass their time in differing ways. There are really professional staff that genuinely care and provide good service all of the time, but there are some, generally the blokes who are distracted and pass time in other ways. I must admit professionalism has improved greatly from when I was first admitted 14 years ago and so too has the general environment. Clatterbridge used to be smoke filled corridors of hangers on and loungers. Your nostrils would clog with smoke residue after spending more than a week there. The fact that there was a high percentage of drug and alcohol abusers meant their families and friends invaded the corridors and stayed throughout the day and until late at night. Over time this changed, there are notably less people admitted and the corridors became non smoking and visiting times were more strictly adhered to. On the whole the patient environment has improved greatly over the time I have had the need to use it.

Staff though, there's usually table tennis and a pool table on the ward. It's no coincidence that some of the male staff are particularly adept at table tennis and pool. While I was on Kensington Ward for the first time a couple of the male nurses decided to set up a game of cricket using a piece of wood and the plastic centre of a used cello-tape roll. When one of the nurses bowled from the table tennis end, the crack of the nylon on wood was like a flash to me, breaking the air making a bright spark of clarity. I wanted to join in get close to the snap of the nylon. So I stood in the slips blinking and jumping each time the cello tape centre was smashed against the walls. The game went on for at least an hour much to the nurse's amusement.

I suppose I've spent many hours in Clatterbridge so I'm bound to have experienced the odd unprofessional behaviour. One time there was a bank nurse on who used to be in the paras. The nurses were often aware of potentially unruly patients and I was being a little reticent to return to my room. This nurse said something like I'll sort you out and he grabbed me by the balls and squeezed. I didn't react much at the time, but I don't think it was sexually motivated, I think if he was where he said he was from, then that kind of behaviour happens, designed to intimidate. I do however think it was highly inappropriate for the circumstances.

In the same vein, I had admired one of the female nurses and saw her watching me do it. One of the symptoms I have, and it's quite common with this illness, is that I lose my inhibitions and chase after women. This will become apparent later when I describe some of my other experiences. On this occasion the nurse was leaving the central nursing station, there was no-one else around, just me and her. She was a very fit lady, lean and strong. As she came off the station I was walking towards her and as we almost collided, she grabbed my head and rubbed her breasts against my face. I was gob smacked and even in my state I was never going to complain. (Curiously this was not the first time a woman who I had no physical relationship with, had done this to me, it also happened at a team building day organised in work, when one of my female colleagues took advantage of a situation when I was unable to react to get out of the way. I can't think what is on a woman's mind in this respect, but at least she must not have felt threatened by me at all and I quite liked it).

Indeed, from the very first episode through to the last there was occasion for me to believe that either everybody, or people who knew me could read all the contents of my mind. This is probably one of the most frightening and unnerving feelings I have experienced and also in the case of 'female voices' the most erotically embarrassing experience I have ever felt. Thankfully through luck, more than any other process, the embarrassment and consequently the perverse attraction has diminished, or more correctly is diminishing through understanding of the motives, drives and initiating experiences that can lead to submissive thoughts and behaviour. Previous to being diagnosed I had been a fan of erotic literature and had a small collection of books purchased from book clubs or mail order advertisements in national newspapers. I enjoyed stories of women dominating men either for their own pleasure or because circumstances allowed them to. Suddenly every female I had ever come into contact with knew my most secret thoughts (Imagine you find you're most secret fantasies have always been common knowledge and suddenly you become aware of the fact that you are trapped by your own thoughts). The voices teased and tormented me and promised to help me understand the sisterhood. The activities were extensions and developments of the situations I had read and also my limited experience of such activities. This did not include elements of pain or suffering, just erotic humiliations by beautiful women.

Of all the experiences I have had, this has been the most difficult to come to terms with and to accept. Both in manic and healthy periods, usually in lonely drunken evenings, I would scour the internet for similar stories and pictures. I visited numerous adult websites, although I never subscribed to any, and as anybody who has ever done this knows, there is a limited amount of free pornography available. I did however sign up to an alternative lifestyle dating sites and chatted and emailed with numerous women. I have almost come out of the other side of this particular journey. I very rarely use the internet for this purpose now unless I am particularly drunk when these desires usually manifest themselves (I have had little female contact for the past 8 years and little opportunity for regular healthy sex, as a result of my medication regime, since the age of 29. I believe this has a positive correlation with what I would describe as destructive sexual feelings and desires. In a healthy relationship, and I still hope to find one, I don't think there would be a need for my fantasies).

On the plus side I have never taken the step of turning such an adult dating contact into a reality, keeping contact to the internet. It doesn't work in a manic frame of mind, nor in reality, if the woman is not drop dead gorgeous (it is in the eye of the beholder though), online, I can always imagine they are and therein lies the safety net I suppose. I do not, in everyday life, walk around with the urge to obey women in any shape or form, the thoughts are just sexual stimuli that help me sleep at night.

I have moved from a starting position of being ashamed and embarrassed by my thoughts, through understanding and acceptance and in the main managing my feeling better than I had previously. It has enabled me to put my issues into some form of context. I am certainly not alone in finding this kind of thought stimulating. By and large I have found, through talking to women on adult dating sites, that they do not share the same general fetish thoughts as men or at least not in the same way. For example, there are many submissive females; it would seem a good deal more than dominant women. There are also many females who understand the male submissive psyche, but in the vast majority of cases it is their job and their enjoyment is based on their remuneration, not the experience. Another built in safety factor I suppose; it's almost irrelevant if the woman doesn't actually enjoy what she's doing for its own sake. I think life is designed quite cleverly at times with temptation on the one side and logical progression to do the right thing on the other.

Needless to say, I have been totally screwed up, in some respects, as a result of my illness, although I do not know how prevalent these desires would have been without my experience of mania, it could just have easily have been the same I suppose. I would like to think I'd have still had some of the original thoughts, but it would have never escalated to the proportions it did under normal circumstances.

Pornography can be addictive as we all know, but together with the stimuli for my thoughts, it also denigrated the character. Whether this process happened gradually, or whether it impacted immediately; it is not conducive to building self esteem and a healthy lifestyle. My conclusion on this matter is that my thoughts started out as fantasies and should have stayed as fantasies, which I do not believe are harmful. My mistake was bringing them into the public domain, but I'm not sure whether I would have had the required control in times of mania, even if I wanted to. Once I had started it was addictive. Alcohol abuse on the other hand, is not an adequate excuse as I can choose not to indulge and could virtually eliminate my fetish thoughts, or more precisely, the destructive need to share and discuss them on the internet. Alcohol also has the effect, in quantity, of increasing instances of involuntary thought, so I think it is possible that my reasoning process is also affected, probably more so than when people lose their inhibitions after a drink, I should leave it alone, but hey, I enjoy the buzz and I don't have many pleasures at times.

To continue with examples of nursing staff, they are often in the position of facing off violent behaviour from patients. It's surprising how very few actually end in corrective action. But on my second visit one of mine did.

Simon was about 5'8" medium build and bald. I had spoken to him when admitted because I thought he was one of the voices I had been communicating with in my travels. He said to me "Ok boss, what do you want to do now "and settled me down in the common room. He had a slight interned foot which gave him an ever so slight limp as he walked. Paul was about 5' 10" curly hair and glasses. He was often on medication and I'd sometimes refused medication. I was held down by 3 or 4 male nurses at one point, they take you to your room and one takes an arm each while the others just keep you subdued, the real force is in the arm holds. I was injected in the top of the leg just below the backside.

On this occasion I was quite high and laughing with the other patients making fun and walking up and down in front of the station Paul was manning. I blurted out "this is Simon" and did a limping walk down the corridor. Paul said "Right that's it, in your room. " I said no and carried on laughing. Paul walked towards me and put his hands up to meet mine. Our fingers locked together and Paul tried to push me back towards my room. I'm quite a strong person, or at least I was then, quite fit and had always been involved in one form of sport or another since childhood. I stood my ground even though Paul was pushing me back, then I began to bend his hands back and force him down. He called for help, the male nurses raced to help him. Paul took one arm and Simon took the other. My arms were held straight at the elbows and my hands were forced backwards as if they were trying to rest my palms on my wrists. The pain was excruciating but I wasn't shouting out. They held me in that position with force on my wrists for about five minutes. I was in agony and couldn't move, but because I didn't cry out in pain, the pair kept the pressure on their hold. When they released me the pain abated but a numb pain remained in my wrist and was to remain there long after I left hospital three weeks later. I used to shake my hands back and forth to feel the retained pain in my wrists and I thought I'd been damaged for life. This is not an uncommon practice on a mental health ward. I have experienced people being held in theses holds and crying out in pain, or more correctly cursing the staff, on various occasions.

It wasn't the first time I had shown aggression to Paul, we were talking amongst some patients sitting in chairs on the ward. The heavy wooden framed chairs you get in hospitals, with foam cushions for the seat and backrest. They are quite low with short legs in front and legs extending from the frame at the back. For some reason I had a disagreement with Paul and became angry. I moved forward and picked up an empty chair by its front leg and motioned to hit Paul with it. I remember him raising his feet to protect himself. I don't think I actually hit him with it, I think I put the chair down because it seemed ridiculous trying to hit his feet. The fact is I can't remember, but I'm not surprised he was wary of me and more than anything I was astounded in retrospect that it had been so easy for me to lift the chair in that manner. It would be quite impossible, but I did it with ease.

So they had what they thought was a potentially violent person on the ward and they dealt with it, I suppose they do.

Kensington is the secure ward were the most disturbed patients are treated, as you progress, you are moved off into the more open and relaxed wards. The ward you went on was dependent upon where you lived. It's changed somewhat now, all the wards are quite secure with electronic doors and procedures but Kensington is still the place where people with problems needing special attention are taken. The next place for me was Windsor ward.

The wards are built in rectangular shapes, a corridor runs around the central block containing a large common room, storage cupboards and a kitchen and meeting rooms along the short leg of the rectangle. Down the back straight there's a utility room and toilets. Around the outside of the rectangle is the nurses office and work station, communal wards and along the back a number of private rooms, and more wards and a games room down the back straight. Windsor and Buckingham wards are adjacent and mirror each other in their layout.

The corridors are brilliant for walking in, and I walked and walked. The medication made me feel edgy and I had to move so I just continued my walking routine from Kensington.

The ward was full, new faces to me, but as I watched and got to know them names sprang to mind, not their real names, names of characters I had known previously who resembled them in some shape or form. Calum the school teacher, Peter a childhood friend, Liam, and so on. There was a very tall, overweight lad stalking around the common room, going out through one door, walking around the corridor to the other side and coming in the other door. As he walked you could hear his footfall and it sustained as he walked all around the building. I was sitting in the common room as he did one of his stalking walks around the ward when he stopped in front of the TV.

"Don't think I don't understand messages from the television" and off he walked again. I was getting better but still experiencing the usual thoughts, but this made me think, it's not just me.

Another big difference about the open wards is that you have your meals in the canteen, on Kensington you are confined to the ward and they send them up to you. I passed my day by meal times, something to look forward to. Don't know if it's the medication but I ate and ate and ate, First time in the canteen was unusual though.

Patient 1: I just sit and stay quiet, keep myself to myself
Patient 2: How are you Kevin the foods good if you can taste it?
Patient 3: It tastes good it's not what it seems
All 3: haahaa
Patient 2: The tea tastes of kippers
I tried my cup of tea, they were right it tasted of kippers
B: You're not going to put me off, you won't bend my mind
Patient 3: Hahaaaa, Your pie's got snot in it

I looked down at my shepherd's pie and there was a green foreign body in the pie, I pushed it with my fork, it blended with the pie and disappeared.

All 3: Continuous loud laughter.

The mental goading and actual laughter continued throughout lunch. I was determined to enjoy my food, my mind was stronger than theirs, I had to overcome their networking and feed them thoughts of enjoyment. So as I ate my food.

B: This is beautiful, mmm, can get enough of these chips. The gravy is superb ....

That was my approach every mealtime, the goading abated and gradually as I became more and more stable, the involuntary thoughts receded and I approached normality again. If a little heavier with all the food I was eating.

Episode 2

I HAD RECOVERED slowly from the first episode. The medication starts high when admitted to hospital to bring you under control and is slowly reduced over time to a lower therapeutic dose. I was initially on a drug that made me want to get relief by pacing back and forth, I couldn't keep still. I can't remember properly the one that had this effect but I later got to grips with one of the drug names and called it the Stellazine shuffle. I used to just take the drugs and not really take a great note of their name or the amount in milligrams I had to take. It was just two of the white torpedoes and one of the little blue ones to me. I was also really low. I just wanted to lie down whenever I could and sleep, over medicated as far as I was concerned. Tricia wanted the old me back and decided we needed a holiday. She booked us some time away in Fuerta Ventura.

By this time Mark had been born and was about six months old. It was a really nice break, but I was still tired, wanting to rest all the time. My facial expression had changed from happy go lucky to dour and miserable. My psychiatric nurse referred to it as a masked effect and said it sometimes happened with medication. Over the next few years my character also became dour and miserable, constantly running over the unexplained nature of what I had experienced. I was no fun to be with and it just exacerbated my feeling of isolation.

I returned to work after six months and set about picking up where I left off. There were changes, I hadn't been made redundant, there was no fraud investigation, and I was working for Jayne on the corporate database. I was having difficulty thinking properly right from the off. My decision making was not as easy and I mulled over trivial things for hours on end. In fact I never regained my ability to operate positively in a work situation. Any sign of stress and I became paranoid, couldn't think clearly and made poor decisions. It's never enough to be perceptible to outsiders, they just thought I was incapable, so my prospects were limited and my confidence has generally slipped away. I talked quietly were once I was an outgoing person,

Socially, I couldn't face 5 a side or the Thursday night game, I just didn't feel good, but a couple of the lads used to keep in touch and invite me along. If you've ever been involved in this kind of activity you'll know how difficult it is to get ten or more people turning up every week, so I suppose in some instances I was making up the numbers. There was a couple though who were trying to get me moving again though and one who took his chance when it came. Where I grew up, you gave 100% in football and that includes in the tackle. Because everybody is playing the same way it's hard, but mainly fair, it's all about body weight, balance and timing. We played regularly as I mentioned with roughly the same 10 people. One of the lads was a southerner and always used to say in jest I kicked him. As far as I was concerned I didn't, I was just more physical than him. Indeed one of the regulars was a friend whom I had known from as far back as primary school. The most enjoyable games for me were when we faced each other, if anything, I played harder and more physical against him than anybody else on the pitch and he gave as good as he got. After a few weeks of ambling around, not really getting involved, my southern friend made his presence known with a stiff challenge from behind, the first time I'd ever felt his presence physically, in all the time we played together. Even in that situation, I just carried on thinking, there are more games. There were many more games over the years when I was in better health, so in that respect he wasn't a coward at all, usually they kick you and don't turn up for the next game.

The times I did play it was hell. I was just waiting for the final whistle. I was slow and laboured and just wanted to stop. The only thing that kept me turning out was the memory of what I should be doing, thinking if I try it will get better, but it didn't, I just felt awful.

A good example of this was a game of squash I had with Andy, my brother in law. He was being supportive encouraging me to do something, that's the kind of thing we used to do. I remember taking him out for a run when he felt down one time (before I was ill). That's a laugh; he used to lace me every time, me taking him for a run. I'd played squash quite a lot by then and I was fairly good at it. I'd had a game with Andy when he was starting out and beat him easily, understandable. Squash is definitely a game where the more you play the more you improve. On this occasion I didn't really feel like playing but I was always caught between the "I should be doing this" and "it'll make you feel better" syndromes.

Well, we played and I hardly hit the ball at all. My co-ordination was not great in terms of ball to racket and I was thinking I don't want to be here. I didn't win a game and scraped no more than 3 or 4 points per game. I said to Andy, I can't do this when I'm drugged up. He laughed a little and said "what do you mean drugged up?" It's not apparent by looking at somebody that drugs have an impact, but when you have experienced life without them and know what it feels like to physically push yourself, then try the same on medication, you are very aware of your limitations.

Within a couple of months I had decided I couldn't live with the side effects of medication any longer and weaned myself off everything. I was missing my competitive nature, missing the relaxing burn you get after sustained physical exercise.

When I was a child or at least up until the age of 16, I swam about five and more times a week. Mornings before school, at lunch times, at various clubs in the evening. I used to push myself hard but it was only in the last 18 months or so that I felt the real burn. I suppose I was coming to the end of my time swimming seriously but I got involved with Everton Swimming Club twice a week. I had swam since the age of 7 and always thought I'd trained hard. The introduction to Everton was stepping up a gear. We swam further, for longer, and faster. If your stroke wasn't right you were taken to a practice pool to correct it. If you were taking it easy you were placed in sequence next to somebody who would push you. You trained for stamina to start with and finished off the session doing series after series of sprints, you felt like you were dropping and you did some more. You exercised you're not only your body but your heart and lungs until you thought they were about to burst.

Then getting changed after the session, my skin would glow, I would have to dry myself three or four times because I was sweating so much, I'd get dressed and sit in the changing cubicle and for those few minutes, relaxation was complete, the feeling was so good, so calming so attractive, like post sex without the urge to sleep.

That was the feeling that drove my approach to sport, whatever it was. I may not have been as good as some people, I may not have had the skill levels or physique to excel, but I enjoyed the endorphin rush of exertion and the subsequent total relaxation. So the sports I chose to play in were mostly fast and required physical effort. Swimming, Football, Basketball, Squash, Jogging (well I'd say running but my running is jogging to everybody else). I played Badminton and Volleyball too over the years, they are demanding in their own way and very good games, but they are not lung busting. I played Badminton badly when I couldn't manage anything much else due to the effects of medication, enjoyed it, obviously not as much as I had when I played without medication, but it's a bit of a girls game. You can keep Cricket, Golf and Snooker.

On medication my buzz was impossible.

I had a re-match with Andy after the drugs had worked their way out of my system, he hardly won a point.

I thought if I could manage my stress levels, there would be a good chance that there would be no repeat of my manic episode. I also thought that the depression, lethargy, reduced mental dexterity, weight gain, oh yes and the sexual dysfunction were a high price to pay for feeling like shit. The repetitive movements on the early medication I was on, pacing back and forth etc where hard to live with. I don't care if it's a psychiatric nurse or a consultant or anybody else that say's that you feel less like exercise as you get older anyway, or in time you'll get used to the dose and you'll feel like your old self again. Or you forget things and slow down mentally as you age anyway.

It's not the same thing. I've been on various medications, felt the side effects of each of them. I've taken myself off them and returned to my usual self. Returned to medication and felt the same effects.

It's the drugs, I know it's the drugs, I know they are a lesser evil than mania, but I won't be convinced they allow me to function effectively in a work context. I find it difficult to concentrate in stressful work conditions, I make mistakes, I forget important facts, and I become irritable and paranoid to the point of being a liability. It didn't help that I was not a popular person in work anyway. I obviously don't know the reason why I felt I was marginalised. Well maybe it stemmed from my approach to work.

My ambition on leaving school was to work within the business community and to rise to a position where I could make a difference, which I never quite made. In my final year of school I was advised by one of the sports teachers to go to P.E. College and become a sports teacher, something I would have loved. My history and politics teacher thought it was a ludicrous idea given my potential. He was always objective and balanced in his teachings; even though I knew we were being taught by somebody who was prepared to discuss the known facts, not merely the preferred spin. Unfortunately I wasn't balanced, being brought up in a house were any television programme showing officers as heroes (again) or a middle or upper class actor playing a working class role, would lead to a twenty or thirty minute diatribe on the class system and its inequalities. As you can imagine, this happened quite frequently from as far back as I can remember. My father also had other pet hates, like me waiting around for friends, "just go out and do whatever you want to do, don't wait for anybody" and "never trust anybody, never look for anybody when you are in trouble, sort it out for yourself". These and other examples of his parenting are things I would never wish to pass on to my children in that manner. But, I would never like to be without the character they have made, as in difficult times, I don't think I could have coped without being singularly independent.

I failed to reach the grades required for Essex University, my first choice to study Politics (even after my teacher's attempts to validate my application retrospectively) and found a place at Teesside Polytechnic studying business studies. Considering the course had a heavy content of statistics and accounting, it was a bad choice for me. I am not naturally good mathematically, too slow and I'm sure I'm numerically dyslexic, if there is such a thing. I transpose numbers in all kinds of situations. So once again I took the difficult route but thought, 'If I apply myself I can do anything ', it's what I had been brought up to believe. I hated being a student, resenting many of the people around me and did so little work even I was surprised to receive just a pass. The final year was good, but it was too late in my course to make a difference. I took the marketing option and for the first time stumbled across a discipline I enjoyed. My study was inadequate, but still a passport to a marketing role and for the first time I was really enjoying myself working. Unfortunately for me (well I'm not so sure), I was still full of resentment and bitterness and also emotionally immature, something which is common from my upbringing (Probably the reverse scenario is very true too, providing a double conflict). At times unable and unwilling to accept, different points of view and personalities. From very early on colleagues decided not to work with me on projects and after my first psychosis, I seemed to remember why I had started out in the first place, publishing "Biographical Paradox" whilst not completely stable but very emotional about life, the final poem said it all. I was a different person and my conscience couldn't bear the fact I had changed. I suppose that was it for some colleagues. I had outlined exactly what I thought of them in two or three of the poems. So I suppose it's not a mystery that I wasn't popular in work, I compromised in some respects, like deciding to work for my manager, but lost credibility in my own mind for capitulating on important basic skills I had learnt at Polytechnic, all in all it was a disaster. I can laugh too, not unlike me to take on insurmountable odds and think I can win. In a funny sort of way I have won, I've found a balance and contentment in life I never expected. Maybe that's just what happens with maturity. I know for certain I will find peace when I go, I've been so tired of this life on so many occasions it will be a welcome relief.

I would have made a good P.E. teacher, but I would never have had this journey. I'm great with my kids, but find other people's children a challenge. At the end of the day, none of them would have deserved to have been subjected to my insecurities. I made the right decision based on good advice.

With increased stress levels paranoia grew and I often thought people that disliked me had spread vicious rumours that were without foundation. I thought this was the reason I found it difficult to build working relationships. More likely it was just the fact that I was quite open about my Bipolar and some of my experiences, I don't suppose that helped.

Well I have to admit, in the last two years or so, I have begun to regain some of my old sparkle, and that's on medication. So I will contradict myself almost immediately here and say maybe there is some truth in the medic's pronunciations that it will get better in time, although it was a struggle to convince them of the effects of the medication they were prescribing. Time is relative though and in long periods of depression you see no end to the misery. Waiting 13 or 14 years to feel comfortable was not in my expectation level. It could be argued that if I stayed on the medication regime longer it would have been achieved earlier, to my mind there didn't seem to be any great acknowledgement of the difficulties my medication was causing, just, it will get better in time. Basically I couldn't cope, I was over medicated at times, my thoughts were suicidal and my quality of life in terms of mental well-being was very poor. Yes I didn't have involuntary thoughts, but I slept at every opportunity possible, in the car park at lunchtime in work, even on the toilet at work, at my desk and profusely at home, all I wanted to do was sleep.

A measure of how people react to a situation that is not apparent was my supervisor's intent to instigate disciplinary proceedings in work for my poor work rate and apparent disinterest. Whilst all around me, I was being ignored, socially and in a work context; one of the lads who worked in the post room offered me coffee his sorting room on our floor. We knew each other from passing the time of day and playing a little five a side in the evenings. A number of times I escaped to the sorting room and he tried to chat with me, I was there, but not quite with it. He never knew how much his friendship meant.

On this particular occasion, in a little while, I began to feel like my old self and if it meant I had to do six months in hospital to get 18 months feeling like this again, I'd take it anytime. I even got discharged from outpatients at the hospital, it was looking good. Sometimes it happens that a person can have an instance of psychosis, then nothing for the rest of their lives. My hopes were up and I was enjoying life again.

There was no particular focal point for what happened next, it just happened. It would have happened in any circumstance as I was no longer medicated; it was just a question of when. After the initial instance of a manic episode, the next can happen just as a matter of course, even if you are taking medication it can happen by all accounts, although in my case I have never experienced an episode when I have been properly medicated.

At work I was involved in making use of the corporate database for marketing activity. The database had initially been designed for extracting names and addresses for direct mail activities using Boolean logic. There were political reasons why this had to be treated with caution. Historically the customer had always belonged to the adviser doing the business. At one point the Company had a different division for each of the sales channels, Tied Agents, Direct Sales Force, Corporate Sales, and Direct Mail. Although the Divisions had now been merged back to a single Company, the originators still existed, so the Tied Agent still believed he owned his customer and so on.

My main task, along with a colleague was to set up a system to manage 'orphan clients' or customers that were no longer linked to a current adviser for servicing, the same functionality basically as the bureau service I had set up previously. This time however we were to use the IT department as a resource. So together Viv and I produced a system specification from Jayne's brief and the IT team built the system, drawing on the Company databases and linking it to the corporate database.

It was cumbersome and had inappropriate output, not wholly because of its design, but because of the input in terms of data files and administration systems used to make it work. It teetered for months and became unmanageable and useless.

When it fell over it came down to IT saying it does what you asked it to do, me saying you said it would be able to do this. I remember saying "ok I said I wanted it to do this, but you said it would do that" that's fair isn't it. I was stonewalled.

Gerry never confirmed or denied, just let his line Manager give the departmental line, just doing what I suppose is company practice.

I can't play the office politics game, I say what I think, don't build bridges, don't network, I can't be bothered with the game as it's often unscrupulous. I work on the assumption that I progress work to the best of my ability, if you can't judge me on that alone and need to judge me on my personality, then I'm not really concerned how you feel. So I suppose my work experience is a product of my nature.

I can live with that too. Work colleagues didn't trust me, didn't know my motivations couldn't understand where I was coming from. For my part I have a creative mind, I solve problems in my head, I communicate my solutions, usually to my direct manager, sometimes the ideas are good, sometimes they are not. I need a manager that knows this, can filter the good from the bad and give direction on how to progress.

If there was one thing I can say about Jayne, she knew this very well and used it to her own and my advantage. She always ensured I was rewarded very well. She was a master at the politics game. So while she understood the drive and possible benefits from a bureau solution, she also had an ear to the IT lobby, its management and the company view on in house development. I take my hat off to her. I've seen her go into meetings in really tight situations and wipe the floor with people. Not in a nasty way, just her command of how to present a proposal.

For example she would listen to advice from her team in preparation, from a wide source of people in the company, she would gather background information.

I'll use an example of me, not because she used my advice often, or because it was necessarily that good, just to show how her mind worked and the fact that when her meetings were relevant to my work she would always take me along - so I saw the evidence at first hand.

On databases, I would give her the ins and outs of how the proposal would work, descriptive mainly of what it needed to do. I would use a little jargon because I was dealing with technical people all the time. I'm no means technical, but Jayne would say "your far too 'techy' for me" she even put me on a technical grade in work which was crazy, but the pay was good. I'd marry the information up with my marketing training and say this is the system, this is how it works and here are the benefits.

I was never sure how much she'd taken in, but she'd come to the bit in the meeting where it fitted, strip it all down, say some wild generalising things (she did this with many things she didn't understand in detail) that made my ribs ache inside, nail the point and look for comments and a chance to move on to the next point. She was brilliant.

I had argued with Jayne at the outset that a bureau service would have been a better solution until a flexible true marketing database had been built by the company. I arranged for a demonstration of such a tool for the marketing manager. The research and the proposals I was putting together were really immaterial. Interested groups had more sway, so I was more task orientated than project manager. It didn't stop me trying to influence things as best as I could, but my opinion is that the raw database materials used were flawed for the problem we were being asked solve. When it became unmanageable the people who were involved in the design and build, and who had lobbied strong for the right to do it because they were company experts said it's your specification that was wrong. That's all they could say because that's all I did.

I can live with the specification, I thought I had done a good job on it; it was the interpretation that was wrong in my opinion.

At work I was occupied with the database, but I was also becoming more and more paranoid. Things were not going right and I thought people were conspiring against me. I'd come home and watch the TV and I started and smile at programmes that were not amusing.

"You are going funny again aren't you?" said Tricia.

"No I'm fine, he just said something that reminded me of work that's all"

Indeed he had, it had no relevance to work at all, but I'd interpreted it that way. Even Johnny Bravo on the Cartoon channel made me laugh about what was in my head.

Tricia said "What are you laughing at now" "Johnny Bravo has just made a joke", which was really plausible being a cartoon, but not so plausible he was talking about the database in work.

I always got up for work with just enough time to get ready and get out of the door. Suddenly I was getting up before 7am, to get showered and changed and down in time to see The Big Breakfast.

I'd never watched it before and didn't know the Ginger bloke, was amused to see Keith Chegwin and was knocked out by Ulrika Jonsson. I didn't know that Gaby Rosalyn was the usual presenter, she was on holiday and Ulrika Jonsson was standing in for two weeks.

Ulrika was on doing a piece to camera, she was smiling and giving eye contact to the camera as she talked, she looked absolutely gorgeous.

Ulrika: Can you see me Kevin?

B: dead right, you are beautiful

Ulrika: I know, I've been listening to you, do you think I suit this job?

B: Well it's better than the weather, I get to see your personality, your mad as a hatter.

Ulrika: Careful now, you know us stars don't talk to just anybody don't you, you have to be one of us before that happens.

B: well I'm not one of us.

Ulrika: You will be, sorry I'm a bit busy I have to go now.

Ginger: Yes she has to go now, stop distracting her

B: What do you mean distracting her (laughing?)

Ginger: (Laughing) who are you calling ginger

B: I don't know who are you?

Ginger: (still laughing) Well that's nice you interrupt my show, call me Ginger and pester my guests.

I'm rolling on the floor nearly at the thought.

B: It wasn't me it was him

Ginger: (laughing more) what? That's a poor excuse. So you're talking to me, Ulrika Jonsson and you think you can pass the buck to someone else? Like I don't know who you are?

B: Well it was, it was him, the one in the jeans and white T-shirt.

Cheggers: What about me?

B: You still got your ringmasters outfit from Junior Showtime?

Ginger and Cheggers: Laughing

Ginger: What?

B: Where's Ulle?

Ginger: How do you know that's what we call her?

B: I just do, must be leakage?

Ginger: leakage? leakage? What's leakage? (Laughing)

B: Well you know now don't you, no need to explain.

Ginger: I see why she's seen you, you'd better watch out she'll devour you.

B: I'm a stag, is she an animal too?

Ginger: You're a stag hahaha. You'd better believe it, she's a star, she'll pick you up and discard you when she's done, you can't cross over.

Ulrika: No I won't Kev, your safe with me.

B: You're beautiful.

Ginger: Crikey he's lost it (laughing).

Tricia was on her way down stairs.

B: Have to go now someone's coming.

Ginger: (Uncontrollable laughter) What do you mean you have to go someone's coming, we're live on TV watched by millions and your going because someone's coming. (Laughing) Who's coming? The Queen? Where are you going? Do you think I won't hear you (laughing)?

I was stifling laughter and had to walk into the kitchen away from the TV. I walked into the Kitchen and closed the door just as Tricia walked into the front room.

Cheggers: Where's he gone? (Sniggering)

Ginger: Who, the bloke in the Jeans and white T-Shirt? (Sniggering)
Ulrika: Oh Keeeeviiiin, I know where you are.

I'm about to burst in the Kitchen, the door opened and I pretended to be occupied making a cup of tea.

"What are you smiling about?" "Just thinking about what somebody said in work yesterday. They were talking about having a night out drinking just shorts" I struggled to make something up.

"Do you want a cup of tea?" She did and I was able to control myself for the moment.

I was still going to work at this point, I was often preoccupied. I found it easier to try and keep my mind on my work. I was feeling paranoid and every time somebody asked about my work or involved me in part of theirs I thought they were doing it to be purposely awkward. I am convinced some of these thoughts were in fact true. Dean worked on the legal side and liked to curry favour with some of the young girls on the section, He involved me in his work so that he could basically use his seniority to point score.

Dean didn't realise he was pushing a bit too far, he didn't realise the thoughts going through my head.

Dean was older not far from retirement, so even in my thoughts, and I did have a manic episode when in contact with him, it was,

B: he's seen his best he's not a threat.

Dennis on the other hand was about my age, but big both in height and frame, a rugby player, been in the local paper for punching someone at a game so wasn't averse to letting his passion get in the way of etiquette.

When we first worked in the same area he was a bit dismissive of me. In the peaks and troughs of my moods over the next few years I thought, when I'm not all there one day I'm going to take you out, the restrictions of employee behaviour won't mean a thing to me then. I was no pushover, although I'm small at 5' 6",

I was quite strong and surprised many people in the sports I was involved in.

I don't think many people who I came up against knew that I wasn't physically scared of any of them, even if they were twice my size. In retrospect probably a foolish outlook from myself, but I suppose I rarely had the thought tested and the older you get, the less physical confrontation becomes an issue as it's not the way to settle differences.

Work was always a stress to me in terms of not being able to say what you feel about a person, where I grew up most people just said what they thought and got on with it. If it bled over into violence, then you got on with that too. Mostly, it would be forgotten about after that and things would be normal again. That was my great regard for where I grew up, none of the bitchy backbiting that goes on around the office. None of the talking behind peoples backs and the petty bitching. The girls at home were allowed to do that, but didn't to any great extent. The blokes would say what was on their mind and you either dealt with it or you didn't (In a work context, it's an uneven playing field due to seniority and the consequences of disciplinary action) but it was over with and you moved on. I valued the honesty of the people I grew up with in that respect. Obviously work doesn't operate like that. I thought at times that this was a contributing factor to my isolation in work. In general, I don't gossip about people, if I have something to say to somebody, I say it to their face. Gossip is where some work colleagues gain their confidences, they talk about people, they give their opinions to other people they trust and in turn trust people who give opinions back about others. I said almost nothing to anybody about anyone, so I suppose in that respect I wasn't trusted at all.

I contented myself in thinking, if I ever get to the point of not caring about the constraints of work again, I'm going to try and have Dennis on my mind.

I even said this to one of my colleagues one day, adding, "He'll kill me anyway, I won't stand a chance." But in my head I was going to have a really good go at it.

I worked with Dennis quite closely over the next few years and while we never really gravitated towards each other, I felt he actually understood some of the things I was going through, he was surprisingly supportive in some circumstances and not a bad manager. I suppose it was just his approach to work and it did him credit. I wouldn't admit it but I didn't feel aggrieved by him for very long once we had worked together for a time. He was crossed of my mental list of retribution.

Dennis wants to see you?

I can't remember the reason why but I was not in work, I think I'd taken some holidays to try and relax and calm down. I was still aware that stress made me ill but didn't have the insight at that point to realise I was actually quite ill.

Ginger: You coming out to play yet?

B: No not yet I've got something to do?

Ginger: What are you up to?

B: Got to see somebody he thinks I'm scared of him.

Ginger: So ever thought of doing a broadcast to him let him know (laughing)

B: I don't understand how it works, I don't know who can hear me and who can't. They don't speak in Greasby, Upton and West Kirkby.

Wirral Voice: We don't speak on the Wirral you're a dog. You speak to the stars (laughing). No-one speaks to the stars, they just use you for fun (laughing).

Ulrika: Don't listen to him Kevin, your special, you're going to be one of us.

B: Hi Ulle, your special, you're beautiful.

Ulrika: Will you watch me in the morning.

Dennis: Kev, what's going on I can hear you.

B: I'm coming to see you Dennis, apparently you think I'm scared of you.

Dennis: What are you going to do Kev?

B: Nothing, that's all we do, I'm coming to see you and I'm going to knock on your door and ask for a cup of tea.

Dennis: What's the point in that?

B: There's no point, you just meet me eye to eye and I ask for tea.

Dennis: What if I don't invite you in?

B: That's not my problem.

Dennis: I'm not in, I'm away on holiday, and there will be no answer.

B: I'm coming tonight Dennis, I'm going to knock on your door and ask for a cup of tea

Ginger: (Laughing) you what, let me get this right yeah. You're going to your boss's house in the middle of the night; you're going to ask for a cup of tea and for him to look you in the eyes? What are you two bloody policemen?

B: Nope I'm a runt, my eyes are not piercing blue the madness shine on through?

Ginger: Unbelievable, you believe all that (laughing) you'll believe you can talk to the stars next.

B: Well you wait until I'm a star; I'll be coming for late night cuppas at your place too.

Ginger: (Laughing) I'm not looking in your eyes I'm telling you that now.

Ulrika: I will Kevin

Chegger's: Can I come too?

All 4 (Laughing)

Dennis: Rowan you're off your cake, don't come near my door

All 4 (laughing)

The rest of the day for me was consumed with what was going on in my head. Flirting with Ulrika; laughing with Ginger and trying to keep it all secret from Tricia.

Ulrika: She can only hear you Kev, nobody else. That's how it works when you're a dog. People call it love; they get so close together and then find they can read each other's minds. They live their lives believing they are special together. In truth, they are controlled by networking interest groups. It's mass manipulation, it's been dressed up as various things over the centuries, religion, political persuasion etc. Some talented people are let through to entertain the masses, these are the stars. Stars can hear dogs, we don't know if Dogs can hear us because everybody thinks it's a game. They don't talk to stars because stars only play games, but we hear them all. So when you began talking to me I thought here's a stag, a dog in transition.

People laugh, stags are a joke. They are supposed to be irresistible to women and sexual perfection. I believe Kevin. I believe in you.

You only get to be a star when you have skeletons in your cupboard that can be used to control and manipulate you, you either accept the job, or you are exposed to ridicule and debasement. Nobody knows who is truly in charge because it's all controlled by the mind.

Over the years as you live with your loved one, you become more and more tuned in to enlightenment. As you don't know what it is, the net workers, suggest and impute thoughts into your head, the power of suggestion leads many people into crime and debauchery at the very least shameful thoughts about themselves.

Finally, when you are in the last quarter of your life, you are allowed progressive enlightenment and you are given the truth. By this time most people are so ashamed of their past that they are bound to continue the drudgery of their life for fear of exposure and they understand the full truth of their servitude and oppression. This enlightenment comes at different times for different people but it is no accident that age is associated with wisdom in all the cultures of the world. Why do you think your life passes before your eyes at the point of death? It is the final blow by the net workers. Showing your humiliation and servitude in what you thought was a rich and wonderful life.

You and Tricia were too good together; you were too strong a unit, the net workers worked hard to break you down from an early age. You should have lived a long productive life together, but you decided to have a child, you were breeding power and strength. The *family unit had to be broken before it grew strong. They worked on you, they worked on Tricia and they will work on your offspring.*

Follow my guidance, we stars are allowed to enjoy the benefits of free love, material wealth, but we are on a treadmill of responsibility. We work when we are told, we are inspirations and lessons to the masses but we never know if or when we will be destroyed and sent to live back with the dogs.

We will help you, you are to be a star, we will bring Tricia through when she is ready, until then enjoy the life, that's all we can do as stars.

B: That is absolutely mind-blowing; I can't comprehend the significance of it. I will never know if I am having imputed thought's or thinking for myself, I never know I've got free will or a conditioned mind how can I carry on living?

Minister: You know in your heart Kevin. There is truth in some of the things Ulrika has said but you are aware of the way to keep your sanity and your dignity.

B: Who are you?

Minister: We are the balance of the network. We are the spiritual conscience of the world. We are fighting the same as you, we are an uncomfortable alliance of disparaging thought, but we douse the network and give hope.

B: Isn't the network overbearing and all powerful.

Minister: Not at all, as they impute thoughts and destroy self belief, we gather minds and repel their thoughts; we are the organised religions of the world. We are weakened by our differences but strengthened by our membership. The ancient books are full of examples of fortitude and virtue. They are the basis of healthy living, common throughout the known world. We know how to treat our fellow man, we know how to lead good lives, our ancient ancestors documented the way to balance the world and put it in harmony. As with the network and ourselves, the message has been amended by unscrupulous minds and interpreted for selfish purpose, but don't read between the lines to find the truth. Open your mind to the truth; you will understand the wisdom and spirit of God. You don't need to read, you need to think, it's very simple, you know the difference between wrong and right, all you need to do is do what is right.

Ginger: I heard that Kev, religion is dying, the power of their network is diminished, Save yourself the grief, cross over with us and become a star.

B: I will for Ulle, she is beautiful, I can't help being spellbound by her. She is very special

Ulrika: Thank you Kevin, you are special too, you will make a good star.

I watched TV blankly as I continued chatting with my friends. Tricia spoke to me occasionally and I answered and went back to the more interesting thoughts in my head. Trish went off to bed and I continued to watch the television. I needed to walk again, so I put my white denim jacket on and set off on foot.

B: I'm on my way Dennis.

Dennis: It's no good coming here, I'm on holiday.

B: I just want to ask for a cuppa.

The conversation continued as I walked. I'd been in work at Christmas time when Dennis had a day off. Our Senior Manager was Geraldine. She'd worked with Dennis for many years and had bought him a Christmas box of bottled beers. I was walking by her desk and said I'll drop that off he lives near me (even then there was madness in my motives). She gave me his address and when I drove home that night I dropped it off.

That was some time ago, but I knew where he lived now. I walked from Upton through Greasby to Pump Lane and down the country lanes heading for Hoylake, just over the hill after the station. I was wearing a white denim jacket but the traffic on the country lane wasn't impressed, plenty of blaring headlights and horns. I would guess it's about three miles away maximum, but early hours of the morning, with no street lights in the middle of a country lane, it was a bit spooky at times. I imagined seeing shadows and figures in the dark, was aware of the animal noises about me, but walked undeterred.

As I walked I talked with Dennis, Ginger, Cheggers and Ulrika. I was intent on testing the eyes, the cup of tea was just a polite way of saying I'm coming anyway. As I walked down the hill with the station on my right, Dennis's road was one of the ones leading off to the left. I couldn't remember which one it was. I walked down one of the roads and didn't recognise anything, I knew it was about four or five houses down but it wasn't looking familiar.

Then one of those coincidental events happened. Somebody in the distance, returning from a late night out, started singing very loudly.

"Kumbya, M'Lord, Kumbya. Kumbya M'Lord, Kumbya"

I remembered from primary school it meant draw nearer, I thought people were listening and starting to help me.

I walked towards the voice and out of the road I was in and turned left and headed to the next road. I never saw the singer and he only sang those two lines.

In the next road I noticed a hedgehog walking across the road, it curled up when it saw me.

You can't go in anybody's house, you need to be invited

A door opened, a cat came out and the door remained ajar for some time.

B: Dennis, are you going to invite me in for a cuppa.
Dennis: I'm on holiday

I couldn't remember for sure if this was the house or not, wasn't entirely sure I was in the right road and I stood and chatted with my mental friends for about an hour.

Stu was the owner of the Advertising Agency that we used in work. He was responsible for all the brochure design and promotional copy used in the product literature we produced. He was good friends with Dennis and I had known him for some time too. He had worked on all the literature that I had thought was being investigated for misuse of Company money in the first episode.

Stu: Kevin what are you doing outside Dennis's house?

B: *I'm waiting for a cuppa.*
Stu: *He's gone away on holiday, he's not there.*
B: *Can't seem to be sure of the right house.*
Stu: *Well he's not there, if you want to make your way home I'll keep you company.*

I began to walk home. Stu and I talked of the literature I'd been involved with back then, the fraud investigation, the way things were turning out. I was tired and hungry and it was getting lighter. The conversation kept going all the way home. I crashed out in bed and slept.

Sleep didn't last long; I had to be up for the Big Breakfast. Ulrika was on and she was smiling at me and saying.

Ulrika: you're going to be a star, we are going to make love
B: *Do you like sauna's and massage*
Ulrika: Oooh yes
B: *and roll mop herrings?*
Ginger: What (laughing) what are you talking about Rowan? You're supposed to be seducing her you Stag. (Laughing)
B: *Well I like roll mop herrings, but it's probably the wrong country, my history teacher always said I was illiterate.*
Ginger: (falling about) what's roll mop herrings got to do with literacy.
B: *Don't know I've never read anything by them.*

I'd get the giggles when something amused me like that. Real belly laugh till the muscles ached and if I was out people would look at me concerned but move on.

The thoughts continued through the morning and I acted as normally as I could on the outside.

You didn't let on you could hear and talk, if anybody suspected you did, they would call a doctor in and you would be locked away until they drugged your mind into a dog's state, were you were easily controlled and conditioned. Pavlov demonstrated the theory well with his meat paste; only human dogs had imputed thoughts for stimuli from the net workers to control their responses. That's what the term means, workers caught in the net of their masters.

As the afternoon drew near, I began to think I had another tea party to attend.

Bill and Julie lived directly opposite our first house in Greasby. They were a pleasant couple and we often passed the time of day with them. Bill was into martial arts, a black belt at Jujitsu or similar. The catalyst for my stored up vitriol was Jim, our next door neighbour. It was 1985, I was 23 and Jim was in his early 30s and boy was he a party animal. Every Friday and Saturday night without exception, he and his wife Kay would go out to a pub with their friends and then he'd invite them back, and usually anybody else he met in the pub for a few drinks. The music was loud and it went on until 2 and 3pm in the morning every weekend without fail. The summer was even more fun because he'd barbeque in the garden all afternoon first.

At the start Tricia and I used to go next door and relax and enjoy the weekend that way too. We had stretched our income to buy the house so there wasn't much left over. We had no carpets, no telephone, no cooker, (we used a camping stove) curtains only in the front of the house for over a year, but it was good being together and it was a brand new house and I thoroughly enjoyed my life with Tricia there.

I used to make home brew beer and wine because I suppose we couldn't really afford to spend much on alcohol and because we liked getting smashed occasionally. When we went around to Jim's there would often be drink about so I'd say I know it's only home brew but it's all I've got. Either we got used to my beer and wine or some of it was actually quite drinkable, I suppose it's for others to pass comment on that.

The black spot was Jim's partying. The semis were nice but the walls paper thin, you could hear everything next door. A combination of the same thing every week and getting too close to somebody meant we stopped going around to Jim's, but he continued to party like there was no tomorrow.

Tricia is not a patient person and with the music thumping through the walls she would toss and turn and complain to me. I have a higher threshold but when I blow I suppose I blow the same as Trish. Tricia would complain to me while we were in bed with the music going on, she would huff and puff repeatedly. I started going in after midnight to complain about the noise. Tensions grew over the weeks and culminated one Sunday afternoon when I went around complaining about the noise. Jim had his friends around Terry and Sue. He'd been drinking and must have felt I'm not going to lose face here. Jim was a big bloke, over six foot.

He lunged at me and we fell on the coffee table, it broke. He started saying I had to pay for the table. Kay said "Don't be silly Jim it was already broken". We moved outside and his friends and Kay formed a barrier between me and him, I thought at the time they were holding me back but retrospectively they were probably just blocking my way to him. Jim on the other had been moving freely behind them raining punches down towards my head. I don't remember anything but seeing Jim's face in striking distance and I let a punch go. My father used to box in his army days and from very young he would raise his palms to me and say get your stance right, get your balance right, use your shoulders, get all the weight of your body behind the punch. And I did.

Jim's nose split across the bridge and blood spurted out. He fell backwards against the garage door and slowly slid down the door to the floor.

Terry said to me "You weren't going to stop until you hit him were you?"

I didn't answer. Tricia and I walked back into our house. I said to Tricia ""He's damn lucky it was me and not one of the lads from home because they would have finished him off" I didn't need to say that to Tricia.

Jim came to and after half an hour or so he appeared at the front door, He was saying we can't go on like this we have to be neighbours. I let him in, I was laughing saying "Did you see that couple driving down the street viewing the houses for sale", some advertisement. I've never seen the point in prolonging things so I just said fine by me. Jim never changed though, we still had the partying, but I retaliated playing loud music when they were in bed first thing in the morning, things got strained, they decided to move on but didn't, I got a better paid Job and we moved on to a detached house.

Bill and Julie had been out with Jim and Kay one night. This was sometime after Jim and I had had our altercation. Our windows were only a matter of feet from the sidewalk, no more than 15ft. The two couples were standing beneath our bedroom window. Bill started mouthing off about going to a house party and bringing home brew wine and laughing loudly. Jim was joining in but rather quietly as if he was not entirely comfortable, you knew Jim when he was having a laugh he was loud and brash.

My adrenalin kicked in, I was bouncing, my heart was pumping, and I started getting up. Tricia said don't Kevin, leave it. I argued but I lay down and listened, each word making my heart pump harder and faster. Adrenalin only lasts for a relatively short period, that night I must have exhausted my supply ten times over. The high, the readiness passed, but the heartbeat pumped on and on, leaving my body feeling inadequate like retching to vomit and there is nothing there.

It was one of the most frustrating feelings I have ever felt in my entire life and I have even considered it was the catalyst for what happened to my mind because it was an unnatural reaction. I know that this is not the case. Experiencing an adrenalin rush prior to a possible physical confrontation is a comforting feeling, knowing that your body is primed for action one way or another, the fight or flight syndrome. Another side effect of the medication I take that is not widely recorded is the loss of the adrenalin rush. This to me is a worrying scenario because I no longer re-act to situations; they just happen at an even pace, there is no instinct about it at all.

Anyway, I had a tea party to go to.

B: Can you hear me Bill?

Bill: I can hear you Kevin, I've been listening all week, you're the new entertainment around here. The Stag is coming out to play with the stars.

B: I only want a cup of tea

Bill: You're not going to stare into my eyes then and take the evil out?

B: I'm just going to knock on the door and ask for tea.

Bill: Your not very good at this are you, you have to be invited in, it doesn't work if you make the first move.

B: I just know I have to come and meet you face to face.

Police: He's right young runt, from eye to eye only does its stuff by the rules and you're following our rules on this one or you're off the streets for good.

B: Fuck off plod; you've sold your soul.

Police: Yeah we know, why do you think we sing Blue Moon? We lost our love and our hearts. We are heartless bastards akin to mechanised authority. Our network is dour but efficient and we won't stand for you waking people up and encouraging them to use the airwaves, it's our control point not yours. People don't talk straight because they know we can listen, so nobody say's what they mean everybody says something different to the truth so nobody's mind can be read. And that's the way we like it. Now you're talking straight and people are listening and the fabric of society is being challenged.

B: I just want a cuppa with an old mate, what are you talking about?

Ulrika: Kev we are nearly ready to pick you up

B: What do I have to do?

Ulrika: Don't worry about it, we will find you.

It was only about a 15 to 20 minute walk from where I lived to where I used to live. I walked and came into the Crofters by the public footpath at the bottom end of the estate. You can't drive in from that end it's just a footpath. Our old house was about 5 semis up on the left. I stood at the end of the path of where I used to live and faced Bill's house. I looked directly through their front windows and stared.

B: *I'm here Bill, are you going to invite me in.*
Bill: *No I'm not, you're going to have to come across and knock.*
B: *You know I can't do that*
Bill: *Then you're going to have to stay there until you get tired.*
B: *I'll stay until I get picked up by the stars.*
Bill: *Please yourself, but I'm not inviting you in.*
Ulrika: *It won't be long now Kev, someone you know will come to pick you up.*

I could see the outlines of Bill and Julie occasionally looking out of the window and I just stood and stared. I continued to talk with both of them, with Ulrika and with Ginger. I was there for over an hour, just staring. The door behind me opened, it was my old front door.

You can come in if you like

The door was ajar, but there was nobody around.

B: *Thank you but I have to wait for Bill to invite me in.*

A car had been making its way down the road in stages, it was somebody collecting money, a milkman or a window cleaner, and he parked about ten yards to the left of me on the opposite side of the road. I looked closely; it was Eric Clapton in disguise.

Eric: *Just get in the car Kev, this is what we do, we have ordinary jobs too like everybody else.*

He got out of the car and went to knock at his next call

Eric: *Just get in the car Kev.*

I crossed the road and walked up to the passenger door and tried the handle.

The bloke flew back to his car "What do you think you're doing, what are you up to? Stay away from my car, stay off it"

"I'm sorry mate I thought you were someone else"

"I don't care who you fucking thought I was, keep of the car"

"Made a mistake mate that's all"

He went back to his collection round shaking his head in disbelief.

I went back to my previous position and stared at Bill's.

Ulrika: I'll tell you when Kev; don't give up, we'll be there soon.

I'm not sure exactly how long I stood staring into Bill's but I think it was considerable.

In the end, I understood I wasn't going to be invited in. My chat with Ulrika had changed too; I was going to be picked up by Chris Eubank on a Harley Davidson. I spoke with Chris Eubank and he told me he was going to be with me soon. I moved to the end of the road where it meets Hambledon Drive and sat on the Road Sign saying "The Crofters"

I sat there for about 20 minutes waiting for Chris Eubank and Bill came past in his car. He pulled up next to where I was sitting and wound down his window. "Kev, are you alright, what are you doing here? "

"Yeah, I'm fine I'm just waiting for a friend"

He wound up his window and drove off.

Bill: Well that wasn't too hard was it?

B: You know you were supposed to invite me in, why didn't you invite me in?

Bill: We're not supposed to meet.

I sat on the sign post for a while longer, the Police turned up.

Police: "What are you doing here?"

"Just waiting for my friend Chris, he only knows my old address so I said I'd meet him here"

B: not you Chris (I was talking to Chris an old school friend I'd known for years)

Friend Chris: I know Kev, I've been listening, all your friends can hear you, that's how it works, that's your network, although yours is very small because you've never spoken to anybody and when you did you said "Fuck off you bastard."

I stifled a laugh in front of the policeman.

Police: "We've had a complaint about somebody hanging around in the area and I'm just advising you that if I come back here on my next patrol and you are still here I'm going to have to take you in for questioning".

"It's ok I was just leaving, I don't think he's going to turn up now anyway".

The policeman drove off and I started walking again. It was getting colder, nearly dusk and I wished I had brought a coat with me.

I remembered the words of the mentor and I questioned the stars as they had let me down twice today.

Ulrika: Don't worry; we are sorting it, we will be with you soon.

I walked towards Pump Lane, through the housing estate. I remembered one of my work colleagues lived in a close on the left as I walked. I tried talking to him but got no reply. He wasn't really one of my friends but a decent sort of person, I wanted to talk to somebody and see if they knew what I thought. I walked into where I thought he lived. The houses seemed different; I couldn't make head or tail of what I was looking for.

He's moved, he's gone away, and nobody knows him here anymore.

I was tired and cold and confused I turned around and continued to walk towards Frankby.

I carried on walking until I reached St John's Church and walked up the driveway. It was completely dark. There is a large hut to the right of the church, the church hall no doubt. The lights were on and there were people inside. I needed to talk to somebody; I was feeling very insecure and lost for ideas about what to do next.

Walking up to the church hall I rapped out S.O.S on the door. There was no reply. I waited for a response but nothing. I tried again and got no reply.

Walking across to the church I sat down on a bench facing the graveyard and listened with my mind. There was nothing, just peace. I don't know how long I sat there. A car drew up and a young couple got out and walked around the graves as if it were the middle of the day. I sat some more, feeling the cold but not wanting to move, enjoying the calmness. Another car pulled in. It was my brother in law Andy and his wife Sally. I don't know how they thought of looking here but they did. They walked over and asked me if I was ok. I said yes, I was just relaxing, so after a few minutes they got back in the car and left.

Soon after I began the walk back home, 20 minutes or so and I was there. Tricia wanted to know what I'd been up to. I just said I'd been out for a walk. "You've been gone nine hours Kevin, where have you been?"

"I've been for a long walk."

Tricia:" I'm not putting up with this tonight Kevin, you're not well and I don't want to be here. I'm taking the baby and going to my mum's, I can't put up with this anymore."

"Why are you going, I've only been for a walk, just to clear my head. There is nothing wrong with me. It's you that's stressing me out, always going on at me. I can't move without you saying "what are you doing that for?", "where are you going? ","why are you smiling? "You just go on and on. I don't care if you go to your mums just let me get some peace. I'll be ok in the morning

Tricia gathered some things together, loaded them into the car with the baby and drove off.

I looked around and thought 'I've got to get out and walk'. I remembered the peaceful feeling in the graveyard and decided to head back there. I picked up my flying jacket, put it on and walked out of the door.

My flying jacket was something I never thought I would have. I used to make airfix models when I was a kid. I was interested in old planes and dreamt of being a pilot. The WWll flying jackets were really cool. Even when I was at Polytechnic I remember Andy McCluskey from OMD wearing one while singing Enola Gay and thinking, that's cool.

I had worked on some project or other in work and I got a £500 bonus. I'm pretty stupid with money, If I get a windfall like that I just think I wouldn't normally have that kind of money so I do something with it that I wouldn't normally do.

There was a leather sale on at the Leasowe Castle, just along the shore from Moreton. Trish and I took the short trip from home to have a look. I'd already decided what I was looking for. Sure enough there was one there and it was brilliant, just short of £300. I'd never spent that much on any item of clothing before. The most I'd spent was about £150 on the catalogue for a suit for work and I thought that was expensive too. I bought Trish a leather jacket for about £180 and we went home. I wore it whenever I could, but I always felt self conscious in it. I always felt it was too expensive and I could never settle if I ever took it off while we were out anywhere. I said "this will be my Jacket for the next 20 years." Stranger things are said in jest. I still wear it today on my motorbike, even though back then I was a 40" chest and now I'm a 46 it's battered to hell but still does a turn.

Minister: Is that the Golden Fleece you're wearing?
B: I'm a biker that's what I do.

I didn't have a motorbike at the time, I had always wanted one since being a teenager and I wasn't to get one until my early forties.

Minister: I know the way it makes you feel.
B: I just wear it and it keeps me warm.
Minister: You are warm but you don't feel comfortable. The jackets comfortable but it hangs on your soul.
B: What do you mean I just wear it, I'm a biker without a bike, I wear it because it's warm
Minister: It's expensive, it's not you. See how people's heads can be turned, you buy something you think you need, you spend more than you think you can. You enjoy the feeling you enjoy the fact that others know you can. The feeling grows, you want more, you change your life, your needs, and you lose your sense of direction. You lose your soul materially.

B: *It's just a jacket; it's not a status symbol where do you draw the line.*

Minister: *That's where it all starts; tell me why it makes you feel uncomfortable.*

B: *Because it's new. I like it new, I like the look, but I will be more comfortable when it has shown wear and tear.*

Minister: *Why is that?*

B: *Because it will not matter.*

Minister: *See the way significance makes you think, see the way a mind can build insecurity and insincerity through avarice at the same time. You can't rest when you don't know where it is, you feel smug when others see you in it, and your heart is cold when you wear it.*

B: *it's just a coat.*

Minister: *What if it was a brand new sports car, a gold watch, a fine house. Would your insecurities and your vanity change you as a man?*

B: *Yes they probably would*

Minister: *Then know yourself Rowan, know the simple things in life are meant for you, know they keep you well and know they keep you true.*

By this time I was walking along the footpath in front of the ex RAF houses, I think they were, somebody told me that once, about 200 yards from St John's Church. I took off my flying jacket and threw it on the grass verge.

B: *Don't need that anymore!*

At the church I sat down on the bench I had visited earlier that night.

Minister: *Do you know? When people pray in church, their minds are as one and their prayers reverberate around the world. Christians unite in their millions and the word of God fills the earth dispelling evil thought and cleansing the souls of sinners. Listen Kevin, there is always somewhere in our network were prayer is taking place.*

I heard the sound of a church service. It was a full church reciting prayers and saying praise be to god.

Minister: The service is for you Kevin, the return of the prodigal son, you were wearing the lamb your father slaughtered for you and you have discarded it. The service is taking place at St Mary's Church in Upton, you are awaited. Bring the Golden Fleece to show your penance and present it at the altar before the congregation.

I got up off the bench and started to walk back the way I came. About 200 yards down the road I came across my flying jacket lying on the grass verge. I picked it up and put it on. There was the sounds of a church service in my head and I visualised an alter scene and could see the minister with his arms held open.

Ginger: Where are you going now Kev? Going to make up for lost time in Church? You haven't been in one for years. Don't you think if prayers could be heard the world over; they would have let you into their secret when you used to go.

B: Don't know, don't know what to believe so I'm going to go and see.

Ulrika: Can we get married in a church, when you're a star.

B: I'd marry you anywhere your special, but I'm already married.

Ulrika: Dogs don't count when you're a star

B: So I'm not a dog then?

Ulrika: You're a stag, mmmmmm, the best to have.

Ginger: See Kev she wants to own you, I told you she'd devour you.

B: I don't care, just looking at her makes me feel good.

Ulrika: Wait until you see me in the flesh.

Minister: Don't be sidetracked Kevin, remember the lesson about insecurity and vanity. The stars will only lead you down that path and your soul will be lost forever. You still have a chance to redeem yourself and you will be welcomed back into the flock of Christ.

I walked for about 25 minutes reaching Upton Cross. The bell of St Mary's tolled and I thought that was for me. It was a short walk through the village to St Mary's Church. My head was filled with encouraging comments in my head.

Voice 1: Have you got the fleece?

Voice 2: Don't worry we won't look, just come in and walk to the altar, we know your coming.

Voice 3: We've been listening to you all week. Don't worry you're going to be safe now.

Reaching the church gates, they were locked. There was no sign of life anywhere, the church was in darkness.

Minister: Don't worry Kevin, it's going to happen soon, we had to be sure you were going to arrive. We'll ring the bell soon to summon the congregation, it is all for the best.

B: What do I do now, when will I know you are ready?

Minister: Use your instincts; we are blocking malevolent thoughts from your mind, feel the peace and walk with the wind.

I closed my eyes and concentrated, he was right, it was calm, I felt the wind brush me on the left side of my body, turning and facing Church Road, I walked and as I walked I was guided by the wind.[1] If it blew me left I walked left, right and I walked right. I walked amongst the housing estates crossing roads back and forth, turning back on myself, retracing steps, and then walking again. My thoughts were of friends and relatives and people I grew up with. I began to think they lived in this locality, they had moved without my knowledge. I spoke with them in my mind and understood they were either in or out by whether the lights were on in the porch or not. I stood in front of houses and enquired who was home from the driveway.

We're home but you are not welcome, you are trouble, you're a stag, you talk to the stars you're not the person we knew.

I was turned away and lost and I didn't know what to do.

The church bell rang out, it was 2 am. I remembered the service, the congregation had been summoned, and I made my way back to the church.

---

1 The inspiration for the poem "Walking With the Wind" first published in Biographical Paradox 1997 Avon Books.

It was as before, cold, dark and deserted. I walked across the road and sat down on the bench facing the church on the opposite side of the road.

Ginger: Well what did you expect Kev, what do you know about religion, what do you know about the church. It's failing badly, nobody goes anymore, if they ever did have a powerful network, it's diminished somewhat now and by the way where do you get off calling me Ginger (laughing)

B: What (laughing), yeah I saw you in the paper; its Chris Evans isn't it?

Ginger: Well, it's my show, I'm known to millions and you call me that ginger bloke. (Laughing) It wasn't me it was him

B: who?

Ginger: Cheggers, I never said any of that pretentious stuff (laughing).

Cheggers: It wasn't me it was him.

B: Come on folks, that's an old joke and it isn't even funny

Cheegers: Who said that?

B: It wasn't me it was him.

I sat on the bench with Chris Evans and Keith Chegwin in my head and it was one of the most genuinely funny hours of my life. I was sat at the junction of Church Road and Ford Road, Upton facing St Mary's Church from 2am until sometime after 3 am and I rolled around laughing. I can't remember what was being said, I just remember being in fits of giggles. No-body saw me, nobody came near. The lights flickered above me occasionally, sometimes I spoke with the minister who was asking me to go home, but there I sat and enjoyed the conversation.

I eventually headed home with the thought of being picked up by the stars uppermost in my mind. It was only a short walk home and I was home in less than ten minutes. I carried on the conversation with Chris Evans and Cheggers and Ulrika kept me up to date with how I was going to be picked up. I was to expect a transit van with blacked out windows and it would pull up outside the house. All I needed to do was to get in the van and we would be on our way.

Tim was one of my close (proximity) neighbours. It was a small close which split into two. The branch I lived in had five houses in it, three detached and two semis, all small three bedroom houses. I could see Tim's house from our front windows, it was about 15 or 20 yards away on the right hand side, set just in front of our house, but facing directly down our branch of the close. My house was at ninety degrees to the road.

Tim was a big man, over six foot and built like a bull. He would often talk to me about people who annoyed him in work, and people he met during the day. He was a truck driver and always had an opinion on everything. He was fond of saying how tough he was and how he scared people when he was angry. I used to stand and grin at him while he related his stories and Tricia would say, "What is it with you and Tim, why do you look at him like that?" "I don't know what you're talking about, we just chat. In a future manic episode I was to come out of my house and walk up to Tim and slap him across the face. He knew something was amiss, he didn't react but my unpredictability meant we were never friends.

On the other hand, he had a good heart and helped me occasionally in difficult times. For example after the first episode I was struggling with my medication and sleeping most of the day. I was disinterested in life and it was an effort to do anything. The position of our house meant that there was a very long wooden fence running down the boundary of the left hand side of the property. There was a small service road to the left of the house with two more houses facing it and then Tim's house, all three facing the same way.

Graham was Tim's friend, I didn't have much to do with him but he lived next door but one to Tim at the top of the service road. The wooden fence was falling down, the posts had been sunk into the ground untreated and had taken maybe three years to rot. The fence was hanging towards Graham's property and the house in the middle. It needed replacing. I arranged for the delivery of concrete posts and cement. I also ordered a fence post screw and a supply of concrete. The intention was to use the existing panels to build the new fence.

I began shaping up to remove the old stumps and to dig the new post holes. I was totally inadequate. I'd never done this kind of work before but crucially I had no stamina and no interest in progressing the work. Tim came across as he did with anything going on. He just looked at what I was doing and took charge. He had put the fences up of his two neighbouring properties when he moved in. He had the knowledge and the ability to do a pretty good job. Graham came out and got stuck in too. We had the mixer going, holes being dug and fence panels being cut to size all at the same time. It took about a day and a half. Tim had no idea what I was dealing with at that point, that would change over the next couple of years but I was really grateful for his help. He also helped me with my car on occasions. If you were ever working on something outside, Tim would be there and he was always an expert. It was part bonding and part annoying but we rubbed along.

I tried to pay him back in kind a couple of years later. He was a mad bastard and once he got something in his head he just set about doing it. His back garden was slightly higher than the level of his house and he decided he wanted to dig it out to make a hard standing for keeping his boat in the backyard. He filled two large skips with earth he removed from the back garden. It was heavy going, the earth was thick clay. I spent a full day with him filling wheelbarrows and running them up planks into the skip. It was one of the occasions I was off my medication and I had been working out in the gym. We just did run after run until all the earth had been moved.

Tim was proud of his army training. He often talked of his experiences in the army. One night about 2.30am he knocked on my door. Kev, I think someone is trying to break in to the houses at the other end of the field at the back of my house. Are you coming with me? To this day I don't know if it was a piss take or not, but there we were stalking across open grassland at 2.30am in the morning looking for burglars. Tim didn't realise I couldn't see anything because I'm short sighted and obviously take my contacts out before I go to bed. In retrospect, I think he was having a laugh because when we first moved into our house, I disturbed somebody skulking around the back of my house at night, it was only teenagers but I set off after them and followed them into the field backing on to Tim's house, he either saw me running across the back of his house after the lad, or I'd told him about it.

My best memory of hanging about with Tim was the day we were having a barbeque in my back garden. Not sure if Tim was involved to start with, but there were a small number of people around. It was easy to walk past our back door and into the garden. Tim strolled in playing an accordion and singing. It was magic, he'd never mentioned he could play before, I had no idea. He just waltzed in playing. Surreal!

I was standing at the bedroom window looking out onto the close awaiting the arrival of the blacked out transit, just standing, no movement and waiting.

Tim: Hi Kev how's it going

B: Not bad, what you doing up

Tim: Couldn't help it really, been listening to you, Yeah right, you talk to the stars. There's a pint of piss on your doorstep. You can take it when you want it.

B: I'm just waiting Tim, just waiting.

Tim: Well don't wait too long it's nearly four o clock in the morning, people will be going to work in an hour or so.

B: Only nutters like you, most get up at a reasonable hour.

Tim: Yeah right, you won't be going anywhere see you later, I've got another hour or so yet.

B: See you Tim; I'm a bit busy just now anyway.

Ulrika: We'll be there soon Kev, hold on we are on our way.

I waited until 7am, staring out of the window.

Ulrika: Sorry Kev I have to go on air in a minute, we'll catch you another time.

B: You're not coming, are you? Tim was right, you're not going to turn up.

Ulrika: Come and tune in downstairs and believe my words.

I went downstairs and watched the Big Breakfast. I chatted to the presenters and talked about joining the stars.

At 9am I took a shower and a shave. I remembered something one of my friends had said at a scout camp when I was younger, there was no shampoo and he was washing his hair, he used washing up liquid and said it's all the same stuff. We were out of shampoo, so I used the foam bath, tried some soap and laughed manically in the shower.

I filled the wash basin and looked in the mirror to shave. I was thinking my mind was merging with my father. Dad had been wearing a beard for some time now. I imagined as I shaved I was compelling him to shave too. As I shaved I laughed and saw my dad looking back at me clean shaven.

Somehow, I can't remember how, I ended up in Kirkby that day. I remember walking along County Road towards Tower Hill and subsequently on to my parent's house in Melling Mount. I was going to see if my dad understood what was happening, to see if he was clean shaven.

My mother was expecting me and started questioning me about the things I had been up to. My mum could be really irritating; she often had things in her head that defied logic, about how I was running my life, who I was involved with and how I should think. She would just continue to nag on and on if she believed that it was true. She was also the closest person to me in terms of understanding, not the same relationship as Trish obviously, but just always there. She was a little bit potty, but I knew she cared and I loved her, well, because she was my mum. We could have raging rows and quite literally sit down five minutes later with a cup of tea and chat as if nothing had happened. I used to go across to see my parent every weekend,

Tricia did the same with hers, so I'd drop Trish off at her mum and dad's and I'd go to mine for a couple of hours and pick her up on the way back.

On this day, mum was aware I'd been walking the streets at odd hours and through the day. She was trying to work out what was going on and she was just getting casual explanations from me giving wholly inadequate reasons for the way I was behaving. Oh yes, my dad still had his beard and remained his usual contained self while all this was going on.

I shouted at my mum, I've had enough of all this interrogation; I have to get out to get some fresh air. I went to open the door. My mum had locked all the doors from the inside and hidden the keys. I was feeling suffocated in the house, pacing backward and forth and needed to get out.

"Mother, give me the keys I need to get out."

"No you're a danger to yourself you need to be with someone."

I grew angrier and angrier and started to think of how I was going to get out. I tried the doors again. My dad just sat impassively, my mum ran upstairs and hid.

I was at bursting point; I picked up one of the metal dining chairs and said I'm going to throw this through the patio doors. There was no re-action. I have no idea why I didn't put the chair through the patio windows, it's what I wanted to do, I just wanted out and I was bouncing off the walls. I put the chair down and went into the downstairs toilet and locked the door behind me. The window was open, it was a top light and I thought I'm out of here. So I balanced on the toilet seat and tried to ease my body through the open window. Of course I was too big, all I succeeded in doing was bending the window frame on its hinges and after 15 to 20 minutes of trying to get out I gave up.

As I came out of the bathroom, Tommy came in through the front door.

Tommy is my mum's brother, ten years older than me. My mum and Tommy were quite close. I became quite close with

Tommy too. I can see where the possible beginnings of this came from; it was probably my mum's work initially. Tommy services canal boats and engines on the Leeds Liverpool canal. He became involved there after purchasing an old wooden canal boat in the mid 70s. He repaired it, worked on the out board and used to take his sister's kids along at times, just because that's what he did. So to start with, myself, my sister and cousin's, Alan his brother, and his partner Mandy. Not all at once, just enough that could fit in the car, any combination of, would accompany Tommy and Mandy to the boat and spend the day there.

He got to know the boatyard owner, ended up working for him and subsequently ran the business, first with a partner, then on his own. I can imagine this conversation going on with my mum and Tommy.

"Tommy, can you take Kevin up to the Marina and keep him out of my way for a few hours?"

"Yeah he's no bother, I'll pick him up."

I can laugh now; I know he does too, because we get along. Tommy had to put up with the intransient nature of a willful teenager and it wasn't always easy for him when he had other things on his mind. It's not bad when the child is your own, but other people's children are a different kettle of fish. Tommy' response with every problem I've taken to him is, "That's what families are for."

I can imagine my mum roping him in, especially in the school holidays and at weekends too.

I could be doing a massive disservice to both of them, but it's exactly the kind of thing she would get up to, so even if it's not true it's an excellent example of the way my mum worked.

Anyway, the facts are that I spent a huge amount of time with Tommy from the age of about 10 or 11 until about 17 or 18. Most weekends, school holidays. It was no big deal, I used to meet him as he drove past our estate, or if he wanted to speak to my mum he'd collect me at the house on the way through. On the way back he'd say, I'll drop you by the bollards and we'd chuckle, same joke every day. One day he did actually say by the bollocks and apologised which was ridiculous. Like everybody else in Kirkby he used to swear in his everyday language. I swore like a trooper in school and with friends but at home and in front of the family I never did and neither did my parents. I thought Tommy's apology was amusing and I didn't realise why he did it until a good few years later. I was in my mid twenties to late twenties, I was talking to Tommy about something, and I was angry and blurted out "it fucking gets on my nerves." He looked at me and said "that's the first time I've ever heard you swear."

Mum: "Go up to the Marina with Tommy"

She'd been on the phone to him while she was upstairs asking him to come and get me.

B: Tommy, I've got to get out, just get me out of the door.
Tommy: It's ok Kev, just come with me.
B: I'm not a dog anymore I'm changing.
Tommy: You're not a stag you're in trouble.
Dad: You're a gent son, like your dad.
B: What do you mean?
Dad: We don't talk much, but when we do we talk straight. Dogs talk backslang in variants, so each clan has its own backslang so nobody knows what they are talking about. They hide their plans from others and more importantly the police. They talk openly in secret, they are dogs. Gents well, everybody understands them, they talk straight all the time. It's a throwback to ancient times when there was peace on earth; everybody knew what was on everybody's mind because we all spoke with the same language. You have heard the biblical phrase, 'speaking in tongues', it means understanding with the mind. No matter what the spoken language, people who talk straight understand with their minds. Networks were still important, nobody fully understands why you become part of a network, or why you can be part of one and not part of another, and they are as individual as you. But vested interests and criminality grew and people conditioned their own minds away from straight talk. In

Liverpool they use backslang, but in other parts of the country and indeed the world there are other names and variations.

I was vaguely familiar with backslang and how it works. In essence words are changed by either changing a vowel or consonant adding a small phrase consistently to the spoken word. So "How are you? "would turn into "Howagu areagu yaragou that's about the level of my understanding, but the principle explained. If such a treatment was practiced and continually added to language, it would be unintelligible to those that did not understand the code. The very sounds of the dialect made me shiver, giving a subversive feeling and suggesting an ignorant approach to life. That was a dog in my book.

Tommy: Your dad's talking historical, people have changed, they use some of this, some of that, there are pedigree breeds, we have jobs and we do them well.

Dad: They're all dogs, you have to talk straight, and you have to continue to do the right thing.

Tommy: "Come on Kev, let's get in the car."

"Ok where are we going?"

B: I just need to get out of the house just drop me around the corner.

Tommy: Whatever you want

Tommy: I'm going to work are you coming with me?

B: Just drop me at the corner.

I jumped into the car with Tommy and he turned it around and headed off Melling Mount. At the end of my parent's road there's a left turn and you follow the road to a T-junction. Turning left again you would head down the main road and can turn either left towards Tower Hill and Kirkby or right towards Maghull and Ormskirk. We stopped briefly at the first T-Junction.

B: I'm getting out thanks Tommy.

Tommy: Ok Kev, you know where I am.

I opened the car door as it briefly came to a standstill and got out. I walked off away from the direction of the main road.

"Kevin, what are you doing, where are you going?"

Tommy was half in, half out of the other car door.

"I've got to walk; I've got to see people"

"Come back Kevin, get back in the car and we can talk"

Tommy: I have to do this, were not supposed to talk like this and your making me talk straight because you don't understand my slang. People will hear me, I won't be trusted.

B: I have to walk, I have to listen to my senses, I don't know where I'm going or who I am.

Tommy: Get back in the car Kevin, your family; I need to know you are safe.

I turned around and walked back to the car and got inside.

We didn't talk much as we drove along the Ormskirk road, heading towards Burscough. The car was a red Volkswagen Jetta, about 10 years old and well worn. Right from his early teens he was into motorbikes, old cheap British bikes, he and his mates cobbled them together and hung around in groups. They all learned to maintain and service them to varying degrees. This was a passion for Tommy. He progressed onto all things mechanical, cars, boats, tools, gadgets. I suppose you can only call it self-taught, or at least the meeting of minds with likeminded people. It's amusing and mind blowing to watch him work. He understands engines, but if something won't work, he'll come up with what seems like a hair brained solution and makes it work.

I was with him one day when he was trying to get a 1950's petrol air compressor to work. The bore for the spark plug was worn, either been cross threaded or some other mal-use. Tommy decided to make a sleeve that fitted inside the original bore, I want to call it a heli-coil, but my ignorance is showing I think, out of a piece of tubular aluminium. The engine hadn't fired yet in all his other attempts to get it to start. He made this insert and fitted a smaller bore spark plug into the cylinder head. The compressor had a pull cord to start it. Tommy wound the cord around the flywheel and let it go. There was a bang as the compressor fired and the spark plug launched into space. The aluminium was too soft. I was dumbstruck. Tommy had had his head just over the cylinder head before he pulled the cord, it could have been the end for him. His reaction was a grin and acknowledgement that the metal was too soft, but "It fired though didn't it?" and set about finding something more suitable. He found a brass pipe joint that he could work with and completed the job. The compressor worked fine. He later used it to spray my first car.

I have some understanding of mechanics and it's mostly down to him. The times he's helped me with my car, he'd say "Well you strip it down until you need a hand, get the manual and follow it. It makes me smile thinking about what he gets up to, it's not text book stuff but its effective most of the time. The most amusing part is; if it's something he really wants to do, if it doesn't work, he just tries something different until it does. He'll persevere with the job he's started with, until he knows he has absolutely no chance of making it fit for purpose. I'd lose patience and kick it long before that and give up. He just tosses it to one side and starts again with a different approach. Loads of patience and know how, masses of trial and error and fearlessness about tackling almost anything mechanical. "Think positive, it's going to work" he says.

The Marina is a canal boat mooring site situated next to a pub. The quickest way to reach it when approaching from the Ormskirk direction is across land that used to be a British Naval Airbase during the Second World War, locally known as the airfield. I gave Trish her first go at driving there. At that time, the old control tower was still there and the roads were little more than wide potholed tracks. Tricia nearly wrecked the car driving fairly quickly through all the deep potholes. "How was I to know to drive around the potholes?" she said, I suppose she was right. It was a poor decision on my part, for choosing a potholed road in the first place. Well she was always right anyway, like any woman, so what the hell.

These days the airfield is an industrial estate with well maintained service roads. As we drove through the industrial estate, I was listening to the engine and feeling the gear changes while discussing with Tommy the work that needed doing to get it back to A1 with my mind. We talked but we never spoke a word.

The workshop is an old container filled with an inaccessible workbench, tools, outboard engines bits and pieces of anything that might conceivably have a re-cycle value in the world of marine engines and boat fittings. The office is a caravan that previously provided many years of family service on a caravan site in Towyn North Wales, before being transported up to the Marina.

The first thing Tommy does when he arrives is have coffee between 10.30am and 11.00am. Then after a couple of hours work he has his lunch break, coffee and sandwiches. It's at these times he gets regular visitors who persist for years at a time, even when they stop, there is always somebody to take their place. They come in, have coffee, chat, talk about work they are doing or have done on engines, bikes, cars etc.

This day one of Tommy's regulars was chatting about their mutual interest of country music, they used to go to Pontins for the country and western week and wear all the costumes, hats, shirts etc. Fred was in his late sixties or seventies, white hair, small man, a little overweight. He pulled out a blue cowboy shirt with a white bib on it.

Fred: Tommy would look good in this bib don't you think?
Tommy: It's not my bib it's yours.

There was a tension about the way they were speaking, not in reality, in their minds. There was one-upmanship going on.

Fred: I let him into my secrets and he uses them for his own benefit
Tommy: That's the way it goes, you scratch my back I scratch yours, I take your junk and put it to good use.

Fred: "Bought this shirt down at the market, what do you think?"

Tommy: I like the colour, did you see the stall at the last convention, they had very similar stuff but it was really expensive.

Fred: It's all banter, it's all vying for control, and I'll teach you how to defend yourself so you can join the fun.

B: I don't want to join the fun, I'm happy the way I am.

Tommy: If you want to get through life you have to learn to give and take, let it all wash over you so it doesn't drive you crazy.

Fred: "I saw that stall, but you know me for a bargain, had my eye on these for a while, wasn't sure about whether they would fit or not."

Tommy: He's going to look a prat in that one.

Fred: At least I'll be a happy prat. What are you going to wear next time, or are you just not going to play.

Tommy: I'll be playing the disguised cowboy.

Fred: I can teach you, I'm taking my boat out for two weeks, come along I'll help you cope with the world.

Tommy: It would do you good; you'll have time to learn with nobody around.

B: When are you leaving?

Fred: In about an hour or so. I have some things to do but then I'm off for a secluded boat trip, just me and my thoughts.

B: Will it help?

Fred: what is your alternative, where are you going to go, what are you going to do?

Tommy: It's up to you, you never know in this life what's around the corner.

Tommy and Fred chatted the way they do and I listened and waited, thinking I may be going on a boat trip, not sure if it was the right thing to do.

If you want answers, I have answers for you?

B: Who am I speaking to?

You don't need to know just now, all you need to know is that I understand

B: How do you understand?

I'm the pivot in your network, everything goes through me, and I have knowledge and understanding.

B: So where am I heading, why is this happening to me?

Well you are not going on a boat trip, you will learn little from the mundane dross of everyday chit chat. Haven't you learned anything yet, it's not happening to you, it just is, we all experience it, we are just at different stages of development. Some have learned by choice, some by birth, some by experience and some by oppression.

B: *And what of me? What path am I walking?*

Like everybody else, you are walking your own. You have to find a clear space to talk with me, you have to be alone and you have to have only my voice in your head. I will help you to see the way forward, I will give you purpose and I will give you clarity of thought. Find that place.

Fred had gone off to attend to something or other. I don't even believe he had a boat; he was just a caller at the Marina and a friend of Tommy's. I spoke to Tommy "I have to go, I don't know where I'm going but I have to go and I am not sure when I will be back"

"You can't just wander off Kev, give me a minute, I've just got a couple of things to sort out"

Tommy was busy in the workshop. I turned and walked off across the car park to the pub. I crossed the swing bridge to the far side of the canal and headed towards Burscough, all the time the anonymous voice in my head encouraged and guided my thoughts.

I was about half a mile down the towpath when I heard a voice shouting behind me. "Kev, Kev, stop wait a minute" I turned and stopped waiting for Tommy to catch up with me. He took a minute or so to catch up. When he eventually stood before me he could hardly speak. He was not one for exercise and had basically done none for most of his adult life. He was really out of breath and distressed. "Where are you going, come back, we can work things out" "I have to go, if you don't leave me, I will dive in the canal and swim to the other side" "I know you can do that Kevin, you need to come back with me and we can talk" "I'm sorry I have to go" Tommy knew I was serious and that if he persisted I would have swam away from him. We exchanged no other words and he turned and walked slowly back to the Marina. Later I found Mandy was incensed I'd put Tommy through this ordeal and her words to hand were always "As long as your alright" with the emphasis on your. Typically the kind of reaction I received from friends and family who know there is something wrong, but can't bridge the gap of believing the grasp of the rational can be lost in some-one seemingly functioning in all other aspects.

I carried on walking into Burscough, talking all the time to the anonymous voice. Joining the main road I headed towards Rufford. Before you leave the town there is now a Tesco on the left hand side. I turned right approximately at the same point and just kept walking. I walked out of the town and into the country and came across a railway bridge. Climbing the embankment I lay down close to the rails. It was a hot sunny day, it was peaceful and still. I chatted with the anonymous voice for what seemed like ages and fell asleep.

It was still mid afternoon when I woke up. Gathering my thoughts I headed back the way I had came. I was telling Tommy that I would call by soon and chatting with the anonymous voice. Our conversation had explored my current situation and where I was heading, but I was not convinced there were any answers for me, all I had was the comfort of somebody being there and answering my questions. I began to think that I had to travel again, maybe catch a train, possibly to Middlesbrough to start my quest of re-visiting the past.

When I reached the Marina, instead of crossing the bridge and walking across to the workshop, I stayed on the opposite canal bank and walked on by in the direction of Liverpool. At the next swing bridge, about half a mile down the canal bank I crossed back again and took the road towards Southport. After a little while, I came to a pub on the left hand side of the road. By this time I was weary from walking, hungry and thirsty.

Ordering a pint of lager and a toasted sandwich with chips, the barmaid said she would bring the food over. The bar was sparsely filled with people going about their business.

Regular 1: Here's the stag come for watering ha ha ha.

Regular 2: He's not a stag, he's a dog, look at the way he's sitting and the way he's dressed

I shifted in my seat and sat upright

Regular 3: That's right lad, make yourself comfortable

I looked around the bar to see who was talking to me, people just seemed to be getting on with themselves, and I slumped in my seat again, tapping at the base of the table with my foot.

Regular 1: Yeah, he's definitely a dog, see he can't help himself.

My drink was about a quarter gone and the food had not yet arrived or been paid for. I stood up and walked out of the bar heading towards Southport. I had to get to the railway station and jump on a train to Middlesbrough. The sun was still shining and it was a hot hazy afternoon, I walked for about twenty minutes or so down the narrow lane and a police car appeared on the horizon. I thought nothing of it as it was a straight road, no other way to go for me or the car, but when it drew near it stopped and the policemen got out.

I can't really remember what they said, I was assuming somebody in the pub had called them because I hadn't paid for my meal. The truth was that Tommy had been on the phone to Tricia and between them they had been in touch with the police who were out looking for me. I was taken to a local police station, having no idea where it was and waited for Tricia and her brother Andy to come and pick me up. Tricia and Andy spent a good time trying to persuade the police to transport me to Clatterbridge Hospital, but they were adamant it was not their responsibility and advised them they should do it themselves.

So under duress, Andy, with Tricia in the passenger seat, drove me to Clatterbridge Hospital. I sat in the back saying nothing, but both of them were extremely nervous because they were aware of my state of mind. At one point I appeared between them and greeted them with a loud hello. Retrospectively, they both said this was one of the most nerve wracking moments they had experienced, a bit like the "here's Johnny" part from the Shinning.

On reaching the hospital, I jumped out of the car almost before it had stopped and without looking back or acknowledging the pair walked into the hospital. They were expecting me and I was admitted.

The first person I spoke to properly was Simon in Kensington ward, the guy who had almost broke my wrists the first time I was admitted. I thought he was the anonymous voice from Burscough and he greeted me with the words "You're the boss. We chatted for a while and he led me to the common room to sit and relax. Another nurse was there but we didn't speak out loud.

Nurse: We want to test you, how you've developed.
B: What do you mean?
Nurse: Mixing minds, I have experience and you have yours, do you want to try?
B: yes.
Nurse: Focus on something nearby and relax.

I stared blankly out of the window. After a few moments I felt like my mind was reviewing everything I had done at an immense pace.

Nurse: Hold it there, you're doing fine.

It was as if my thoughts were being checked, reviewed and downloaded. Then the reciprocal transfer started, the guy was an artist, I could see beautiful shapes and images played out on the glass I was staring at, not in true vision, in the form of coloured suggestions of images typical of when you can see colours glancing off the floaters in your eyes when you aren't looking at anything in particular. Or maybe that's just my experience.

I was convinced our minds were being mixed and I sat until the feeling drained away. One of the staff brought in a bag of chips for the nurse and he spread the bag open on the table started to eat with his fingers saying, "Help yourself Kev." So I did.

I suppose the times spent re-cooperating in hospital are pretty much similar. Having to establish yourself with the other patients; having to protect yourself in some ways. I would break into song un-expectantly, walk up and down continuously until I was settled and able to chat with the other patients, but it is a very difficult environment. Everybody is ill, to one degree or another, and everybody is coping in their own way. You often feel very much worse before you start to feel better due to the interaction with other patients. To start feeling well you need to feel secure, but that's the very last thing the situation allows, the feeling of security only comes with experience of the situation and knowing what to expect. As every time you are admitted there are different people with different problems so you learn to cope and eventually the medication starts working properly and you progress. By the time you are ready for discharge; things have calmed considerably. In my case, every time, it is the prelude to over six months of a morose depression, as the medication is managed to a therapeutic level.

Episode 3

I can't remember very much about the build up to episode three. I do remember a sunny morning and I had gone out for a walk on my own which was an unusual thing for me to do. I would normally have been with Tricia and my son, or just my son, but this day, I was walking around Upton on my own. I walked towards Saughall Massie, passing a large tree I noticed it was growing at an angle.

Trish is bent.

I started thinking Tricia was keeping things from me and she was out to deceive me. Walking around I thought about the ways in which Tricia and her family were plotting against me over my son. It was never a difficult jump to make in my mind as I had lived all my married life with Tricia despising my mother. My father had lost contact with his family when I was about five or six because his mother and my mother could not get along. The only contact I had from then on was from my maternal family. It was something that annoyed me for many years. History was now repeating itself. I knew my mother was the common denominator but I couldn't understand why Tricia couldn't just do as I did when I met her parents, be civil and get on with things. After all I had no great affinity to them, although in time I came to respect Vera, her mum, just because of her grasp of life. Pretty typical of Liverpool women from her background I suppose. We never had a great deal of contact. Sometimes you just know when people mean well, without ever doing a great deal to try and say they do. Anyway, not only had I lost a large part of my family, my son was about to experience the same.

As I said, I can't remember much about how this episode progressed. I know for some reason my sister found out that I was not feeling too good and she came across to visit. Tracy had been working for some time now with her friend Gina, who was a professional Michael Jackson tribute act. The pair of them had worked in numerous places with other tribute acts and Tracy's conversation was about meeting these people and chatting with them. She was using their stage names and giggling saying things like "I was talking to Tom Jones and Shirley Bassey came over and asked to borrow a pen." She named about ten different stars with stories to match and laughed repeatedly. While all this was going on I had the voices of the real stars in my head and I was laughing along too. I thought Tracy was laughing at the same things as I was laughing at, the joke being she could talk about all these tribute acts in reality, because they were real events, but she didn't have to acknowledge the voices in her head and my head in reality as this was not common practice and a sign of madness. So we chatted and laughed about her experiences on the tribute circuit. At the same time, I thought we shared conversations in our minds with the actual stars. Tricia knew I wasn't re-acting normally yet Tracy never seemed to notice any difference.

When the weekend came, I got out of bed quite early. It was a sunny morning and I decided to go and see Andy, Tricia's brother. I was following through the scenario of Tricia and her family deceiving me and I rang him to arrange to go to Southport. I can't think of any reason why I chose Southport, it just seemed like a good idea on such a sunny morning.

Andy and I had always got along quite well together. I accept we were in each other's company because he was coming to see his sister, but given that, we rubbed along quite well. Andy and Sally, his wife, had visited regularly over the years and we'd often have food and get drunk together and Andy and I occasionally played football and squash together, so there was no reason for me to have any malicious thoughts hanging around in the back of my mind towards Andy. Here I was though, knocking on his door at 9.00am on a Saturday morning. I was invited in and we walked through the house into the garden. Andy and Sally both acted their usual selves and we chatted for a few minutes in the garden. I then asked Andy to come to Southport with me. I can't remember the reason I gave, I just know he agreed and we set off in my car.

I remember I didn't speak too much on the way, my mind was focused on how close Andy and I had been and why things had changed. He stretched his hand out near the gear stick I was holding and with my mind I asked him if he was homosexual.

Andy: What kind of a question is that?
B: Well either you are or you're not?

The communication was stilted and uncomfortable, even in the mind.

When we arrived I parked the car on Promenade about 250 metres south of the junction with Nevill Street. We walked in the direction of the Southport Theatre. In my mind Andy and I were commenting on the females walking past. They were answering his thoughts and he was flirting with them all.

Andy: See Kev, anyone can do it. You're not the only person that can talk to people and chat up the women.

B: So why didn't you tell me this from the start, how was I supposed to know?

Andy: You can't be told, it just has to happen, if I had explained it to you, you would never have believed me.

We had walked past the theatre and turned and started to walk back in the direction of the car. It must have been really strange experience for Andy, first of all I'd asked him to come out here which was unusual, it was still quite early so there wasn't a great deal of life about and I wasn't talking much at all. He was obviously trying to work out what was wrong with me or probably thinking I was building up to sharing something I needed to get off my chest. In any case he showed no sign of frustration or wanting to hurry me along. We walked back past the car still heading south on Promenade. Without warning I turned to Andy and said let's sprint the rest of the way down the road. Andy said he didn't want to run, "What's the matter with you, come on it'll be good" with that I took off down Promenade sprinting as fast as I could. I ran about 200metres and stopped resting my hands on my knees catching my breath. I was thinking this is good, it feels great.

B: *Are you watching Southport?*

Going into a football training routine, I started doing star jumps and then clapping over my head. Side stepping back down the Promenade in the direction of Andy. I stopped and looked at him, raising both arms as if asking for the ball in an attacking situation. I was thinking 'this is what footballers do'. I was getting attention from passersby and I was roaring at Andy occasionally to come and meet me. Running and jumping doing imaginary headers and then I'd stop and raise a hand signaling wanting to be played into the game.

After a while I met up with Andy again. He was looking concerned, I confronted him almost immediately. "What's it going to be Andy, me or you? It's fifty-fifty, who's going to come out on top? Come on me and you now" "I don't want to fight with you Kevin" "Come on Andy, hit me, fucking hit me we'll see how it turns out" "I don't want to hit you Kev" I started pushing him in the chest "Fucking hit me you twat" I pushed him in the face. Two policemen emerged from the direction of the marine lake. They had been notified of somebody running up and down Promenade shouting and had come up behind us.

"What the fuck are you up to?"

I turned and walked directly to the policeman who had shouted and stood in front of him.

"Who the fuck wants to know"

"What are you doing here?"

"I've just come for a trip out with my brother in law and we are just having a walk"

"We've had complaints about your behaviour; you are going to have to accompany us to the police station"

I didn't argue I calmed down quite quickly; the policeman handcuffed me and put me in the back of the Landrover while he talked to Andy. When we set off for the police station, the two policemen started chatting. I joined in, they completely ignored me. At the police station I waited to see a doctor, the police were in my head.

Police: You will learn about the power of the mind, we don't play games here.

B: What do you mean?

I asked if I could get some air, I was led to an area in the station yard it was enclosed by bars. After staying there for about 15 minutes I tried to return to the station. It was blocked by bars. The police had blocked my mind from seeing the bars on the way in, I had no idea it was enclosed, now I was locked in. In my mind the police were instructing me how they used their powers based on the strength of their network. They listened and monitored communication with the mind. They placed ideas in people's heads; they could make people see things that are not there and in some instances control body movements by suggestions. In different circumstances I should have been a policeman as my mind was conducive to control and a potentially good conductor of the will of the police network.

After some time I was let out of the yard area and placed in one of the cells. At about 2.00pm I was brought a meal in a take away container. Feeling hungry it looked appetising but I couldn't help noticing it was upside down. The rice was on top of the curry. I thought this must be a standard joke to prisoners, upside down meals. Apparently, I could not be moved until late afternoon because I had chosen the day of the Apprentices March (A march of some description anyway) to take Andy to Southport. The police thought we had been there in connection with the march and had just arrived early and got out of hand. So it was about 4.00pm when I was loaded handcuffed into police transit van with four policemen on board. On the way out the policeman who had arrested me was sitting by the doorway, he opened his mouth and stuck his tongue out pointing to it. "Your tongue.... it was blue" I took this to mean I had spoken the way policemen speak and I was one of them. The police chatted all the way, eyeing up the female talent and commenting on them as we went. I sat quietly listening to their instructions in my mind.

At Clatterbridge I was taken to Buckingham ward to be checked in. Carrie, a nurse was on the door. She spoke to the policemen bringing me in, "You don't like it when one of your own is on the streets do you?" I thought she referred to the fact that I could communicate with people with my mind and I understood about how it could be used. The handcuffs were taken off and I was admitted to the ward. Walking around the ward I assessed the people that were in it. There was one man who was quite vocal, he had a range of drawings, he was copying Slavador Dahli from memory and saying how intellectually superior he was to all the staff on the ward. I thought this was the source of the atmosphere and began to 'cut' it by walking swiftly around the ward. It wasn't long before I was transferred to Windsor ward where I eventually reacted to treatment over time and was discharged.

Episode 4

IN THE RUN up to episode four I had been slowly losing my grip on reality for several weeks. I had taken to writing poetry as a way of expressing the feelings I had about my mental health condition and about life in general. Some of it was thought provoking but much of it was over sentimental and not particularly good. I became engrossed in writing and shared my output with my immediate managers in work. I don't know what they were thinking at the time, but my mind was not right at all and I was having involuntary thoughts throughout the build up to becoming seriously ill again. I eventually published my collection of poems with a vanity publisher, Biographical Paradox, something I thought I would treasure for the rest of my life. In fact it is something I was more embarrassed about. Like this book however, there are elements of mania in the things I have put down in writing and to understand them properly, it is important to recognise the output is coloured by an unstable mind. Mentally, I am passed the embarrassed stage because I can appreciate now the circumstances of writing. At the time, when I was publishing my work, I didn't think there was anything wrong with me. I may not have been in a full blown manic episode, but my decision making was poor. I read all the revues about vanity publishing, understood that I was very unlikely to get my money back at all and still I carried on. But then, that has not been an isolated example of my indifference to the loss of money. I have paid out over £2,000 to enroll for training to become a driving instructor and left the course after two weeks, bought a franchise that was impossible for me to break even and bought a brand new van to run the business. All in all, in the space of 12 months in 2006 I lost about £20,000 and chalked up another £24,000 worth of debt. In terms of how I feel about throwing this money away, it is indifference. I tried to achieve something whilst not accepting the limitations of my condition, so I put it down to experience. A costly one at that, but one I have never really lost any sleep over. I have a destiny that is beyond my understanding and I am just going to follow life and see where I land. For one short period in 2006, I lost the will to carry on and I overdosed on my risperidone. I know the thought was that it was a cry for help because I told my ex-wife I had done this, but in truth nobody puts large amounts of any substance into their body, with no knowledge of what effect it may have, if they didn't have a desire to end it all. For all I know it could easily have been an irreversible fatal dose.

This was 1996 though; I had been trying to manage without medication for some time. Fitness wise I was in good shape. I had trained for and completed the London Marathon in April and was playing five-a-side about three times a week. Mentally things had slowly worsened and on this day, Tricia had taken our son and left the house the night before, she was probably staying with either her mum or with Andy because she knew I wasn't well.

In work I had become paranoid, one day when I was sitting taking a brief from Dennis, my manager, Geraldine, the senior manager came over and started to talk across us. I was sure she was being vindictive and smart in her conversation, although this was imputed by me, her actual words did not have the meaning I was taking. I became very irritated and then for no particular reason I passed out, my head banged down on the desk in front of Dennis. The next thing I remember was the nurse coming into the room shouting "Who needs my attention?" or something similar. I was taken to the medical suite and sent home for the afternoon.

On a daily basis in work, I was getting bogged down with repetitive tasks; I thought I was being deliberately targeted to stop me having the time to think things through properly. If you are constantly answering the telephone, managing data, proof reading etc, you never have the time to consider project work and develop new procedures or come up with alternative solutions. I even reported Dennis to the product manager for delaying progress. Stuart was the overall Project Manager, as he was the Investments Product Manager. I grabbed some time with him while he sat at one of the free desks in the open plan office. I was speaking really slowly and really deliberately in a low, monotone, not a quiet voice. I was outlining my reservations and saying what I thought needed addressing. It must have been really strange because it was not a natural way of communicating. I was obviously troubled and the things I was talking about were not the issues for me that needed addressing. The fact was that after it became common knowledge amongst the management team about my illness, I had been demoted to a lower level and I was unused to the administration side of the work I was now expected to do. In my own little world I was trying to think tactically about the sales support material we were producing, both in its design and usage, but I was in fact on the production line. I used my poetry to distract Geraldine. She showed some interest, but knowing the sequence of events I think Geraldine had more than a little feel that something was not quite right. In time she was to instigate the best help I have ever received by getting me put on LTD or long term disability. I received 2/3 of my income whilst on LTD and remained on it for over three years, but as usual with myself, I fought to come of it to go back to work instead of accepting it was probably my best form of financial security and I self destructed as usual. Geraldine and I were never friends but she was in my opinion professional and I can appreciate the help she gave me now. When she was reading my poems I thought 'It's me that's usually proof reading, now you can do it for me'. Ridiculous, I know, but that's how my mind was working.

I remember sitting at my desk trying to proof read a product brochure I had been working on. It was a new product launch and I had been coordinating all the promotional material. I got up from my desk and walked across to Geraldine and just said, "Geraldine, I can't do this anymore" "Take a seat Kev, do you want a drink." I turned and pointed and said "I have one on my desk" "Do you want me to go and get it?" "No thank you, I don't need it "I need to go Geraldine" I spoke to her and tried to explain. "I'm not feeling too good and Tricia has moved out." The previous night Tricia had told me she wasn't staying in the house with me in the condition I was in and she had taken the kids and gone to stay with her family. The outcome was that I left the building and headed for Kirkby to see my Mum and Dad.

Driving up towards Melling Mount the local lads started pulling my leg.

Kirkby lads: Going to your mum's for tea and cakes?

B: We always have tea and cakes.

Kirkby lads: (laughter) we know, go on have some, it's nice you know (more laughter)

B: Well it is that's what mums do (laughing).

Kirkby lads: They don't speak to us you know.

Dad: Who said that?

Knocking on the door my dad answered.

Dad: Oh it's you. Your mad, what's all this about?

"Hi dad, how are you?" "Ok your mum's inside"

"Hiya Kev, I'll just put the kettle on"

Kirkby lads: (laughing): tea and cakes is it?

Dad: Yes

We chatted as usual, I told them I had come out of work because I didn't feel too good and I told them that Tricia had left home for the evening. After an hour or so I told them I needed to go out for a walk. I set off towards Tower Hill dressed in my office clothes, I walked around Kirkby talking with my mind to the people I passed, listening to a whole host of people but also including a number of schoolboy bullies who had been around while I was going through school. I never really had any problems at secondary school, no more than anybody else. At primary school, I was a little vulnerable as I had grown up in what people used to call the posh part of Kirkby. I didn't experience the rough and tumble of living in Kirkby until the age of 5 and it was a bit of a shock. From the age of six I used to walk home from school in the evening about a mile and a half. Nearly every night I used to get chased by a group of boys the same age as me. They never caught up with me so it must have been half hearted because I was really slow, but I was terrified. You can't exactly call them bullies though I wouldn't have thought. Even in junior school I was naïve and took a little amount of stick. There was one lad who I thought was really evil and thought if I ever meet him as an adult I'll lay him out. He was in fact a member of the group of friends I used to hang about with. You have to laugh, he's a catholic priest and I don't suppose he did anything much worse than any other kid, but even into my late twenties if I had seen him about I would have punched him. Anyway, apart from those minor instances when I was very young, I never really suffered at the hands of bullies. But they were about and some kids had a hard time and I always felt they would pounce if you gave them an opportunity.

So I walked about, the voices from the past filled my head with the mindless minority were goading and threatening to make my life hell. In the meantime I was also chatting to my family who were asking if I was going to call in. I walked about for some time before heading back towards Melling Mount. On approaching where the railway bridge crosses the road a police car pulled up next to me. My mother had called them to say I was wandering around on my own. They asked me to get in the car and drove me to my parent's house. I was wondering what the fuss was all about and also a bit nervous in case the police decided to take me to hospital. As it was I settled down at my parents and had something to eat. It was decided that I would stay the night at my parents as Tricia was not at home.

Throughout the evening I was constantly distracted, not in an agitated way. I would just stare blankly at the TV. I was in concentrating on the conversations in my mind rather than what was going on around me. My mother continued to make conversation with me and I reciprocated without really acknowledging what she was talking about. I was just on automatic, answering as best as I could while keeping a closer track on the exchanges going on in my head. This behaviour was fairly typical at this stage of mania. I think it was one of the main pointers Tricia used to decide if I was well or not. I could snap out of it for periods and appear normal, but it's not like the pre-occupied male syndrome women usually deal with, its more intense and I am totally engrossed with thoughts that do not relate to my surroundings at all. The malevolent exchanges with what used to be kids at my school increased and the threats were getting heavier and heavier. That's the way they worked at school, they'd threaten you and see if you showed any sign of being scared of them, if you did, they would move on to the next level, controlling and manipulating. This wasn't schoolyard stuff though; it had gangland connotations and threats against my personal welfare.

My parents went off to bed at about 11.00pm; I stayed up running over the things in my head. I'm not sure how long I waited but at some point I just thought I've had enough of this and I walked out the door.

B: I don't care who you are or what kind of gang you think you are in, you're the same old individuals to me. I'm out on the streets and I'm going to walk wherever I choose, this is my home and I'll meet any one of you.

Police: Watch it Rowan, we don't need any trouble here.

B: I'm just walking around, no trouble from me.

Police: We've brought you in once today, we'll take you to the station next time.

B: You'll have to have a reason and I'm not going to give you one.

Police: We are watching you.

I walked all around Kirkby that night starting with Tower Hill, both the electric and the gas side. In my youth it was a dilapidated area with deserted flats providing sinister walkways which I used to visit Tricia, either riding my racing bike or on foot. Moorfield also had a number of houses demolished because of subsidence and the walkways were often used by joy riders in stolen cars. It had changed for the better and today you can't even recognise the place as the same. I called out with my mind as I went.

B: I'm here in Tower Hill if anybody is interested?

Walking through to the town centre I noticed how quiet it was. There were a few youths shouting in the distance and then silence. Walking towards the Golden Eagle Hotel remembering the first time I got served at a bar at 16, I turned right and headed off towards Westvale. I headed straight for Susan's house, my first real girlfriend, I was about 14 at the time and it only lasted a matter of weeks but it took years and years to get her out of my system. She was brilliant, two years younger than me, but taller and loud and robust mentally. She was pretty too, must be true what they say about first love. I stood in front of where she used to live.

B: Susan, remember when I came and asked you out for a second time here and you said no?

Susan: Go away Kev, it was a long time ago.

B: I'm not here to see you tonight, I'm just here to walk about and see if anybody wants to meet me.

I walked around stopping outside houses where old friends used to live, acknowledging the changes to the environment and telling anybody that was listening where I was with my mind. Walking passed Helen's house I stopped to think. We both swam for Kirkby and trained together regularly, well with everybody else in the team of course. Helen was a good looking girl; one or two people suggested we should go out together. I had a mental block, she'd been a girlfriend of one of my close friends previously and she was to go out with another of my friends as well. I could never quite get to grips with seeing a girl who was with or had been with one of my friends and it's something that lingers even today. It's crazy I know but it just didn't seem right to me. I stood outside Helen's house and made my apologies.

From there I walked through the narrow lane between the park and St Chad's Church. It was dark and the graveyard was a favourite place for kids to visit in the night, not en-mass, just kids seeking a bit of a thrill occasionally, being in a spooky place, or at least I did with a few friends when I was younger. I didn't hang around there, never did, and just passed through mostly at night. Northwood was next and then Southdene. Anywhere I could ever remember for any reason. Anyplace I thought the sinister voices in my head said I couldn't go, I walked there and broadcast my whereabouts. It was well into the early hours by the time I got home and I slept.

Returning home the following day, the house was still empty. It was about 10.00am and my mind had turned to work. There were a couple of lads in their early twenties at work who both worked in the same department as me. They were good fun and the banter was quite good. Both lads were called Terry and they were in my head giving me a hard time about why I was not in work. The conversation turned to manipulation of the mind as they understood it, after all they were communicating with me now. For some reason I was saying I believed the world was about to end and I was laughing. They laughed along too saying 'oh yes the worlds about to end so you're lying on your couch at home waiting for it to happen'. I was laughing a real manic laugh and it made my stomach muscles ache. They could hear the laugh and feel the ache in their stomachs and became agitated. This wasn't supposed to happen, they could feel my feeling and they became scared and stopped communicating with me.

Getting up from the sofa I decided to go to the gym. I left the house and walked through Upton. It was deserted. I thought this is it; it is true about the impending end of the world. People had gone away to prepare for the end.

At the gym I walked into reception and Lisa was on duty. Lisa had really taken my eye; she was about 30 and very pretty. She was demonstrating exercises in the reception area to a bald middle aged man. She knew she was teasing him and he was almost salivating as she opened and closed her legs in front of him. He pestered her for some time after she finished. He had a Morgan sports car in the car park. I walked up behind him and encouraged him to go out to look at his car. When we were alone, I told him to stop pestering Lisa. Back in the reception, I walked up to the desk; Lisa was still alone. "Would you come out with me for a cup of tea and a chat some time?"

B: Will you marry me?

Lisa: Yes

Lisa looked at me and just said "More sugar" I didn't put two and two together and was confused by her response so I repeated "Will you come for a cup of tea somewhere with me?"

She just replied again "More sugar."

It was only after, I thought about the situation after I had recovered that I realised what she meant, it was just an alien thought for me that she should be interested in predominantly tangible benefits before getting to know somebody. Well, naïve I've always been. As I was not getting anywhere I left the gym and walked home again. When I arrived home Tricia had returned and wanted to know where I had been and what I had been up to. I told her about going to my parents and I told her about going to the gym, I said I had just asked somebody to marry me and she had said yes. I didn't say I had done this with my mind and been answered in the same way. Tricia was furious and went up to the gym to confront Lisa. I don't know what she said exactly but I think she explained that I was unwell and also had words with her.

That evening I set off for Ormskirk. I had been chatting with work colleagues in my head. There was a lot of laughing and joking and we were going to meet up at a restaurant and have a meal. From my mental arrangements, we were supposed to meet about 8pm and I was running about 5 minutes late. Parking the car in the first available space I found, I headed to the main shopping area. I didn't know which restaurant we were supposed to meet in, but I found a nice cozy place and broadcast to my friends where I would be. I entered the restaurant and waited for a table drinking bottle of beer. Before long the waitress asked me what I wanted to order and I looked at the menu and couldn't make my mind up. The waitress chose for me recommending one of the platters. Asking if anybody wanted to share the meal I'd chosen, in my mind, I got a positive response and I ordered the meal for two, some form of nacho's and dips, I can't remember now. I sat eating and communicating, waiting for my friends to arrive. It dragged on and on and one by one they made their excuses and said they were not coming. Unabashed I finished up, paid for the meal and left the restaurant.

Walking around Ormskirk, I became very aware of a 'force' that was directing my movements. I could override it if I felt like, but if I left my senses open, I could feel my body being urged to go in one direction or another. I walked around for about thirty minutes just following this 'instinct' sometimes just walking around in circles, other times crossing roads when I felt the direction to do so, or turning down a particular road or street. When it came time to return to the car, I had forgotten where I had parked it. I walked around the town centre two or three times trying to remember where I had left the car. I started to panic thinking I would not find it at all and then I stumbled across it when I had almost given up hope. I travelled home and went to sleep.

The next day Tricia would not let me settle, she kept asking me about my behaviour trying to impress upon me that I was not well. Towards the end of the afternoon she was at her wits end and she contacted a family support group to arrange to come and take me to Clatterbridge Hospital. I think they were social workers and they came and chatted at length trying to persuade me to accompany them to the hospital. I thought I was reacting normally to their conversation and indeed they were not entirely sure of themselves, but maybe in hindsight this was because I was not reacting as expected. Eventually I got in the car with them and chatted along as we made our way to the hospital. On arriving at the hospital I walked quickly away from both of them, trying to get as much distance between me and them as possible. They tried calling me and tried to speak to me further, but I just wanted them out of the picture. It was arranged that I would have an interview with one of the doctors to see if I needed to be admitted. The social workers stayed outside the meeting room. The doctor was speaking slow and deliberate, I mimicked him only spoke much slower and deeper. "W---h----y a---r----e y--o---u t---a--l--k--i--n--g s---o s---l---o---w---l---y?" and then I said "If I talk quickly does it make any difference to the way you understand" and I speeded up my speech until it sounded like a long player record played at 45rpm. The doctor was sitting in his chair and I had got up from my chair and perched myself on a desk alternately speaking slowly and then more quickly, questioning his interview technique. Not un-expectantly I was admitted to the ward.

I was given a bed in one of the communal rooms and settled down for the night. In the morning I was up about 8am and decided I wanted to leave. I started exploring the ground floor, the main door was not yet open, and the windows only opened a fraction. I had the computer game 'LittleBigAdventure2' going through my head and imagined trying to find a solution to a problem by trying different approaches. Giving up on the window, I walked into the gym area, there was a fire door by the snooker table, I pushed the bar and walked out of the building.

It took me a couple of hours to walk home. Tricia had been warned I was coming and was at the police station. As I walked past the station I saw her car in the car park and I walked in. The police showed me to the room she was in talking with some police officers. I started talking to them saying, "She thinks I'm crazy, it's not me that's mad it's her" I was a little convincing or more likely the police were making me feel comfortable because they started listening to me for a while. Tricia couldn't believe it and became agitated. Eventually common sense won the day and I was taken back to the hospital. That was not the first nor the last time I walked home from Clatterbridge but once admitted you were never allowed to stay away for very long, I suppose that's the beauty of being sectioned.

The stay in hospital escapes me for the most now but towards the end of my stay when I was going home on leave to get used to everyday life again, I went out and bought a mountain bike. One of the nurses used to travel to work on a push bike and had come in one day when it had been pouring down with rain. She was alive with the experience and I thought I have to do that, get out on a bike in all weathers. My next weekend leave, without telling Tricia my plans, I took a bus into Birkenhead and jumped the train through to Liverpool. Heading for Halfords on Hanover Street I went straight to the bicycle section picking out a mountain bike. The salesman was really helpful suggesting I needed a luggage rack and he fitted it onto the machine. Choosing a protective helmet and paying by credit card, I took the bike outside and set off for Kirkby to see my parents as usual at the weekend.

It was a sunny day and as usual I wore a T-shirt so my arms were bare. I happened to be on largactyl (I think, a drug that was solar sensitive anyway.) at that time and the sun caused a reaction to my skin. My arms itched and became red in the sunlight. I had always loved getting out in the sun and I couldn't imagine living with that as a side effect for any length of time. I called in at my grandparent's house, my cousins who I never visited, the next door neighbour I used to live by when I was a child and eventually my parents. My mum was worried I had cycled all this way and suggested I should get a lift back from my dad. He just shrugged and smiled saying "You've started something you should finish it." After chatting for a while I got back on my cycle and rode home the way I had come. On reaching Upton, I stopped at the fruit shop at Upton Cross and bought a bag of plums. Balancing the bag of plums on the handlebar and freewheeling down the short distance to where I lived I turned into our estate and bumped into Peter from work. I was hyper about my journey and animated. We exchanged a few words and I went home.

It just illustrates really the fact that with this kind of illness, you don't get treated and then become better overnight. I was on the verge of discharge and my mind was not working properly and didn't for some time yet, but it was enough to appear in control, and enough to make the medics relaxed enough to allow me home.

I used the bike again the following weekend, after discharge, to go and look at a caravan I was considering buying to live in out Heswall way. I still wasn't stable, but there was an improvement. Soon after the medication took hold anyway and I had no desire to use a pushbike and the slow recovery started all over again.

Episode 5

1998 WAS NOT a great year for my immediate family, my mum, my dad and sister. My mother was diagnosed with ovarian cancer. She had known for some time that things were not quite right but she had an aversion to doctors and hospitals not wanting to get checked up regularly. Indeed she had had a test previously which drew concern from the doctor but refused to follow it up until it was too late. I suppose it was the last quarter of the year when it was acknowledged that mum was seriously ill. In October or November I can't remember exactly, I went to the Royal Liverpool Hospital with my mum and dad for her blood tests. From that, she was booked in for a scan at Clatterbridge Hospital. In the short time to Christmas she lost a considerable amount of weight and was booked to have treatment the week before Christmas. For some reason this was not possible and a new date early in the New Year was suggested.

Every Christmas since I was born, the family had met in my grandparent's home that they now shared with their son Tommy and his wife Mandy. This Christmas was for me was a poignant one. My mum was looking frail and her sister Elsie, who had been ill for some years and was being treated for bowel cancer and complications, greeted my mum with "You're not happy unless you've got the same as me are you?" They both laughed. We had an almost usual gathering, spent maybe an hour or so before going our separate ways. On leaving my grandma's house I was behind my mum and she said "I'll be dancing down this path next Christmas."

I was not taking any medication at this time. I was in one of those periods where I believed if I could manage my stress levels, I would remain well. Consequently, when it came to liaising with the Doctors about my mum's health I left it to my sister to deal with them; I also thought it would be better for the doctors to deal with a single contact point. My father had had a stroke a few years before, he was recovering well but he was not up to dealing with the doctors. So my sister managed the information flow. I trusted her to be open and honest, but Tracy was Tracy, I should have guessed. She put her particular spin on it, even with me, in an attempt not to worry people. I even repeated her stories to family. So right up until close to the end, mum was going to have chemotherapy and she was going to recover and everything would be fine. Then suddenly, the chemo was not going to happen and people had to be told the truth.

So early in January 1999 mum was admitted to Clatterbridge Hospital. My dad still lived in Kirkby and my sister in St Helens. It was easier for me to visit the hospital as I only lived 10 minutes away in the car, so I visited more and my dad and sister visited less. At the time I was signed off work on long term disability, I had been for two years, so I could visit during the day and used to take my daughter, who was still using a pram, to see her. I think it was for about two weeks. The Doctors had decided that the cancer was untreatable and mum had been fitted with a feeding tube.

From Clatterbridge, mum was transferred to Fazakerly Hospital. She was admitted to one of the wards. I travelled across daily, Tricia asked me to slow down and I took an evening cooking a meal and relaxing with her. Just as the meal was ready to be taken off the cooker, Tracy called. "Kevin, I'm at the hospital and we need you here. I can't cope with this, I don't know what to do" She was in tears and inconsolable. I dropped everything and jumped in the car and made my way to the hospital as fast as I could. When I arrived Tracy was with my father and she was all smiles as if nothing had happened. I couldn't believe it. She had faked being upset to get me there so she could leave. We went to the canteen and sat at a table with a cup of tea. "I rounded on her and spoke my mind about what she had done and told her I was trying to keep my stress levels down. My Father and sister just shrugged at each other. Neither had ever understood fully what happens to me. Their reaction is 'you should just pull yourself together', as if I can somehow reason myself to think right. Obviously, on their mind was 'there are more important problems than yours to consider at the moment' and I suppose it was understandable.

I left the hospital, I was fuming. Driving to my grandparent's house I was quite distressed and spoke with Tommy and Mandy and my grandmother. I asked Tommy if he would come for a drive and with some encouragement from Mandy he did. We parked up just around the corner and I just vented my anger and he listened.

I can remember the first signs of when something began to go wrong for me. I continued to spend a lot of time going to and from the hospital. My cousin's wife, Sue, worked at the hospital in the mortuary. She decided to pop up and see how my mum was getting along. However, she wasn't prepared for the sight she was about to see. My mum had deteriorated considerably and was very thin and frail. Debbie's face dropped as she turned the corner to greet mum. I was not present at the time, just Debbie and mum. The next time I came in my mum told me Debbie had visited and how she had seen the look of shock on her face. She told me she didn't want any more visits from Debbie, or anybody else and would I go along to the mortuary and tell her. Of course, I went as asked. I'm not the most diplomatic of people, just say what is needed so I told Debbie mum didn't want her to visit anymore and left it at that. Debbie never spoke another word to me and completely blanked me whenever we met ever since then. Curiously until recently at my grandmother's funeral and it was if nothing had happened.

Very soon after, Bob, my mum's sister's husband visited. He always liked to think he was capable of understanding situations and in his carefully chosen words, not meant to be offensive, but having enough edge about them to imply he knew what was going on, he would say his piece, often cased in a humorous manner. At this point the family had still been told mum was going to get better. Bob was always one for silly jokes and had a mischievous laugh. He had been telling mum some jokes and then it was time for him to leave. As extended family, Bob and his immediate family had been distant from me for many years. He could never resist the inclination to have a pop and so he did and I laughed, then he parted with the words "see you in passing."

The next time I saw mum alone, she was recounting a joke Bob had told her. I remember it had the term gatekeeper in it and I started thinking about the term meaning somebody who filters messages from the mind for somebody. So who was the gatekeeper in our family, who was filtering the messages we received and controlling the information we had. I started searching for the gatekeeper with my thoughts. The joke itself was as silly as expected and I sat with mum laughing at the absurdity of it. In fact I laughed and laughed and my mum giggled too. My mum enjoyed shared laughter and it was weird seeing her in her condition laughing along. I had Bob's voice in my head re-counting the joke and I couldn't stop myself laughing more. I had to get out of the room. I told my mum I needed the toilet and left her. I sat on the toilet one floor down stifling laughter and I couldn't stop myself. I was there for about twenty minutes trying to regain control and eventually I did.

When I returned to the ward, the nurses were making my mother comfortable and I sat in the waiting area. The waiting room was quite busy.

Hospital Visitor: Are you special?

B: No I'm not special, who said that?

Hospital Visitor: We think your special, getting special treatment.

B: who's getting special treatment?
Hospital Visitor: Your mum's getting special treatment; she's getting a private room.
B: She's very ill; it's not special treatment at all.
Hospital Visitor: All our relatives are very ill.
B: Well my mum is special to me, maybe it is special treatment.
Hospital Visitor: That's a smart answer, you should be careful.
B: Careful of what?
Hospital Visitor: Careful we don't make you regret it
B: Do what you please, I'm here, not going anywhere, and I'll be waiting
Hospital Visitor: You won't be waiting long.
B: No the nurses are done, I'm off.

I returned to my mum's bedside and we chatted for a while. She seemed a little more comfortable and I left for the day. The following day I started driving towards the hospital and my mind wandered. The threatening behaviour of the "voices" in the hospital waiting room had started me thinking about loutish behaviour and the use of mind control. I thought back to a couple of years earlier when my grandmother had been mugged whilst returning from the Post Office with her son who is downes syndrome. I was searching the airwaves for the person who did it. I was talking to people in Kirkby, trying to find information about who it was and where he was.

Kirkby voice: He's not here, he's gone.
B: I hope he's gone because I'm not going to rest until I find him.
Kirkby voice: What are you going to do?
B: Just look him in the eyes.
Kirkby voice: We sorted him out, he shouldn't have done it.
B: How do I know?
Kirkby voice: It's not your patch anymore, not your responsibility, you left it all behind.
B: I have no patch, I just come and go.
Kirkby voice: Well it's done, he's been corrected.

B: *I'll keep listening and watching.*
Kirkby voice: You know it's done.
Containing my anger whilst driving was very difficult.
Police: We're watching you Rowan, one slip up that's all it takes.
B: Fuck off plod.

I carried on past the hospital and on to my grandmother's house in Kirkby. It was only a ten minute drive from the hospital and I popped in regularly. All the time I had the conversation with the Kirkby lads and interjections from Mandy like;

Mandy: Oh yeah Kev what are you going to do?

On arrival it was surreal but expected, Mandy was talking to me about what I was doing here today and smiling and joking. It was just her friendly way but I thought she was taking the "mickey" about what I was going to do to the thug who mugged my grandmother. My grandmother's name was Katy.

Katy: What's it like to die Kevin
B: I don't know, I think it's just blackness and peace
Katy: Does it hurt?
B: I don't know.

I was talking to Mandy and communicating with grandma for about half an hour or so, then I said I had to get back to the hospital. Mandy quoted Red Dwarf, "Smoke me a kipper and I'll be back by morning." I'd come and gone so often in the past few days and was about to do more. We laughed but she didn't have any idea at that stage I wasn't with it, or at least I don't think she did.

I had also been having conversations with Sally, my sister in law.

Sally: Hi Kev, I'm here if you need me. I know it's a difficult time for you.
B: Hi Sally, thanks, just getting on with things the best I can.
Sally: Come and see me if you need to talk.
B: Thanks, I'll catch you soon.

With driving backwards and forwards from Upton to the hospital and on to Kirkby and back I had imagined that I was talking to people with my mind on the way. Mostly people passing in other cars, family, people who were visitors in the hospital, people living in the surrounding areas etc. There was an element of trying to remain calm in my thoughts under threats of violence, elements of showing my fearlessness under these threats and acknowledgement that people understood who I was and why the things that were happening to me were happening. All this, with a backdrop of being watched and monitored by the police. I was broadcasting messages constantly and a measure of my defiance to the police and was my constantly broadcasting of beats and rhythms, entertaining people who were tuned in and wakening others that had not heard before.

Typically if a song came on the radio, or I had a cassette playing in the car, I would take up the drum beat and project an image of myself playing the drums. It would be interspaced it with fireworks going off around me and then change the image to animal from the Muppets, looking up and laughing, then it would be back to my silhouette. I'd add a bass line, so the image would contain myself playing drums with a base line over the top and the lyrics to the song, broadcasting to the world. If the song had meaning to the situation I was thinking about, all the better. Later on I would have 'guest' appearances from rock and pop stars that would help out with the arrangement. When I was tackling the problems of sectarianism in my head, I'd add the sounds of a marching band and an image of some-one throwing the mace. I'd imagine I was getting help from a childhood friend Michael, who used to throw the mace brilliantly for the Boy's Brigade. I started broadcasting two songs at once. I knew that if two songs are written in 4:4 time, or in equal time anyway, you could basically splice them together, so I'd broadcast the sound and images of one song and interlaced it with the lyrics of another. I could only do this with one of the songs on the CD or the radio, but the people I was broadcasting to didn't know this. The reaction of the people in my head was incredulous:

How does he do that, projecting images as well as sound?

Are they really the people he says they are helping him out?
How do you manage to play all the parts of the band?
Police: We are watching you Rowan, you slip up just once and you're in.
B: Ok Mr Plod, I'll be good.

All this was going on while I was driving my car. I had a distinctive Mini Cooper. It was a look-alike, not an actual Cooper. I had travelled to Oxford to buy it from somebody who specialised in restoring Mini's. I tend to trust people and take them at their word. This chap said he would prepare a Mini Cooper for £2,000; it would be rot free and finished to a high standard. I ordered the car and went down and paid my £2,000. It was the worst car I had ever bought in terms of value for money. The paint job and the chrome work and alloys made the car look the business. The engine leaked oil and blew black smoke from day one. I had the engine re-conditioned within six months costing a further £500. The bodywork was in poor condition. The complete front panel had to be replaced at the next MOT. I probably paid about £1,200 or more than the car was worth. I loved it though. When I'd get thoughts of people wanting to know who I was, or threatening thoughts, I'd blast out my number plate GUR 70Y and say I'm not hiding, you know where I am.

Being back and forth all the time there were many occasions when I was hungry, I used the hospital canteen, called in at my grandmothers were Mandy would ask if I wanted some food, indeed we had joked I only had to ask, so one day (must have been more) I turned up and asked. Also I used to go to the Chip Shop in Kirkby Town Centre I used as a child and sit and eat pie and chips in the car. I had really enjoyed eating a meal one time, sat in the car close to Kirkby market.

Kirkby Chippy: Who makes the best chips in the country?
B: Kirkby do.
Village Fryer: That's not what you said last week.

The village fryer is my local chip shop in Upton. I think it's the best around for English meals.

B: Well it depends on what kind of mood you are in.
Kirkby Chippy: What like what you fancy for having a drink?
B: Exactly, the Fryer's steak pies are better than yours, but your meat and potatoe pies are better.
Village fryer: So what about the chips
B: the chips are perfect but the gravy makes a difference.

And so it went on, the next time I passed the Village Fryer I popped my head in the door and shouted, "Who makes the best chips in the country?"

The man behind the counter was about 5'8" stocky build and with very short clippered hair. He was a happy go lucky sort of person who had a word to say to everyone. He doesn't work there anymore, but he laughed and carried on with his work. I shouted at him on a couple of other occasions and he just acknowledged me. I think the people I acted strangely to, just assumed I was on illegal drugs of some kind.

The next time I was in the hospital, Tracy and my Dad were there. They had already moved my mum into a private ward. One of the nurses was talking to us and she said my mum probably only had three days left to live and it would be wise if somebody could stay with her. Her body was closing down and she was getting a buildup of fluids in her back. Tracy volunteered, and I said I would stay as well. There was little sense in us both staying so it was agreed that I would stay with my mum. There was a room adjacent to the mum's private room with a sofa bed in it. In addition my dad gave me a set of keys to his house as it was only a matter of minutes away from the hospital.

I remembered my thoughts relating to Sally and I called on her needing to talk to somebody about what was happening.

When I called she was alone, Andy was out. She invited me in. There was washing around drying on the radiators and she cleared it away. We sat for the most time not speaking; I just looked at her as she sat with her feet tucked up on the settee thinking she looked really good.

Sally: Do you like what you see?

B: I do, it's very nice, very peaceful.
After some time Sally broke the silence.
"Are you hungry?"
"No not really"
"I'll make you something to eat" She made me some tea and toast and I sat looking at her and really enjoyed the food.

Again we didn't say much at all, I finished my food and looked at her and she was comfortable and sat quite relaxed letting me gaze at her. I can remember having a conversation with Tricia, or in company with Sally present, around that time explaining that I never looked at or got to know Sally properly. Tricia was intensely jealous early in our relationship so I couldn't comfortably chat to any female in her presence. It coloured the way I related to women in her presence. Whenever I met Sally, I couldn't converse freely. I don't know how long I stayed, maybe 45 minutes or so, for the first time I relaxed and looked at her. When the time came I got up to leave and we said goodbye.

From what I remember, my mind was mostly clear when I was talking with my mum, there were occasions when I waited in the visitor's room that it strayed and also in the canteen. I was there one time and a group of policemen had come in for a meal.

Police: We are watching you Rowan.
B: I'm just having some lunch.
Police: You know we are going to get you don't you?
B: Well come and get me now.
Police: There is no rush, your coming with us.
Back on the ward, one of the nurses spoke to me.
"Do you think your Mother realises how ill she is?"
"I'm not sure, I think she does."
"I think you are right."
"Do you know it often helps in this situation if the patient understands what is happening to them?"
"I don't know, I don't know what is for the best at all"

"If the patient understands what is before them, they often have the chance to put their life in some sort of order and it is helpful to them"

"It's very difficult though isn't it?"

"Yes it is. Do you think you could tell your mother she is close to death and give her the time to put things in order?"

"I don't think I could do that, do you think my mum knows she is dying?"

"I think she does, but nobody has confirmed it to her"

The thought played on my mind. I knew what the nurse was saying but it would be really difficult in practice and I doubted I could be the one to do this.

I stayed with mum through the night. We talked, we laughed we just spent time together. She talked of the family, she talked of her work and she rested a lot. When the nurses came to make her comfortable, I went to my grandmothers, spent some time. All the time I was broadcasting to people, never about my mum, always some other distraction.

I spent some time during the day with my mum, and then headed home for a couple of hours. Tricia was concerned. "You need to come home Kevin, you can't do this." "My mum is dying Tricia, I have to." I was determined to be there at the end, I wanted to be there and hold her when she passed away.

I hadn't had very much sleep for two nights now, so I crashed out on my bed. When I woke up, I set out for the hospital again. All the time broadcasting my music and images to an ever growing audience who were being turned on to the broadcasts of somebody talking straight, not in code and entertaining with his mind. There was now a running commentary from people telling others where I was on the road. Whilst others were saying;

Anonymous1: We'll look out for you Kevin; don't tell them where you are.

Somebody would identify me and place me on a certain street;

Anonymous2: I see the mini, he's laughing while he's driving,

Which I sometimes did, I ran the whole gambit of expressions dependent on the thoughts in my head, tears, laughter, anger.

Anonymous3: Anyone on the East Lancs watching the mini?

Cars would seemingly hem me in like an escort.

Anonymous4: No he's not here at the moment, must be somebody winding you up!

When I got to the hospital, my mind was on my mum. We chatted and I sat holding her hand for a while. She fell asleep and I wandered in the corridor of the ward for a while. The nurses had arranged for a member of a hospice staff to have a chat with me. We met in the room with the sofa bed. He was very courteous and respectful and explained about the possibility of moving my mum to a hospice. I got the feeling that there was resistance from my mother to move anywhere, but I was not thinking straight and couldn't answer him properly. I think he was aware there was something not quite right with me. When he left, I walked up and down the ward and walked into the nurse's office at the end of the corridor and sat down on a chair that was against the wall. It was quite a big office with enough room for people to walk in and out and go about their duties. I sat in tears for a little while. A couple of staff came and went but nobody spoke to me and I eventually got up and went back to mum's room. She was still asleep, so I went down to the canteen and had a cup of tea. I don't remember much else until the evening. Tracy and my Dad had visited earlier and I returned late on. My mum wasn't sleepy so we chatted into the early hours. She was uncomfortable and would occasionally turn on the breathing aid; I think it was a nebuliser, not sure though maybe it was something to ease the pain or discomfort of breathing. I was at her bedside and held her hand as we spoke.

"We'll do this together mum"

"What do you mean?"

"I'll be here until the end"

In my mind I was recalling the nurses words that my mother had maybe three days to live, that was two days ago.

"You know you are not going to get better don't you?"

"Well nobody has told me that so far."

"Mum, I'll be here with you, we'll do it together."

I was almost in tears, but I didn't cry, I had only done that once when talking to her in Clatterbridge and she had said to me "Don't cry Kevin, I need you to be strong for me."

There was no great reaction; she didn't get upset she just continued to talk. She did however start to do what the nurse had suggested she would. She started to take stock, she started to tell me about her wishes and I sat and I listened. She talked about the people and the activities she was involved in and made a sense of order about the way she saw things after she had gone. For one reason or another, the equipment she used for her work as a singer and a line dancing tutor was very important to her. She had very strong views about where it wasn't going to end up and she said she wanted me to have it. Her fears were because my sister was involved with a Michael Jackson tribute and she was adamant she didn't want the act to benefit in any way shape or form. Professional jealousies run deep I'm afraid.

I had very little interest in any of it as it would be totally useless to me, but my father and sister seemed to think I had tried to snatch it from her on her deathbed. Even years later, my father gave some of it to one of my cousins and said you had better check with Kevin because that's part of his inheritance. Well, you couldn't make it up could you? I know I have my problems but the insecurities and lack of faith in me by my family are breathtaking at times. So the next day my mother spoke with Tracy and my Dad about what we had said the night before.

When I arrived at the hospital, Tracy rounded on me straight away. "I will never, ever forgive you for what you have done. You have taken away the only bit of hope that mum had, I will never forgive you and I will never speak to you again."

"Well that will be a big loss won't it?"

I had never really been close to Tracy at all and only ever really come into contact with her when I made the effort to go and see her. My father stood quietly saying nothing.

"You had no right to tell her that she was dying."

"Tracy I spoke with one of the nurses and she said it was the right thing to do."

"I don't care if you spoke to a nurse, I will never, ever speak to you again and I will never forgive you."

"That will be a big loss then won't it."

She was stunned at my answer, but there we left it.

Of course we spoke afterwards, but mum's wishes were never carried out, there were a few and I was party to them all. It's of no consequence to me, I told my father after my mum died the responsibility for her belongings and wishes fell to him and nobody else. As long as he was happy I was happy. After mum was cremated Tracy took her ashes and spread them alone in a garden of remembrance, curiously on my birthday, nice birthday present. Wouldn't bet against some alternative spiritualist bumpkin going on there. In any case, nobody but Tracy knows where my mum lies, sums her up really.

I can't explain the intensity of the situation; I was malfunctioning and functioning at quite opposite ends of the spectrum at the same time. I had little sleep, was travelling numerous miles in the car. Keeping unconventional hours and was desperate to be at my mum's side. That was the last day I saw my mother. I expected to see her again, so there was no long goodbye, I just spoke with her and left to go home for a while. However, something stayed with me that even now brings comfort. There was nothing left to say between my mother and I. Those last days together and particularly those two nights, we talked, we laughed we remembered and it felt good. Her eyes became bright and I remember them being bright blue even though she had a mixed eye colour like myself. Though her body was weak and in pain, her eyes shone. She was indeed transferred to a hospice and lived for another two weeks or more. I was admitted to Clatterbridge Hospital that night.

On arriving home that evening I spoke briefly to Tricia. I needed some food and left the house for the Village Fryer. They were wary of me in there already because of my previous contact. I walked in and viewed the food behind the glass on the counter. Scallops always look so tempting and I ordered a portion. I must have taken the scallops back to the car, and for some reason placed them on the dashboard and got out of the car again. I went back to the chip shop and ordered another portion of scallops having forgotten I had already taken some back to the car. I don't know whether it was Tricia, or the staff in the chip shop who had alerted the police. The police station was only a matter of 200 metres from the chip shop. A policeman approached me as I was returning to my car and I was taken into custody. I do not remember how I was admitted to hospital on this occasion.

The next thing I remember was being back on Kensington Ward. I was loud and active. The Ward Manager Ged, tried his best to calm things but I would swear constantly at him, calling him a fucking wanker and a bastard. He mentioned to Tricia if anybody spoke to him like that in the street he would lay them out. I continued to verbally abuse him. Tricia brought in my CD player and I would walk around alternatively with headphones plugged in singing and with them unplugged playing the music out loud. Buddy Holly rang out through the ward. Ged confiscated my CD player and I called him a wanker, so I had my sons personal CD player sent in. I dropped it and broke it and blamed Ged. I talked with his deputy, she was really nice and I would tell her she was so much more capable than Ged and should be doing his job.

Then my guitar came in. I bashed noises out of it unmercifully and sang along out of tune. I played Me and Bobby Magee and signed it mentally as a tribute to mum with my mind as it was one of the songs she sang. Not long after, Ged came into the common room and told me my mother had died. I didn't re-act just carried on with what I was doing. In all the times I spent in hospital over the years, I never had very many visitors. My mum and dad visited twice, the first time I was admitted. My sister and her friend once, the second time I was admitted and a childhood friend Sarah, whose parents were at mum's funeral visited once also. Every other time, the only person I saw was Tricia, who I usually told to leave after about five minutes of her arriving. In later years I also got to see my children. I was in hospital for at least a month each time, so for a total period of seven or eight months in hospital, apart from Tricia, I had 4 visits. Mandy and my grandmother would phone occasionally. Mandy called this time to ask if I had any preferences for the funeral. I told her the only thing I would like to happen was for them to play my mother singing "How Great Thou Art." My mother made various studio recordings of her work, but this particular track always meant a great deal to me. She sang it as if she totally believed and it always moved me.

The funeral was arranged and I was to be given leave to attend. I chose one of the young male nurses to take me and was talking to him about going to the wake. He didn't want to tell me he couldn't do it but turned up on the day unshaven and scruffy. I was unperturbed. Ged interjected and said that he would take me, although he had to get back straight after the funeral. The plan was to drive me to my home where I would change.

I intended to wear my black suit and a silk Christmas tie I had received as a present a few years earlier. My dad did not want the coffin coming back to his house (words fail) and planned to have the funeral procession start from Kirkby Town Centre. My Grandmother said she couldn't allow this to happen and decided the coffin should be brought to her home. The words "I'll be dancing down this path next Christmas" came back to me. Christmas had come early and I was going to dance down the path too. I had made my 'tie' plans known to Tricia, in the short time I had to get ready; I couldn't find my Christmas tie. I don't think she moved it, I think it was just one of those things, in the event; I didn't wear it because I couldn't find it.

On arriving at my grandmother's house, I bounded into life. I introduced Ged to Mandy, who was welcoming everybody, and I set about introducing myself to everybody in the room. People mainly I knew of, but didn't know well. So there were a lot of distant relatives. I was not in the mood of the day and mingled unconcerned.

When it was time to leave Mandy said there was a place for me in one of the cars. I declined and said I'll go and see my mum the way I always go and see her in my mini. So Tricia drove me to the crematorium. There was a large turnout of people, not surprising considering my mum's work. I listened intently to the service recognising Tracy's work in scripting of the acknowledgements. It seemed to flash by and before long we watched the coffin disappear behind the curtain. The music they began to play at the end of the service was my mother singing "How Great Thou Art". As soon as the music started to play people began filing away and out of the crematorium. I wanted to listen to the song, so I stayed where I was and Tricia stood with me. The whole of the room had emptied. Judith, my dad's brothers wife noticed. My dad and his brothers rarely spoke. I'm talking twenty years at a time here between meetings or communication. Consequently I haven't had much contact with them at all either. Judith came from behind me and hugged me. Her son Peter was there too, I'd only met him when I was 18 previously and we had got along quite well. Liam, my uncle, also exchanged words. I wasn't really taking it all in, I repeated the phrase given to me by my uncle Bob to Liam, "see you in passing" and he laughed.

Outside there were a few moments of mingling with people waiting to get organised and Ged approached and said it's time for us to be moving on. I said my goodbyes and got in the passenger side of his car. As I closed the door I saw Tricia, her face was crimson in colour and she was crying uncontrollably. I remember thinking 'why was she so distressed?' because my mum and Tricia never got on at all, so I couldn't understand why she was so upset. Obviously it wasn't to do with my mother's death, but I don't know to this day what was going through her mind. I found out later she was driven back to the wake in my mini by Tony, Sarah's dad, who used to be my next door neighbour when I was growing up in Kirkby.

As for me, I was heading back to Clatterbridge listening to people spotting me on the motorway and giving progress of where I was headed. I arrived back on the ward still dressed in my suit and settled down to life in the hospital.

I was always building relationships with the females on the ward. One lady used to be a nurse and we chatted and sang songs together with the guitar. While talking outside her room she took my hand and moved it towards her genitals. Even in my confused condition I pulled back and said it was not appropriate. I think for me, it was more the circumstances, not the thought of doing it. We were on an open ward and although we were alone and in a secluded area, there were staff and patients around. If we had been somewhere private at home, where no-body could disturb us, I wouldn't have hesitated.

After a little time, I was transferred to Windsor Ward and was allowed to wander freely around the grounds of the hospital. As usual I walked constantly and would walk around my own ward and Sandringham and then go down the stairs to the first floor and walk in down the corridor to Buckingham Ward and around the common area in front of the dining room and into the games hall.

The corridor to Buckingham Ward had chairs both sides as it was a waiting area for consultant appointments and the lithium clinic. A female patient from Buckingham Ward, Mary, regularly held court there. She was in her thirties had a pretty face, blonde hair and a tan from spending time on sun beds. She wasn't thin, but neither was she overweight, she was very attractive. There were usually three or four male patients hovering around and chatting to her. I fall for almost every woman I come into contact with when I am manic, the prettier they are, the worse I become.

I spent time chatting with Mary, her and the people that surrounded her. I used to spend the evening laughing, talking and singing love songs to her. Even when her husband was present, I would continue to flirt and have fun. We exchanged phone numbers.

The open ward also meant that you could have home leave. My first home leave was for a weekend. It is how you are prepared for a return to normal life. Tricia picked me up for my first home leave. It was Friday afternoon. That evening, she wanted to visit her mum. We travelled to Kirkby and settled in her parents' house. Andy and Sally were also there and we had our children along too. I was sitting on the settee with Tricia and Sally and Andy were sitting on the floor on the other side of the room. I don't know how the conversation got around to it but I said Sally looked really nice and I enjoyed looking at her, remembering our last meeting. I think this is where I said I hadn't looked at her properly before. Andy was angry that I had passed comment on Sally and Tricia was furious. Sally just said its ok Andy. I think Sally had more of a feel for what was happening to me than any of the others had. Tricia knew, but her jealousy knew no bounds and even given my health and the fact that she knew this behaviour was a common symptom of mania, she could not bear the thought that I could think that at all, reasoning there must be some truth in it. There was in that I thought Sally was good looking, but in normal circumstances it was not something that would ever be said. When we got outside and returned to the car Tricia said "I have had enough of this, you have humiliated me in front of my family, I am taking you straight back to the hospital." So I returned to the hospital that night, my weekend leave turned into a few hours on Friday.

I continued to flirt with Mary. Also there was a camaraderie growing between myself, Brad, Joey and Terrence. We'd all sing together and fool about. I introduced singing two completely different songs at the same time and we had fun playing about. Terrence liked Leonard Cohen and was quite good, but it was all so crazy I suppose people bursting into song around the hospital.

The following weekend, I was on leave and Mary called on the home phone. I took the call and chatted with her. Later I told Tricia that I had spoken with her. She was incensed that I had given her our home number. "Don't you realise she is trash, the lowest of the low, she's probably on drugs and all kinds, that's the reason she is in there" "yeah, I'm in there too" "You don't have to associate with these people, for god's sake Kevin she knows our phone number, what else are you going to tell her"

She cross examined me for what seemed like hours on my relationship with her and asked me if I was having an affair. I told her not to be stupid, how could I be having an affair in hospital "Yes but you would if you could wouldn't you?" "Don't be stupid, how can you possibly think that?"

It wasn't a great weekend and I ended going back early, I jumped in my mini and took myself back. I quickly got back into the routine of eating, walking about, messing around with the lads and flirting with Mary.

The next weekend Tricia called in the afternoon whilst I was sitting in the corridor to Buckingham Ward with Mary and a couple of other people. Tricia came in blazing.

"What are you doing messing around with a married man?"

"What are you talking about we are just friends, he wants to chat with me, isn't that your fault?"

"You don't fool me you, you want to mess with me and I will tear you apart" "I'll take you on any day"

"Can't you see the kind of person she is Kevin? why don't you say something, stand up for me?"

"You are making your own mistakes just now Tricia"

"If you don't stand up for me it's over for me and you, we are finished, you have humiliated me one time too many, tell her to get lost"

"This is your doing Tricia I haven't done anything wrong"

The following leave I drove home from the hospital and walked into the house. Tricia was enraged and started verbally laying into me about my relationship with Mary, she repeated it was over and said she wanted me out of the house. I said there was no way I was leaving and if she wanted to go she could but I was going nowhere. She just got angrier and angrier, she placed her hand at one end of the mantelpiece that was full of ornaments and vases, and she ran her hand from one side to the other trashing everything that had stood there. I panicked, she was about to trash the house and here was I, just finished a section in a mental hospital, who was going to be believed if somebody was called in to remove me? I turned and walked out of the door and drove back to hospital. I had never felt so low and totally alone at that point. I was also probably at the most vulnerable point of my life, my mother had just died, I was being rejected by my wife and being thrown out of the home I had worked hard to provide, for me and my family. I had absolutely no resilience combat the situation. Usually after discharge I spent six months or so in deep depression and this was no exception, I had just been kicked when I was down by the person I loved most in the world and I didn't think I was ever going to recover.

When it came to discharge, Tricia tried to hold out and get me to move in with my father. I was just doing whatever she said; I didn't have the energy to do anything else. I asked my dad if I could move in with him. His answer was he wouldn't come between me and my wife; we had to sort it together.

I had nowhere to go and I moved back home on the understanding I would find somewhere else to live as soon as possible. I agreed I would if Tricia would sort it out because I didn't have the will or the energy to find somewhere new. She agreed to do this. We sourced a place only half a mile from our home in Upton within a month of me leaving hospital. It took until September 1999 for the sale to go through. We talked of still being a couple but living separately, but I knew this was just Tricia's way of easing her guilt and making me feel more comfortable about moving. By December 1999, Tricia was openly seeing a married man she worked with. He was ten years older and she had been confiding her problems to him and getting moral support for some time. They moved in together, first in my house mid 2000 and then on to a new larger house in Heswall partly financed by the sale of our family home. Her story is that it was all in innocence and she only became involved with him after I moved out. I am very sceptical. As far as I am concerned, Tricia spent 10 years with me trying to cope with my illness and the way I chose to deal with it. When I was diagnosed, she loved me deeply, the years of drudgery that followed wore away the luster and I no longer held her heart. At the end she was searching for a release and I gave her that opportunity. I can live with that and wish her well. I know she still cares for me and has been a constant friend, when there have been few.

As for my father and his absurd view that I was trying to get my hands on my mother's belongings, I am speechless. After coming out of hospital, and still going through a period of depression. I sourced a home income plan for him; because I worked in the Insurance Industry I was able to contact a work colleague who was very knowledgeable about financial services products. Through him I sourced the best home income plan he could find to allow my father to maximise his income in retirement using his main asset his home. I was saying to him, look dad, I don't care about my mum's possessions, your possessions, or any other possessions, I want what is best for you and what was best for my mum and I always have. My father has a cynical view of me and it will never change. I met with my father and the representative from the recommended company for an initial meeting. I told my father it was a good deal for him and left him to it. He took the plan and has benefited well over the years particularly with the increase in house prices having a knock on effect to his income. I'm still looking to cash in on him apparently, I have no idea what I ever did to him, but whatever it was it must have been significant. I visited him most weekends for a half hour or so, we chat, we have a coffee. He never phones or visits me, but then he is never in contact with any of his siblings. He has been in constant contact with my sister since my mum's death. When I was younger I used to look up to him a great deal and worked hard to get his approval. He never gave it, but in later years I listened to his opinions and his views on other people, his prejudices and I learned to understand his view of me. I also observed that when I spoke to him about my experiences and life in general, he visibly turned off, looked blankly without making eye contact and changed the subject. I think maybe he thinks I want something tangible from him, when in fact all I wanted was acknowledgement and an ability to talk to him about the things that were affecting my life. It's not as if it were endless sessions of grief. Just an hour or so most Saturdays when we would catch up on football, politics, T.V., the family and then if I'd mention a difficulty I was having in life, cue the non interest. Life is a little easier if you are able to talk to somebody and living on your own there is little opportunity to talk to anybody. In this situation, if it's not your dad, I'm not sure who it is. My dad lives on his own too, I wonder if he ever noticed I was listening and being supportive about his problems as we spoke each weekend. Maybe he has enough positive contact already from my sister, sadly, and it's an acknowledged failing on my account, I no longer really care. I'm just lucky I don't need him, I suppose because it's obvious he wouldn't be there. All in all, he has no interest whatsoever. He mustn't have enjoyed our weekly meetings anyway because he took to going to the pub at the time I'd usually visit. I'm a firm believer in the principle 'if you're not enjoying doing something, then don't do it, go and find something you do enjoy.' Maybe if he had the ability to communicate more effectively he could just say, "Your no son of mine, I'll be in the pub so don't bother visiting". Quite frankly I'm not impressed and no longer visit on a regular basis, but I wish him well. He may be disinterested, but he is my 'disinterested dad'.

I understand he has had a difficult time coping with his stroke, particularly after mum died and I suppose he is just coping with circumstances as best he can like everybody else. Maybe he just doesn't have the mental capacity, as a result of the stroke, to cope with anything other than the things he is dealing with now. He has worked hard overcoming the physical difficulties he experiences by attending the gym and going swimming and has always had the opinion you should have the strength of mind to work through your difficulties. At the beginning of 2007, he had a period of about two months where he was suffering from depression and spoke to me saying "I just don't know what is wrong with me, I can't seem to shake this feeling of being down and depressed." I thought, 'I wonder how you would have coped if the two months had been ten years and at the same time you held down a job, carried out day to day activities, cared for two children, and did all the other things you do in life and all the time all you wanted to do was curl up in a ball and die?' No enjoyment in anything, just an existence. You would have indeed then have had some understanding at last of my experience of life, but I said nothing, knowing it was not worth the effort.

Episode 6

I MOVED INTO my new flat in September 1999 and set about trying to change my routine to enhance life generally and to embrace the new start. This was it I thought, I had to move on and do something positive. I had enrolled for an elementary art class once a week while I was still living with Tricia and decided to look for guitar lessons. Two things I had always aspired to do and thought,' what the hell, if I don't do it now I never will.' I was again trying to control my illness by keeping my stress levels down. I had gone through six months of depression since the last episode and come off the medication because I felt I could not live with the depressive side effects, the slowness of thought, the weight gain and the loss of interest in anything I previously thought of as relaxing.

True enough, once the medication began leaving my system, it all came flooding back and I felt alive again. I became absorbed in my art class; I was going to make a career out of it. It was only an elementary class but I reasoned with application you can achieve anything and I was determined to make this work. I enquired about going on to study at degree level and received positive advice from my tutor. It wasn't going to be an easy course of action, it required studying the equivalent of 'A' level and transferring on to HND before getting access to the degree course but he said it was possible.

In addition I also signed up for evening lessons in guitar at Park High in Birkenhead. I had always wanted to be able to play the guitar to a reasonable level. My ability is not very good. The tunes I can play are self taught in the main and my technique leaves a lot to be desired. However I enjoyed strumming along and singing out of tune for relaxation taking up the opportunity to advance with relish. I surprised myself almost immediately. My ability had remained static for about the last twenty years, all of a sudden I was making real progress. Obviously it was about being shown the correct techniques for improvement.

I was also training hard at the local gym, enjoying being able to push myself again and getting physically in shape. My trainer, Jade, was a young girl just out of her teens or in her early twenties. She was large framed but very fit and athletic. She kept an eye on my training schedule and pushed me without leaving me suffering the next day. My routine was high reps with manageable weights and an emphasis on the cardio vascular exercises to increase lung capacity and stamina. I'd never practised fartlecks before in training and combining them with the running machine was a godsend for me. After my warm up I used to do 15 minutes on the bike, 20 minutes on the rowing machine at level 10 and then 20 minutes of fartlecks on the running machine. It was brilliant; I'd finish off with my weights before warming down on the bike.

Another factor to contend with was my growing interest in religion. I have always had quite a secure understanding of God and what I believed God to be. I often mocked people who went to church, not in a nasty way, just if Tricia and I were travelling on a Sunday and we passed a church were the congregation had littered the road with their cars, I would say "here's the churchy people again." I didn't believe you had to attend church to believe in god, indeed, I thought organised religion and their followers were often hypocritical. Well, I suppose life is a difficult puzzle and in truth there are very few people who live out their existence without an element of hypocrisy including myself.

In November I approached the local C of E Church. I was brought up a Catholic. My mother took me to church every Sunday until the age of about 14 when I turned to her and said, "I'm not going anymore mum." She persevered for a while, but stopped going herself a couple of years or so after. When asked about it later she would say "I'm a 'bit's a', 'bits a this' and 'bits a that'." My father is not religious at all. He was C of E and holds a low opinion of Catholics. Not really surprising. As a mixed faith marriage, my mother and father were very aware of sectarianism in 1950s Liverpool. My father was asked to change faith to marry my mother. Apparently the priest spoke with him and decided there was nothing he could do as my dad was not interested in agreeing to the demands of the church. It was not in him to say he would attend church regularly, guide his children in the faith etc when he knew he could not do it. It was decided they could be married, but at the last minute the plans were changed and the arranged priest was replaced. My parents were married by a zealot at the side of the altar, something usually reserved for women who were pregnant when getting married. The insult lived long and hard with my father, not because the church had insulted him, more that they had not been fair to my mother.

I can see the local church from my kitchen window. I can also hear the peal of the bells when they ring out. It was about November time and I heard the bells while working in my kitchen.

Church is calling to you Kevin

I stopped what I was doing and decided to walk to the church and look at the notice board to see what time the services were on a Sunday. It was a crisp sunny day, so it was a pleasant walk, only about ten minutes away. As I walked up the lane towards the church I came level with the entrance to the Rectory. The Rector came out of the drive and said "Good morning." I asked him what time the services were on a Sunday and he told me 8.00am and 10.00am and I would be welcome at either. "Come along to the 10.00am service and stay for tea or coffee in the church hall afterwards." I thanked him and went on my way.

The next Sunday I turned up at the 10.00am service and listened with intent. The service itself was much of a much ness, no vast difference to the Catholic mass I had been used to as a boy, although I understand the difference in the significance of the bread and wine. I did however take great interest in the sermon. The Rector's name was Luke. Coincidently, in his sermon, Luke made reference to a man in a psychiatric hospital and I took it as a reference to myself even though he had only ever said hello before then.

Luke took up his position at the church door and thanked everybody with a handshake and a few kind words at the end of the service. One of his assistants, Arthur, a retired priest who helped out, was also by the exit inside the door thanking people. As I came close to Arthur, I could see he was warmly embracing people and leaving a few parting words. When I came to him he shook my hand and whilst still holding my hand he moved it in the direction of the door. I thought, they must be taught this technique for moving people along who they do not want to speak with. It was an uncomfortable feeling and I thought some of my prejudices are going to be re-in forced here. Arthur was in fact a jolly sort of chap in conversation but I never did fit with the clergy and their helpers in a comfortable way. They were kind and supportive but it always felt like it was an effort or they were on automatic doing what they thought was right. Natural friendliness did exist and as in every other walk of life it requires no explanation, you just know by the comfort of your communication when you connect with somebody. There is no reason why churchgoers should be blessed with any ability to do this any better than anybody else, so it is understandable. Luke was really nice and he remembered me from the day outside the church. He asked if I was staying for tea in the church hall and said he would speak to me later.

I had tea in the church hall, didn't really speak to anybody, just stood in a corner, sipped my tea and left. When I got home I wrote a letter to Luke explaining about myself and my situation and why I had an interest in visiting the church. I often write letters when I am in the state of approaching a manic episode. I find it easier to clarify my thoughts; it makes more sense for me on paper, as I have more time to think about what I am trying to say. The letters are also unnecessary in many instances and whilst not regretting sending them, I realise life would have continued probably with little change without the letter being sent in the first place. I have no idea their effect on the recipient, but to me, reviewing them only brings memories of a troubled mind. Here is the letter I sent to Luke.

12 December 1999

Dear Luke,

Thank you for welcoming me into your church.

I am not sure if it's for me, but I think you have already guessed that I have things on my mind.

I thought about approaching you for a chat, but some of the things I wanted to say still cause me to lose control of my emotions on occasions.

In the main, I wanted to explore the area of faith as I have come to a point in life were I know where I am, but I don't know where I'm heading. To try and explain this I need to tell somebody (Hard luck it's you) my background to put it in context. Please bear with me; I will be as concise as I can. I do not expect an instant reply; hey it's taken me 37 years to enter a church of my own accord. You may not need to reply, as I feel I am already benefiting from the Sunday Service, but if you do feel you can offer guidance in any way I will welcome it. Sometime in the New Year, maybe after your busy period.

First of all, I am that man from the Psychiatric Ward you spoke about on Sunday. For the last 8 years I have been in and out of Clatterbridge Hospital on average about every 18 Months. I have been Sectioned twice and treated with a range of anti psychotic drugs, which, whilst a necessary evil for treating mania, I find very difficult to live with because of the unsavoury side effects. My last admission was in February (It's always stress related, my

Mother died of cancer). I stopped taking the medication against medical advice (again) in May and I have probably only returned to what I would consider my normal self in the last month or so.

The strain of my illness has taken its toll on our marriage and my wife asked me to leave when I was discharged from Hospital. We have remained friends and I see my children every day.

Two and a half years ago my employer placed me on long term disability and I do not see the prospect of them inviting me back.

Now the positives, I have signed up on a community art course based at Ganney Meadows and enrolled on a guitar course at Park High Sixth Form College. Two things I have always had an interest in. I have already discussed transferring to a foundation course in art with the prospect of moving on to Degree level in two years. Hey presto, I have a goal in life again.

The third avenue I want to explore is my faith, or lack of it. I have always had an interest, indeed I have written some poetry on the subject in an attempt to express my understanding (find samples enclosed). These were published with other meanderings at great emotional and financial cost to me a couple of years ago.

Its bitter sweet this and I find some of my conclusions amusing, I hope you do to. Much of it will be rudimentary to you but I think I've just invented the wheel.

I was christened a Roman Catholic and duly taken to church every week by my mother.

I gave it up as a bad job when I was 14. I thought the mass was just words learnt by heart and the sermons boring. I thought the established Churches were hypocritical in their displays of wealth in the form of real estate and manipulated parishioners in their daily life. For young males, Catholic views on contraception and sex before marriage were both outdated and unrealistic. So I formulated my own moral code.

This borrowed very heavily from Christian values and was underpinned by what I thought was a strong belief in God. I.e. something must have created the universe; this is incomprehensible to man and needed a name, why not God. I also believed that Jesus lived and was a prophet, its history isn't it.

So as long as I went about my daily business, didn't hurt anybody and was happy with my actions, I was a good person and didn't need Religion.

Death in my eyes would be the same as before I was born.

I now know that this is an insular existence. I progressively found it more and more difficult to relate to people.

I have also felt what I believe to be the presence of God when reading from the Bible, discussing belief and most significantly when I was holding my Mother's hand through the night when we discussed her death. I will never know if these feelings are true, or if they are a symptom of my mental illness. Spooky eh.

So, onto today.

Kevin Rowan

I have never understood Christian Faith, but this is where I am.

Belief in God is still easy as before.

I now understand that faith is the acceptance that Christ was born the son of God, died, rose from the dead and will come again.

At first glance it is so much more difficult to understand because there is no evidence, i.e. with God there is the universe, with Christ we are being asked to believe something that is unbelievable.

But I don't think we are being asked to believe that, we are being asked to express faith which is a lot easier than belief.

The expression of faith is following the teachings of Christ, which is really having faith in humanity and that is the difficult part and where my life is empty.

If you can carry out Gods work or the teaching of Christ, then that is showing faith. This in turn leads to redemption which I take to be peace in the after-life. I still can't get to grips with this one. I have a feeling that redemption is a living experience. If you are successful in your expression of faith, then the reward is a fulfilling life with no expectation of repayment in other words no fear of death.

I think the seven churches of the world relate to Religions, proving that there is only one God who is worshipped in different ways, so it doesn't matter which Church I attend, the closest will do fine.

See you on the 22nd at your place, but let's not talk about this, it's Christmas.

Yours sincerely,
K Rowan

    Luke made an appointment to visit me at home. He arrived about 4pm and we had a cup of tea and chatted. I told him why I had been particularly drawn towards visiting his church and that I felt the need to learn more about and develop my understanding of what God means to me. I discussed the history of my illness and how it had affected my life both in terms of my family and home and my work situation. I told him that sometimes I felt sensations in my body when thinking about God and it was in fact happening to me as I spoke. The feelings I described earlier when I had told Tricia that God existed came flooding back to me. As I spoke with Luke, I would get the feeling of a presence down my spine, it was not unpleasant, just unusual, a short spiritual sensation down my spine.

    We talked for about two hours. Before we finished talking, Tricia called on the telephone. She had broken down in her car on Telegraph Road not far from the Caldy roundabout. About 20 minutes away from where I lived. She wanted me to come and collect her. I explained I was with somebody and would be there as soon as I could. Luke was unmoved and un-hurried, he obviously dealt with situations like this all the time and he was intent on finishing his work to his satisfaction. Tricia called back in about twenty minutes time "where are you, are you coming?" I told her I was still busy and she would have to wait. It was incredulous, she was now nothing to do with me by her own wish and she wanted me to drop everything and run around after her. Luke finished up and I set off to help Tricia. I progressed on through Christmas and towards New Year without any great change of mood. I was undoubtedly high with thoughts of excelling in my art classes, practicing my guitar and exploring religion through the local church. Organised religion was never a big thing to me, but like losing inhibitions and flirting with the opposite sex, it's another thing that is symptomatic and can be typical of somebody experiencing mania. I was not at this stage significantly losing control, but the warning signs were there, the unusual interests and expectations, the occasional involuntary thoughts, lots of stamina and unshakeable self belief. The unfortunate thing was, I thought it was all perfectly normal. I thought I was at last putting my life back on track.

New Years Eve came and it was the first I had spent away from Tricia for twenty one years. In recent years Tricia, the kids and I had spent New Year at my friend Dave and Maureen's house; we would usually stay and go home on New Year's Day. We had all been sixth formers together and we had kept in touch over the years. I turned up that night and explained I was no longer with Tricia. They were both a bit shocked. It was usual for the blokes to go for a few pints down at the pub while the women stayed in the house and chatted. I couldn't get into the swing of things, I had drunk two pints of shandy and by about 10.15pm I had had enough. I made my excuses and left. I was very mindful that it was my father's first New Year without mum, so I jumped in the car and headed for Kirkby. I was only in Crosby, so it wasn't going to take very long via Waterloo, down the Dunnings Bridge Road and onto the M57. I arrived outside my father's house at about ten to eleven. The roads had been clear as everybody was celebrating in one place or another. My dad's house was in darkness; he had either gone to bed or was not at home. I didn't hang about and headed home. It was still 15 minutes to midnight by the time I arrived home. Pouring a glass of red wine and reflecting on life. In 15 minutes we were about to enter the new millennium and I stood alone, symbolic of my life now and in the future. My second floor flat has windows that face towards Liverpool, as the fireworks cracked and lit up the sky, the Lord's Prayer filled my mind and tears rolled down my face. I stood and watched the fireworks, listened for the ships horns blasting out from across the Mersey in the distance and cried. The sensation of being in God's presence cursed through my body with shivers running up and down my spine.

I carried on going about my business for a month or so, not really changing very much in terms of mood. Towards the end of January I started to put together a report on the role of the church and how to maximise the number of people who attended from the local community. It was a manic exercise loosely based on marketing principles, taking probably the best part of two days to put together, but I worked on it night and day. In my confused state I thought it was incisive and illuminating. Unfortunately I only have the very first draft I produced saved to disk so I cannot include the final version. Probably just as well as I re-visited the report in a subsequent psychotic episode and it was truly a manic masterpiece at that stage.

However in 2000 it was a low key report which I sent with a covering letter addressed to Luke, the store managers of Asda and Sainsburies, and the Chief of Merseyside Police, with reference to how I had been mistreated when arrested by them previously. The aim of including the supermarket managers and the police was to raise funds for the local churches and their activities. The following is a copy of the first draft of the report.

Kevin Rowan

AN INDEPENDENT REPORT ON THE ROLE OF THE CHURCH AND THE WOODCHURCH ESTATE 24/01/00

Proposal
How to address the falling number of worshipers, at the local churches of the Woodchurch Community.

Scope
All aspects of Community life including public service, religious, and business and leisure facilities linked to aspects of Marketing, Economics, Social Studies and Religion.

Background
In common with the rest of the UK, the Woodchurch has seen a drastic fall in the number of regular Churchgoing population. Most dramatically, in people under the age of forty. This 'lost generation' appear to only need the services of a church for births, weddings and funerals. It has long been recognised that this due to the established churches failure to move with the times. Attempts by the 'happy clappy brigade' to remedy the situation have been well document and recently it has been reported that this form of worship has suffered more than most. Hardly surprising, as it apes the instant gratification of popular culture. This paper attempts to challenge the moving times theory and instead concentrate on the service element provided by the churches aligning religion to marketing principles.

This is not as alarming as it may at first sound. Churches are after all run as businesses with budget constraints and limited resources such as income, hopefully with no profit element. If you take away the profit element from marketing principles it is remarkably altruistic.

To provide:
- The right product.
- At the right time.
- To the right people.
- In the right way.
- To provide profit.

Customer led service at a price.
So what is the difference to the activities of the church if you substitute profit for numbers of worshippers?

The Four Ps of Marketing:	The Four Ps of Religion
Planning	Planning
Production	Production
Promotion	Promotion
Profit	People

So what makes a good service?
- Knowing your customer.
- Listening to their needs.
- Talking to them in language they understand.
- Turning wishes into realities at an acceptable price.

A good product or service will have a unique selling proposition (usp) that people will buy regardless. How this is packaged can dramatically affect demand.

Woodchurch Community Churches

Three churches provide the normal services you would expect from a religious body but what are the usp's:

Births, Weddings and Funerals. But more importantly, an explanation of the fear of death that most people have on their mind. If used constructively this could certainly catch the attention.

Well, this is not very clever, is it, anybody with a bit of common sense could tell you that.

Here's the clever bit, the four Ps.

<u>Planning</u>
Know your audience. How they think, how they communicate, how they understand.

Who is the audience of the Woodchurch Community Churches?

Middle aged to old C2, B1, B2 socio economic groupings of retired professional and semi professional white collar workers half of whom travel from outside the area to their cosy clubs where they can get self gratification from serving the less enlightened members of the community. These are the people receiving the word of God on Woodchurch.

Who should the audience be?

Anybody who lives in the catchment area, predominantly working C1, D and E socio economic groupings or blue collar and manual workers. Why aren't they listening?

It's simple, the message is completely wrong and in a language they do not understand.

There is no lack of goodwill or community spirit in these people, they just do not trust:

a) A service that cannot visibly work as a unit i.e. how can the churches tell me what to think when they can't even agree with each other, there is only one god after all?

b) I may be rough and ready but I am as worthy as the next man. How dare they tell me I am not worthy to pick up the crumbs under a table that I am not even sitting at?

c) What have the trusted lieutenants of the church got in common with me? Who are they to condescend to work for the good of my neighbourhood if they don't live here?

d) Why should they worry about a hypothetical difference in a symbol of celebration? Who are the children here, those who understand, or those who do not?

Remedial Action

Understand the culture. As an extreme example, the use of a profanity can be encouraging, nurturing, an expression of friendship or joy or adulation depending on the context it is used in and how it is phrased. If you understand, it is not offensive. It certainly is not desirable, but should not exclude the user. It is in fact a demonstration of contempt for all things viewed by the moral society as being good.

How can you give unconditional love to somebody you do not understand?

Promotion:

<u>Talk to them in their language</u>

This does not mean ape their vocabulary, it means show them it is OK to mock the institutions and conventions of society that have left them with no great expectation for the future. Agree with them that their community is good and ask them to develop it further. So once again we come to the point of common sense, the next stage is the difficult stage, because nobody knows what will work. It is also a risk because you stand to alienate the cosy world of your congregation.

Production:

<u>Suggested Actions</u>

· Form or use an existing committee to build a better profile of the neighbourhood and target messages at the right people e.g.

· Use the power and privilege of respected church members such as Bishops to contact local radio stations, free sheets etc. for publicity.

· Draw in local Supermarkets of Asda and Sainsburies who have recently been accused of killing the community of Upton Village for sponsorship.

- Request local Police to walk the estate a couple of times per week with Velcro labels on their flak jackets saying proud to serve the Woodchurch.
Print and market designer T Shirts or football shirts with a user friendly message.

- Make the community your football team and show them some respect as they all want to be footballers or footballers' wives and you will earn theirs.

- Offer Church facilities for self motivated leisure groups' for example, many youngsters dream of being pop stars, many parents aspire to the idea of stage schools for their children but can't afford it. Encourage people to run them for themselves at cost, offer training to anybody interested.

- Erect signs saying welcome to the hospitality of Woodchurch.

- Encourage existing churchgoers to stay away and throw the doors of all the churches open on a particular day and invite people to come and see for themselves.

- Recruit willing helpers from surrounding churches such as Upton, Oxton and Greasby to help on the day.

- Contact a local group such as the Christians and ask them to sing *a capella* in each of the churches on the day

- Invite people to attend any Church they feel like.

- Trust a neighbouring Minister to completely take over your Church for the day without telling the Congregation.

- Review your Services

- Contact Arrowe Park Hospital and see if the hospital Workers Union would appreciate some kind of social function or facility.

- Organise fund raising through and by the community

- Take down the security fences that say we do not trust you.

- Ostracise any objectionable activities through a position of strength.

- Break their binding and make it new so that no man can tear them apart, then preach your Gospel at leisure.

Recommendations

Use this document as food for thought and brainstorm, discard or add anything you think appropriate. Thought, talk and prayer are easy; action is the way of the Lord.

I tried to leave the report plus a copy of my vanity published collection of poetry with Luke at the Rectory. He was unavailable, I found out from one of the other priests that his father had died and he was obviously attending to matters. I sent him the following letter that evening.

24 January 2000

Dear Luke,

Sorry about being a pest today. Hope you found the books and shelves to put them on.[2] Here's an idea for you that will be much easier to consider.

Contact the three local Football Clubs, explain your motives and ask if any players can attend a Church Service next summer. Ask if they can come in their playing kit as you will be conducting the service in your favourite team's kit. A Manchester United strip would work perfectly.

Publish the date and ask people to attend in their team's colours, the service to climax with a rendering of God Save our gracious team.

Preach about team spirit, the benefits of controlled aggression, ask the players to contribute with their knowledge of the principles of teamwork.

---

2   A reference to the poem Biographical Paradox "On books on shelves that just grow old."

Talk about how this applies to Woodchurch etc. -teaching a granny to suck eggs now isn't I?

Let the players sit in the special seats reserved for the choir.

I guarantee you exposure, a packed church of new faces and the chance to improve your squad.

Don't tell them they have a manager though or you will get the sack.

Yours sincerely,
K Rowan

I was gradually moving further and further down the path towards a full blown manic episode. My passions and hobbies were the focus of my attention and one by one I ruined my relationships with fellow students and members and instructors and teachers. The first to suffer was my art class. There were about eight to ten regular members, all women except for myself. Most lived locally on the Woodchurch estate and knew each other before joining the course. There were a couple who travelled to the lessons and me. The tutor was very relaxed and the sessions were lively and fun. I had been doing a lot of painting and drawing at home, practising hard on portraits. This was one of my new ambitions, to work hard enough to draw and paint recognisable portraits. There was some discussion going on about what we practised on at home and how much time we put into practice. I took out my A3 pad containing my sketches and paintings and took over the lesson. The tutor remained quite relaxed and I went through them one at a time describing why I had drawn them and adding any comments I thought were of interest. For example I came to the portrait of Debbie Harry and told them she was the first woman to give me an erection by the sound of her voice (well, I was a hormonal teenager at the time I was talking about and she was the sexiest thing on the planet. Her whoa oh s on 'Hanging on the Telephone'just worked for me). There was nothing that was so bad it couldn't be recovered and the artwork was pretty poor in reality, but it is something I would never have done in a stable frame of mind. I was high, I was laughing and joking, I was confident and over the top. There were few involuntary thoughts in my head at this stage but when they occurred I thought there was nothing out of the ordinary and I just carried on taking into account my thoughts.

My outburst at the guitar club, a week or so later was far more damaging. The class consisted of about 15 members, one lady, who sat next to me. We would all receive notes and practice songs at the same time. We probably attempted or familiarised ourselves with about three songs per lesson. The tutor attended local open evenings in pubs and also played regularly at different venues. He interspersed the teaching regaling us about his gigs, concerts he had been to and friends and acquaintances who shared his passion for the guitar. He often dropped into his conversation that he was a Christian and attended festivals and favoured Christian guitar music. In the next breath he would make assumptions about people by reference to the clothes they wore, the language they used and the area they lived in. His attitude had started to grate on me, he was presenting himself an upstanding Christian member of society and yet he had no understanding of people or any indication that tolerance was a necessity in giving unconditional love.

Typically he reminded me of the hypocritical ways of so called church goers. The part in the Marketing Report on the Woodchurch Estate which mentions the use of profanity was particularly written with him in mind. This Thursday then, I arrived at the usual time for the start of the lesson. I handed the tutor a brown envelope and said to him here's the pornography you ordered last time. He took the envelope without saying a word and dropped it into the bin. Inside the envelope was a copy of the Marketing Report, a copy of my book of poetry and a copy of the introductory letter sent with the report.

B: Are you going to speak to me about what's in the envelope?
Tutor: After the lesson.
B: Don't you think you had better take it out of the bin.
Tutor: I don't do porn.
B: That's just like you, first impressions colour your judgement, it's not porn it was just a joke, like the use of profanity can be friendly. Remember when you said the lads next to you at the concert were saying "this is fucking brilliant" and you said what kind of a way is that for people to speak. Just because you think yourself a good Christian doesn't mean the sentiment of their conversation was any better or worse than yours. It was two lads speaking in and understandable comfortable manner to each other. You don't know the circumstances; you don't know the background you know fuck all.

Tutor: I'll speak to you after the lesson.

I was getting annoyed, we had been learning a picking style over the past couple of weeks to the Ronan Keating hit 'When you say nothing at all.' As part of the lesson the tutor usually had a session where he encouraged people to volunteer to play and sing regardless of ability. I sang a few times usually something he taught us to play. On one occasion I played Smithers Jones by the Jam. He was a bit dismissive about the choice of song saying it didn't really suit the acoustic guitar which was true to a large extent, but it was obvious he was not a favourite of music by the Jam. I suddenly stood up in the lesson and began approximating the picking pattern of 'You say nothing at all' to the chord progression from 'Smithers Jones'. I was picking the strings as heavily as I could and began to wander around the classroom, walking behind people and out in front of the class. I totally ignored anything the tutor said. I have never seen so many people in a state of shock in my life. The class was dumbstruck and transfixed, the tutor fell silent. I had responded to his initial attempt to talk to me, I can't remember what he said and I can't remember my response but I think I was swearing loudly, but I do remember the room was entranced and motionless with fixed expressions and wide eyes. Before I sat down I took the envelope out of the bin and emptied the contents on his desk. I said I needed to speak to him privately and he agreed to speak to me at the break.

Walking out of the room I went to the canteen. For some time I waited alone and eventually the class emerged for a break. The tutor was not keen to speak to me and I went across to his table and sat down. I don't remember what I had on my mind. I did try and re-join the class after I had received treatment and was back to normal. The tutor said when I spoke to him in the canteen; he was trying to smell my breath for evidence of drugs or alcohol. He had no idea what was going on. I had packed up my guitar and left the class after we spoke. My attempt to clear the air was futile. He referred me to the course administrator who said they couldn't have a potentially disruptive pupil on the course. I was promised a return of my fees but it never happened. He did however say that he had read the information I gave him and found it to be very interesting. Funnily enough I bumped into the tutor in a guitar shop about four years later. There was only me and him in the shop which was quite small and cramped. He totally ignored me. I don't think he would have forgotten me given the impression I made on him. Another sign of a good Christian, no doubt.

Not long after being rejected by my guitar class, I went on a shopping excursion to Birkenhead. I wanted to buy a new top for training in at the gym. When I go shopping I don't mess about much I go straight to the shop I have identified, find what I want buy it and leave for home. As far as sports tops go, I would never buy expensive branded sportswear, just a good quality t-shirt or if I'm feeling adventurous a non branded training top. I would never think of buying a premiership football kit in a million years. I thought they were an absolute waste of money. On this occasion

I walked into the sports shop in Birkenhead. Co-incidentally, Sue one of the trainers from the gym was in the store. She greeted me warmly. She was in her late thirties and very attractive. At the gym she was always very professional and she knew I fancied her, (but I fancied all the women trainers) because one day she had seen me looking at her and said "I'm married" Today she touched my arm and chatted for a few moments.

After Sue had gone I looked at the displays. Strolling down the first line of racks I took a shirt from the front of each of six rows. I didn't check sizes and they were all premiership shirts except for the Celtic shirt. I chose two different Manchester United shirts, an Everton shirt, a Liverpool shirt a Newcastle shirt and the Celtic shirt too. Only the Celtic and Everton shirts came close to fitting.

At that time my hair was cut in the barber shop at the back of newsagents next door to the gym. The woman who cut my hair was about my age and as is the norm for hairdressers chatty and easy to get along with. I used to enjoy chatting with her and I found her very attractive. I had been getting my hair cut there for about three or four years. I was very ill at this stage but seemingly functioning in some respects. I called in at the newsagents and went straight to the back of the shop. There was a queue of people sitting on the left as I walked in, I said "You won't mind me jumping ahead of you will you lads" and took my shirt off and sat bare-chested in the chair. I had seen a group of school age children sitting waiting as I walked in. The hairdresser later told me they were grown men. I said "I just have to nip next door to the gym" and left. When I returned the owner of the newsagents had taken my shirt and put it outside the shop and not surprisingly didn't want me to re-enter.

After leaving the shop I walked through Upton and onto the Woodchurch Estate. I didn't know where I was going but I passed by the Methodist Church. The Minister was loading his car ready for a journey. I caught his attention and said I was looking for fulfillment and wanted to know more about his faith and how I could become involved. He invited into the church hall and we sat for about an hour discussing faith and how Methodists go about their worship. Later on I came to know him quite well as I joined an Alpha course associated with his church. I reminded him of our initial discussion and explained to him I was having a manic episode at the time. He told me that he didn't notice anything peculiar in my manner or in my conversation. I can fully understand why people find it hard to believe there is not a great deal wrong with me at times. I had had the incidents with the art class and the guitar class and also stripped off in the barbers and yet for at least an hour of conversation with an educated man, I was apparently functioning normally. I got to know the Methodist church quite well and left my poetry and the marketing report I had written on the role of the churches with one of the preachers. It's funny, even in madness, how you can have an impact on people, I know of at least two recommendations that came to fruition in the churches I attended.

I was still attending the gym regularly. Jade had only shown me my training routine at the outset, every four weeks or so she would review it to see if there was a need to change things around or increase any of the exercises or add further reps etc. However, Jade was in my head.

Jade: Come on Kevin, I want those stretches done properly, there's no point in doing them if you don't take it seriously

The other trainers were also in my head, I knew most of them to speak to, they were mainly female at the times I trained, more males later on in the evening and the two Colins who owned the establishment.

I'd communicate with other members too.

B: Ok girls I'm doing my lunges now, no peeking.

Jade: Just get on with it Kevin, I want to see some effort when you get on that rowing machine.

I was there most days and began to have thoughts about working there, not just being a member.

Colin: We don't need anybody else on the staff Kevin.

Female Trainers: Don't listen to Colin Kevin, he may own the place but we run it. We need a bouncer to look after us.

It went on for weeks; I'd train to Jade's cajoling in my head. The other female staff would be there too encouraging me to act as a bouncer and Colin would be sending me messages saying we didn't need any more staff. All the time I was mixing with the other members, chatting in the sauna and talking to the staff as if nothing untoward was happening.

One afternoon I was doing my usual training regime when a couple of new faces came into the gym. It was a couple of young men in their early twenties, they were obviously not physically fit, but they were doing the things young men do, lifting inappropriate weights, building the wrong muscle groups to look the part instead of taking the time to get fit. I started butting in and chatting to them.

"You want to try using smaller weights and more reps and more time on the cardio vascular" "We know what we are doing mate, we've been doing it for years"

They tried to ignore me but I persisted.

"You want to get one of the female trainers involved; she'll give you a routine that will sort you out in no time"

"Honest mate, we know what we are doing we don't need anyone"

They moved off into the room used for exercise classes, there was a punch bag hanging from the ceiling. Obviously they were trying to get out of my way.

Female trainers: Well done Kevin keep it up, we'll make a bouncer out of you yet.

B: *Just doing my job.*
Colin: *You don't have a job here Kevin.*
B: *The girls say I do.*
Colin: *The girls aren't in charge.*
Female trainers: *Colin you know that's not true.*

On walking into the exercise class room, the lads were using the boxing equipment. I started talking to them again.

"OK mate we only came here for a quiet training session, we're going now"

They picked up their things and walked out of the gym. The main gym was down two flights of stairs and I followed them up a minute or so after they had left. Sue was at the cheque in desk with another trainer.

"Well I never, what did you do to those men Kevin" I turned and walked back down the stairs and into the gym to carry on training.

A little while later one of the regular members, about ten years younger than me was talking to somebody else. I butted in and started giving my opinion. The lad was a good way taller than me, but then most people are. He started to say mind your own business "You don't know what you are talking about" I was right up in his face and I roared at him at point blank range. The colour drained from his face and he obviously didn't know what to do. There was a moments quiet as everything stopped. There were only a couple of people in the gym and very soon they were gone. Colin, the owner, came down the stairs. He was very calm and asked what was going on. I said I had a disagreement with somebody. "You can't do that in here, you will have to leave "I'm not ready to leave yet, I have work to do" "I'm afraid you are going to have to leave Kevin" He started to move towards me. I backed off. There were two rowing machines spread out in a small area with access all around. As Colin tried to approach me I kept the rowing machines between me and him. So for what seemed like five minutes or so, we danced around the rowing machines, Colin trying to catch me and me evading him. I left the gym of my own accord, Colin was just happy to see me leave and he left orders that I was no longer allowed in.

After I had recovered from this episode my consultant kindly wrote a letter to Colin explaining my condition. In one of the few cases of understanding I have experienced, Colin accepted the information and sent me a letter inviting me to renew my membership at anytime. He also had a gym in Liverpool close to where I used to work and I happened to bump into him on the street not far from his gym. He acknowledged and greeted me warmly. We never had a conversation, but he probably didn't realise how much a friendly recognition meant to somebody in my position, I bet he doesn't even go to church.

On arriving home I climbed the three flights of stairs to my flat. The flat opposite me was owned by Jacob, who mostly acts in a friendly manner. Among minor irritations, he took in a parcel that couldn't be delivered as I was out. I believed he had opened it, and tried to re-seal it so I wouldn't notice. The box was folded and glued and the glue had been broken to unfold the box. The book inside was shrink wrapped, the shrink wrapping had been split open at one end so the book could be removed and then replaced back over the book. The box was loosely folded back into place. He denied doing so of course and gave me a two fingered salute behind his back when returning to his flat. I obviously couldn't prove whether he had opened the parcel or not and didn't pursue the matter. The following morning however, we came out of our doors at the same time and he blushed crimson when we made eye contact. So as you can imagine, I do not think too highly of him, not because he had opened the mail, he may not have done, but because he had taken small liberties generally, thinking I was unable to react to him. One of my manic thoughts became I was destined to throw him out of our second floor window, or some other form of retribution. I am very slow to reach any level of anger (thoughts bubble along and fester to some extent and either fade away or linger too long), but if the right buttons are pressed I think I probably could snap to my detriment or theirs, at that point I wouldn't really care. I suppose people don't realise the positions they put themselves in at times, but hey it was only a motorcycle manual. Anyway I knocked on Jacob's door for some reason, He was showering or something so only his head came around the door. I thought he was regenerating back to being a sentinel as I had come to live in close proximity to him;

he was getting younger, getting stronger. He couldn't speak for any length of time and disappeared back behind his door.

Nights were really difficult. I was yearning for female company, not as you might expect in a sexual way, although that would have been nice. I needed somebody to hold me close. My body was covered in goose pimples and I needed to feel the warmth of a female body for comfort. I started to call in to the Arrowe Park pub during the day, having a quiet drink while taking in the activities of a large mixed group sitting by one of the windows. I decided they were off duty police and noticed that there was dope being smoked. I got up and went across to the group saying "There's one rule for you and a different one for everyone else I continued to aim comments at them, but they just totally ignored me. In the evenings it was more like a club than a pub. The women would be dressed to the nines and music would pump out. I remember Britney Spears 'Oops I did it again' was popular. I would broadcast it with my rhythms like in the car, standing tapping my heel up and down to the music. The women were fantastic and I never felt self-conscious being there on my own watching them. I was running short of money at this point. I had paid for a pint of lager and I did not have enough for another.

Barmaid: its ok it's on the house, we know you are entertaining us.

B: So, if I come up to the bar and ask for a drink I don't have to pay

Barmaid: Of course not, it's on the house for you; I've been listening to you.

The barmaid was gorgeous; she was wearing a black mini dress and had a golden tan with blonde hair.

I continued to enjoy the music, taking my time with lager and moving with the music. When I finished my pint I went back to the bar. The barmaid I had been served by earlier served me again.

Barmaid: Is this one on the house

B: *No I'm paying for it*

I ordered a pint of lager and gave her all the money I had left. It was about 25 pence short. She took the money and went across to the till. I went back to my position standing in the now crowded floor of the pub. The barmaid came from behind the bar and stood facing me saying nothing. I just looked at her.

B: *You are really beautiful.*

She stood in front of me for a few moments and then turned her back and left, I took a seat in one of the cubicles down the left hand side of the pub. Within a couple of minutes the pub manager was standing in front of me. He was a big man and could handle himself. He took my drink from me and virtually frog marched me out of the side door. I started to walk around to the front of the pub to use the main door. He followed me and said "You're not coming back in." By this time we were on the patio at the front of the pub by the garden furniture. He stood in front of me and pushed me back when I tried to go in. I looked closely at him, it was Jacob re-generated. "Jacob, we can talk about this, let's just go in and have a drink and a chat. The bar manager laughed "You're not going in the pub so I suggest you move along" "Come on Jacob, we can just have a short chat and a drink" The manager was amused I was calling him Jacob but he was adamant. He didn't get angry with me or use inappropriate force, but he did make it clear I was not going into the pub. I felt he had had some form of training, maybe forces, he was too humorous to have been ex-police; they would have remained serious all the time and quoted law or threatened the arrival of the police. If he had had training or not, he was undoubtedly strong and I was no match for him physically. A few weeks later after treatment, I went back into the pub to apologise. I spoke to him and he just said see my wife it's her you need to apologise to and she affirmed I was barred.

That evening though, I wandered off home. The barmaid was still in my head.

Barmaid: I'm coming to see you, I'm sorry the way it all turned out.

B: I'll be waiting.

Barmaid: I know where you live we can be together.

Male voice: She's a bike, nobody would touch her around here, and everybody knows where she has been.

Barmaid: It's true I have been with many.

B: I don't mind where you have been I just want you to hold me.

Male voice: What if she's got the clap?

B: I'm regenerating, I'll regenerate her to, it will be fine, it will be beautiful.

Barmaid: I will be there as soon as I can after work.

I stood waiting at the top of the stairs on the communal hallway looking up the road for sign of the barmaid coming down the hill. For over two hours I waited and to no avail.

Barmaid: I have to go home to my parents; they are worried about me getting involved with you. I need to go and see them.

There was further communication with the barmaid and her parents talk of marriage and organising a wedding, with the goading of the local lads who were divulging her background. I was unperturbed as she was beautiful.

As I had been standing there, I had been listening to the wind. It was swirling around. I listened more closely; it was swirling around inside Jacob's flat. He wasn't in, but I could detect the sound of paper and what seemed like leaves being blown up and down his hall. I became very aware of my surroundings and my senses and was being drawn into the spiritual existence that surrounds us. I spoke with Luke, the Rector, and asked for his assistance. I had a mental image of him running towards the flat in his priest's clothes, but of course he never came.

Jacob has gone; you are witnessing his restless spirit in the flat.

B: Who am I talking to?

It is of no consequence, you are treading closer than ever to a world you don't want to know

B: I have no desire to explore this any further, I may not be able to control how far I fall.
Who can?

Walking into my flat I took my Fender Strat from the wall and walked back onto the landing were I began to play the guitar, banishing the evil spirits from my mind. I walked between the space between mine and Jacob's flat, strumming and finger picking the unplugged strat. Even unplugged the sound amplified in the stairwell and other residents must have been able to hear what I was doing. After about 15 minutes I walked into my flat and closed the door. My sister spoke.

Tracy: You cannot just enter and leave the spirit world Kevin.
B: I didn't enter at all.
Tracy: It's all around you; you are as one and will be.

It was getting late, I had the lights on, no television or radio, just listening; the room was charged with energy. It creaked and groaned. I began seeing dark shapes in the corners of my mind, the fall of silken web against my skin. I was nervous, cold and afraid. I still had the overriding desire to be held closely by a female and right now it was stronger than ever. My body trembled not with desire but with the need for closeness and affection and I was consumed with the thought of holding somebody to ease the feeling of insecurity. I retired to bed and wrapped myself in the duvet trying to abate my discomfort. In the dark, the sounds and images grew stronger and I could not sleep. In fact I hadn't slept for a few days now and at this particular point I was running on adrenalin. Then it happened. I looked across my bedroom towards the wardrobe doors. There were three black diamond's with a faint silvery outline, one on top of the other, spinning slowly in opposite directions and hovering at about head height about 10ft away from me. I looked and thought this is some form of spirit, I thought it was my spirit and it was leaving me, I thought I was about to die. I grabbed my t-shirt and pulled it on; I was already wearing my boxers. The shapes moved towards the door and I followed. They continued through the front door which I opened and I followed them down the stairs and stood by the communal entrance. The shapes disappeared into the night. I returned to my bedroom and got back into bed. I was convinced this was my last night in bed and I slept.

The next day I woke early as usual and made my way to the gym at about 7.30am. Normally I would go to the gym between 9.00am and 9.30am but whilst high I was getting there earlier and earlier. On arrival I was surprised to find the doors were locked. There were staff in, but they wouldn't open the doors. I eventually gave up and left. Not for too long though, I still had work to do, so I returned in the afternoon. When I arrived one of the male fitness instructors was on duty. He told me that I wasn't welcome and couldn't come in to train. I told him I was still a member and walked about down to the common room at the end of the hall. The attendant must have called the police, he didn't try to interact with me, just let me go about my business. I sat down quietly next to the entrance and started reading one of the newspapers put out for members. I sat there for about ten or fifteen minutes. Very soon a police officer came in. He spoke to me and I acknowledged him, he asked me to move outside. I walked outside and we chatted in front of the gym entrance. I remember thinking I've had enough of this and I just turned my back on the officer and walked away. He must have used this time call for back-up and then he followed me down the side of the gym. He took me from behind pinning me to the floor and rolling me around whilst putting handcuffs on me. As he did this I burst out into some form of rhyme, almost like a nursery rhyme disparagingly referring to the police in colourful language. I was shouting and rhyming the words at the top of my voice when the backup arrived. Three police cars with another six policemen on board. There was no need for the numbers, the initial officer had subdued me and I didn't attempt to struggle. I was put into the back of one of the cars and taken to Birkenhead police station. Once there, I was charged with breach of the peace. I was asked to read some form of legal declaration. I remember thinking the police were controlling how I scanned the paper. My eyes moved in a steady fashion left to right without reviewing the words. Given the legalese of the document, it was very difficult for me to understand. When you read a document like this your eyes scan back and forth as you get meaning of the words and their context. The police were in my head, this must be the way they treat criminals, yes here are your rights but we'll make it very difficult for you to understand them, you have to read them as we show you, so you read the words without understanding. I still wasn't sure what was happening to me. I was moved to the cells. It was an old building and it felt like I was below ground level. The wind outside reminded me of the wind in Jacob's flat. The dark images and sound came back. I was lying on a red mattress on the floor of the cell. There was a toilet area adjacent and it reeked of human waste. The panel in the cell door slid open and I could see two female officers peering in to the cell.

Policewomen: We are going to come into the cell and stand above you so you can admire our legs.
B: I think the thought of what you said is already working.
Policewomen: We know how does it feel?
B: I can't help how I feel and you know it.
Policewomen: Yes we know.

The panel closed and they were gone. The night was long and restless, the wind continued throughout and I had thoughts of evil spirits searching for me, trying to find my location so that they could claim my life.

In the morning I was escorted from the cells and handcuffed before being put into a prisoner transport vehicle. I sat in the small cubicle and waited for the journey to commence. When the vehicle eventually began to move, the trip was very short, less than a hundred metres I would say and it reversed into a walled driveway. I was taken from the van and led to another cell in another building. I must have spent the best part of the day in this cell. For the whole of the morning and into the afternoon I saw nobody. I could hear activity going on outside the cell, people walking about, and doors opening and closing. I was confused, my mind focused on when I was next going to see somebody. At lunchtime, somebody came in and left a packet of pre-packed sandwiches and a drink. I can vaguely remember a female doctor visiting a little later on.

Mid afternoon I was moved again, I think I went up a level in the building and was placed in a smaller holding cell. I was in touch with the spiritual feeling from the night before. I stared at what appeared to be the remnants of a metal holder protruding from the wall. I thought it was for holding a glass, and a glass appeared, filled with water.

Go on have a drink, you know you need it

B: *How do I know what is in it, you're trying to fool me, it's not really there*

How do you know unless you try?

I saw images in the walls where they had been marked and aged over the years. The wall was a testament to all it had seen and I was learning about the things it had witnessed.

I remembered my mother had visited Walton jail to entertain the prisoners. She had remarked how sad it had been to see all the men locked up. She also believed that people should pay for their crimes. When I was about 6 or 7 mum showed me one of the steps she had learnt as a child in her dancing classes. She had done tap dancing and clog dancing. The step she showed me was how to mimic the sound of a steam train, stepping back and forward on the spot to the rhythm of the train. I was standing on the bench running across the back of the cell entertaining the people in the other cells by broadcasting my music. At the same time I was pounding out the rhythm of the train with my feet, but also adding with my mind the image of descending stairs with the words "you're going down".

The cell door opened and another prisoner was put into the cell. He was in his late twenties. He looked spaced out on drugs, but then he took one look at me and my antics and became quite restless. He was shouting at the door asking to be moved to another cell. After about twenty minutes or so, the door was opened and he was taken away.

Eventually it was my turn, the door opened and I was led away. I had been entertaining the other prisoners all the time. I had no idea where I was going or what was about to happen next, basically I had no connection with my surroundings or the reason I was there. I was lead up a tight steep staircase, I was in front and I just followed the stairs. When I reached the top of the stairs I stepped through a door and I was in the dock of the County Court. I moved closer to the rail and before anybody spoke began to sing the Beatles song 'Help' at considerable volume. I could see people below me trying to speak to me; I was impervious to any attempt to interrupt my song. I was entertaining people not only with my mind, but also openly with my voice, this was my hour for acknowledging all the things that had happened to me, it was not a secret anymore, I communicated with my mind and I was tired of people pretending it didn't happen, I would answer their questions with my mind, in the meantime I would continue to entertain.

Proceedings went on and I was not a party to any of it. I was still singing when a court official led me from the dock. I was ushered to a waiting area outside the courtroom. It was filled with people some seated, some standing, some pacing up and down. I took a seat on a bench in the middle of the waiting area. There I sat for I don't know how long, I had already lost track of the passage of time from the period I had spent in the cells. All I know is that it wasn't for a few minutes, it was much longer. An embarrassed looking policeman approached me. He was actually blushing as he spoke. You are free to go now.

I left the Court and quickly decided I needed to go home. It was a pleasant day so I began to walk. I'm not sure how far it is from Birkenhead Town Hall to Woodchurch, but it's a good walk in anybody's book, probably about one hour 45 minutes. It was still light when I arrived home and it was early February so I'd guess the time to be about 5.30pm. On climbing the stairs to my flat I reached for my keys, they were not there. The police had taken them along with all the contents of my pockets when I was arrested. I was confused and tired and wondered how I was going to get in the flat. I walked down Arrowe Park Road to the police station at the bottom of the road. Walking into the police station I demanded a lift to Birkenhead police station as they had the keys to my flat. The desk sergeant was dismissive. "Get yourself on your way or you will find yourself in trouble." I was not making sense to him. I was not able to explain the circumstances calmly and comprehensively. All he could see was an angry man demanding a lift to Birkenhead. I remembered I had left a key with Tricia. We had a utensils rack in the kitchen. One of the utensils was missing and the end peg was never used. I had placed a spare key on the last peg of the utensil rack when I was going back and forth between the flat and Tricia's house when I first moved there. I'd left it in case I ever locked myself out of the flat; I'm paranoid about keys and very careful about what I do with them.

Tricia's was only a five minute walk from the police station. I made my way there and knocked on the door. I tried to explain to Tricia that I had come for my spare key. She wasn't aware I had left one there and told me she didn't have a key and if I didn't leave she would call the police.

I walked away from the door.

Kate: You can come in here Kev, come in and have something to eat.

Kate was the eldest girl of our next door neighbours. Her father had been talking to me about getting her first car; she was about 17 or 18. She had been chatty and friendly for a couple of years. Not to any great degree. Just saying hello in passing, smiling, exchanging a greeting and a quick word. The reason she was friendly was because a couple of years earlier I had been buying a paper in the shop she worked in. A man of about 40 was talking to her and she was obviously upset. I hung about in the shop until the man left. Kate was in tears. I asked her if anybody else was in the shop and she replied no, so I said if she wanted to go in the back and sort herself out I'd take care of any customers who came in. She didn't need to and in a few moments she pulled herself together. I waited until I was sure she was ok and then I left the shop. So, we chatted very occasionally, mostly just smiled and said hello.

I knocked on the door and Kate's younger sister Christine, opened the door. "Is it ok if I come in" Christine just stepped back from the door. I walked into the house; there was nobody there but Christine. I went straight through to the kitchen opened the fridge and took out the cheese and margarine. Taking two slices of bread, I spread the margarine on each slice and set about slicing the cheese. I was using a table knife and I cut the sandwich in two and put it on a plate. Later, I found that it had been written up in my medical notes that I had been found in a neighbours house brandishing a knife, I know I was unstable, but was dumbstruck they'd made the leap from making a cheese sandwich to showing some sort of intent with a knife. I didn't say much to Christine; I took the sandwich into the sitting room and sat down watching the T.V. At this point Melanie, Christine's mum came into the room. I don't know whether she had been upstairs or just somewhere local. I had told Norman, Melanie's husband about my illness when I used to live next door. At the time he wasn't sure what I was telling him, but he must have mentioned it to Melanie because she re-acted quite intelligently. When she came into the sitting room she engaged me in conversation, she went to the kitchen and brought back a packet of crisps to go with the sandwich. I was thinking about Kate, I was going to be famous and wealthy and I wanted to marry Kate. Melanie said "Kate's not here" and I replied "What about Christine? This is one of those occasions when I thought I was discussing this in my head.

Melanie later told me I had frightened Christine by saying I wanted to marry her. Sometimes, I don't know if I am thinking something and sometimes say the same thing out loud. Another notable time when this happened was when I was visiting my Grandmothers. Tommy's business partner was a long time friend called Jerry. Jerry moved to Germany after dissolving their partnership. After a few years Jerry was involved in an accident and died. Jerry's brother, Duncan, kept in touch with Tommy and visited regularly. On this occasion Duncan was visiting Tommy and whilst sitting in the company I thought 'he thinks he's Jerry', referring to the fact that Duncan was friends with Tommy. When I was leaving Duncan got up and followed me to the door. "By the way, my name is Duncan, not Jerry" he was obviously aggrieved and I'm not sure whether I spoke my thoughts or I called him Jerry.

Tricia came to the door and demanded I leave the house. I got up and left the house, Tricia and Melanie were talking. I walked down the path and headed towards Tim's house. I knocked on Tim's door and Pamela answered. I walked straight in. Tim was sitting near the fire with his shoes off. I sat myself in the chair opposite, slipped off my shoes and started to chat to him. There was a knock at the door. The police had arrived; I was asked to leave and led away to a patrol car. I was driven to a different police station on put in the cells. The thoughts in my head were about Melanie and her girls. Melanie was coming to visit me in the morning to show me there were no hard feelings and to help with the police.

The morning seemed to take forever to arrive. Outside sounds, when you are in a cell are exaggerated and irritating. The sound of policemen walking the corridors, the sounds of keys jangling are overbearing. I could hear somebody moving from cell to cell opening the hatch on the door. He arrived at my cell. I could see tea being prepared through the hatch, it was painfully slow, the pouring of the hot water and milk, the stirring of the cup, it seemed slow and deliberate and it was driving me crazy. I stayed in the cell for the rest of the morning before being transferred to Clatterbridge hospital.

Apparently it was my own fault that the police had acted the way they had. The fact that I was not following medical advice and taking my medication meant that I was not under the care of the doctors and I had to be charged with a public order offence. The result of the charge of Breach of the Peace was that I was bound over for six months. Well, given my usual recuperation time and state, that was not really going to be a problem was it. It did however change my attitude towards medication. I couldn't afford to put myself in that position again and I endeavoured to find a way of living on the medication regime acknowledging to myself that I would never feel physically fit, or the will to become physically fit, again.

Episode 7

I HAD CONTINUED to petition my employer to be released from long term disability and a return to work. In January 2001, this came to fruition and I was allowed to return into a role that was very similar to the one I had left three and a half years earlier. After a slow start for the first month or so, I settled into the work quite quickly. Before very long I was working on a new product launch, co-coordinating the product literature and subsequently asked to work on a larger project called the SALTR project. Basically this was an industry initiative to plain English product brochures and key features, the two main promotional documents in the insurance world, to help make them understandable and comparable to the general public. In total I had in the region of sixty items of product literature to manage through to re-print in a set timescale. As ever, there was never enough time to allow the relevant approval departments of actuarial and legal and compliance to meet their agreed working standards for approval and so I prepared a project timescale for each item and sought management approval of the plan. There was a requirement for input from the section I worked on and whilst I had no staff reporting directly, I was responsible for co-coordinating the effort of myself and five other members of the section. Given I had only recently returned to work and I previously knew only one member of the team plus the manager, it was an uphill struggle for me to motivate and gain co-operation from the team. I am undoubtedly not a people person to start with. I talk straight and about goals and objectives without little feel for people. To my mind I am logical, 'this is where we are now, this is what we need to do to get here within the time frame given' I've never cared too much whether people like me or not in the process. I suppose that's been one of my biggest downfalls.

The work was going quite well, I was also enjoying it. We were mostly on schedule and although I'd ruffled a few feathers, I was happy things were moving along. As far as the work was concerned, the project began to run into dead ends. There was another highly secretive project going on called 'Project Orange' and it began to impact on the work I was involved in. Senior managers stopped taking an interest in the SALTR project, not just the parts I was involved in, but the whole project. It emerged later that the Company was preparing to close its life funds to new business so the need for marketing literature in plain English was irrelevant. As far as the rest of the Company was concerned it was business as usual, so in a meeting with Trevor, one of the directors (I knew him a little as I used to play in the same five-a-side team as him), he told me to carry on progressing the project as normal. I was then pushing a project that all senior managers new to be irrelevant, so obviously it was fraught with problems.

Against this backdrop, I was working with the lithium nurse at the hospital to try and find a more suitable medication regime. I had made the transition to lithium and was looking for a balance with the other medication. The thought was that I would be able to get by on lithium alone and we were working towards that situation. I was already on a low level of risperidone and I had successfully come off dutonin, the antidepressant without any noticeable drop in mood. The next stage was to get rid of the risperidone.

Looking back my mood was high. The medication was a factor, but maybe the stressful work situation also had its part to play. I was reacting to events quite well in my opinion. If something annoyed me, I voiced my opinion in progress meetings, to my Manager etc. When it came to dealing with problems and sorting them out I tackled them positively and worked my way through them. A far cry from my standard persona on medication, dour and defeatist, frightened to open my mouth in case my opinions are not welcome. I even interspersed project reports with humorous asides aimed at senior managers and other project members and openly took on managers and reported them to their seniors who seemed to be being jobsworths instead of addressing the project. You can say networking was not a strength indeed. My attitude was a good example of the way I used to interact at work before I was diagnosed; only it was magnified in my total abandon of junior employee etiquette.

On reflection, the first point at which I can identify something not being quite right was when Sheila, my manager asked if there was anybody who would like to use the Deacon Blue tickets she had bought for the following evening. I said I would take them and rang my cousin, who was into live music, to see if he fancied coming along. It was at the Royal Court in Liverpool. A good venue, the atmosphere was always lively. I didn't know too much of Deacon Blue's music, just their two main hits. As we stood watching the show, I constantly conversed with the lead singer in my head. It was about him being a star and I was suggesting he thought he was bigger than he was. He was imploring the crowd to get behind him and to show this upstart just how popular he was. During the set images were projected onto the back wall. I had a commentary going through my head explaining the images. It was my thoughts; I was working out the subliminal messages from the band. I can't remember the body of the presentation, but one part sticks out, there were spacemen floating around, I decided they were not spacemen, they were contamination suits and the image was saying don't contaminate my Scottish roots, we'll travel and we'll play, but don't impinge on our legacy, don't leave your imprint on me.

After the weekend I returned to work. I had no worries about anything, talked about the concert as if it had been any other concert. Sian was a headstrong young lady on our team. She was in her early twenties and we hadn't got off to a great start. I had introduced the SALTR production plan to the team and she had basically ignored my input because she was busy with other things. I approached her about it and was quite forthright in my denunciation of her attitude. We did however progress and around about this time we were talking across the section about music. I told her I enjoyed Grease. She joked and said you remind me of Kenicke. My mind was already misfiring and the slightest suggestion could send it bounding down blind avenues. In normal circumstances I would have just taken the joking for what it was as Sian was only very young and just having a laugh. She was also loud and intransigent, something which takes a bit of getting used to in a woman. Physically though, she was very attractive and I thought, Sian must like me, after we started so badly, she must like me.

The project work wasn't going well at this stage as nobody wanted to commit to it. Highly understandable in the circumstances, but a farce to request it should continue. As for myself, I had a little insight into my health situation and asked Sheila for some time off as I needed to relax and wind down. It was agreed, I can't remember if it was a week or a fortnight, but I took the time off anyway.

I thought if I rested and relaxed for a while it would sort out my head and I would be able to return to work fresh and ready to crack on. Once home, started to unwind, then for some reason I focussed on the Marketing Report I had produced a year earlier for on the role of the church on the Woodchurch Estate. I retrieved my copy of the report from my computer and set about improving it, working night and day over a couple of days. I changed the layout and added to the body of the report. I extended the introductory letter with wide ranging observations. For example, I had read an article by Dennis Healey about Oliver Cromwell and remembered my history teacher describing him as a hero. My letter included references to the 'New Model Army' and tied the message of Daily Mail article to my report. I finished off the report by proving the existence of God by logic and turned to spirituality with a poem I had written for the Parish Magazine.

It's funny the way Christians are, I spent two years attending church and socialising with the congregation, even serving time on the Parish Council. In the period since I left it seemed to me that 95% of these 'Christians' ignored me when we meet on the street. I have called on a couple of doors when cold calling for sales jobs I have been involved in (medical history, no matter how its dressed up with equal opportunities, can mean the kind of work you can find is limited, so I have taken inappropriate work in the past, just because I need to work.) and said "Don't I know you from church?" the reply was "No I don't think so. " They even suggested the poem I had written on spirituality had been copied from somewhere. Christians? Who needs them? In reality, I met many good natured and welcoming people and I think at the end of the day I do not share their enthusiasm for traditional worship. I consider myself a Christian, but I'm not keen on organised religion, they seem like social clubs in a time warp to me. The irony of my guilt in not understanding their point of view is not lost.

As I said previously, this truly was a manic masterpiece. I bought binders for the report and printed it off in colour. There were about ten copies and I sent one each to Dennis Healey, My history teacher, David a director of the Company I worked for and a few of my family, the rest kept for reference, but I duly sent them out to people I thought were appropriate.

I was communicating with Sian and the rest of the section in work. My main contact point was Sian.

B: *We didn't get off to a good start did we Sian?*
Sian: *No we didn't I hated your guts.*
B: *So what changed your mind?*
Sian: *Who said I've changed my mind (laughter).*
B: *You know you can only do this because I woke you up with my contact with you. You were on the treadmill like everybody else, working and being directed by unseen forces.*
Sian: *I know something has happened to me since I met you.*

B: *They're frightened of me in work, they know I'm uncovering a hornets' nest, they're going to promote me for weeding out those trying to control events.*

Sian: *Well I'm not on anybody's side.*

B: *You know there are powerful females and their sisters who promote the values of the sisterhood and they are in conflict with the male managers, it is a power struggle of epic proportions and you have just been a pawn in their game. Sheila is one of the sisters, sweetness and light to her male managers, but she is belligerent in her approach. She uses procedures and protocol to slow things down, make decisions take longer, make the business unresponsive.*

I flashed an image of Sheila sitting smugly at her desk working at a snail's pace teaching the male managers the power of a female.

B: *the men saw you as a pretty distraction, to be kept busy, the women as a potential threat with your outspoken attitudes, both wanting your industry, both wanting control.*

Sian: *Ignorance is bliss, I just kept on trying to achieve, but you know I felt like banging my head against a brick wall.*

B: *You know we can be world beaters together, you know we can take on both sides and be successful.*

Sian: *You stupid man, haven't you realised I saw the light before you spoke to me. I have been listening for some time and I know where my path leads.*

B: *You know I am falling in love with you, you know I can't help myself.*

Sian: *(laughter) Yes I know Kevin and I am enjoying the experience.*

B: *Will you come and live with me so that we can love and work together?*

Sian: *Yes I will.*

Jackie: *Oooh Kev you've got a hot one there!*

B: *Stop it Jackie, just like you to but in when I'm about to get serious with something.*

Sian: Get serious with something? What's this something you were about to get serious with (laughter) and who's this Jackie person.

B: Goodness don't mind Jackie, she's an old friend I used to work with, and she's working in another part of the Company now. She's belligerent without being a sister and not too concerned with treading the path others give her.

Jackie: Can I come to the wedding?

B: I want you to take the service at the wedding.

Jackie: Kevin Rowan what do you mean?

B: It's all falling apart around here, I sent a report about a year ago on the role of the church and I followed it up last week. My head is full of messages of support for change. The centuries of vested interest and control are at last being seen as inappropriate. People are demanding a better service from their local churches and we have to organise something credible Worzel.

I used to ask which head Jackie was wearing today. She would change her hairstyle frequently and I would call her Worzel Gummidge.

Jackie: So I can have my Vicar of Dibbley head on then.

B: That's the idea, you can stand up in front of people every Sunday and do a sermon, informing people of progress.

Jackie: Kevin, I'm going to love that.

B: I knew you would. Jackie, "will you marry me?

Jackie: I thought you'd never ask (laughter).

Sian: Hey, what's going on between you two?

Jackie: Don't ask he's as mad as a hatter. Where do I get to live?

B: There's an excellent property called the Rectory next to the church.

Sian: What about us, where are we going to live?

B: I'm bound by the locality, I'll stay here in my flat. It's been a prison for all the residents. They've been identified for serving time for one reason or another by invisible eyes controlling their minds. We are starting to set them free, allowing them to think and progress for the first time in many years. To start with as the flats become empty, we will fill them with friends and colleagues sympathetic to progress, who haven't got the ability or the funding to stand on their own two feet. You will find many of your friends and associates having the rug pulled beneath them with loss of employment, removal of overdrafts, and downturns in business. We will be there to catch them and we will progress.

I had started visiting a local pub, the Stirrup for relaxation. I would buy a pint and sit in a corner somewhere out of the way and watch and listen. All the time I would be broadcasting and entertaining the regulars. The women would be in ecstasy. The older ones, the pensioners, would say;

Older woman: I can remember the days when this was commonplace, it's a lost art, you are a true gent.

The younger ones would say;

Younger woman: Who is this man and how does he do this?

The men would encourage me to keep it up;

Men: Keep it up son, never seen the women so happy.

I'd broadcast my beat, it would start with the beat of the song on the jukebox and then I'd extemporise, add images. I'd sit quietly, tapping my foot and broadcasting my music of love and harmony.

The atmosphere in the pub was always comfortable and when it filled out it would buzz and I thought it was all my doing.

You're a throwback

B: I know, this is the way people were entertained, this is the way order was kept. Every pub had its Gent and they would charm the ladies and watch for trouble, calming nerves and keeping the peace. My grandfather was one of the last. He stood in bars and played his merry tunes. The women loved him, the men allowed him to ply his trade for the good of the community, but despised his very being, just waiting for the day his body became frail and his ability washed away. He'd transmit his tunes and step his steps all for free beer and gratitude. Never veering from the task, unless he had to dance the jig. When two gents met in combat, neither would know the authenticity of the other, until the striking of the first blow, which led to a merry dance and the jig would entertain and captivate all present. This was a shaming of the gents, who should have known better on who the vent their wrath on each other.

Woodchurch Boys (W/Boys): Yeah that's right, we've heard the stories we've heard your kind. You're going to keep us safe keep the women entwined. Your fate is set, you have travelled and found, your home your place, until you reach the ground. We'll let you play your tunes and sing, but remember when it's over where you once ruled, a beaten dog and you're the fool.

B: I play my merry way, my tunes derive from pleasant days. You can't scare or oppress my will. My mind is strong my limbs are still. I will watch and wait for your move and drive your venom into the gutter, don't speak to me because I'm a nutter.

W/Boys: ha-ha, it's true, it's true he speaks in rhymes, you're going to regret all the time. See we have history in this part of the world and you, your crime could not be worse. You stepped you jumped out of your park and you have left without your mark. We can't accept your trade in here; your home has not yet paid the bill.

Kirkby/ Lads: You don't need to ask from us, this Gent is certainly one of us. With consequence and invitation, we send our acceptance of visitation. The Woodchurch Boys are as one, come and go in our land. The Gent you have has grown and flown, let him rest in his new home.

W/Boys: Your own is here and here to stay, he'll work his part for little pay, in our pubs and roundabout, the reciprocation is all about. The Kirkby lads have just been told the Woodchurch is their second home.

There was absolute silence on the airwaves. This had not been heard for centuries. It was the coming together of communities in the old ways. Long forgotten folklore was being reinacted. The people doing it didn't even know what they were about to say next. Rights and passages were being re-formulated.

I sat in the pub and I began searching the airwaves for the Rowan clan, waking the Gents up from their slumber, it was time for those capable to walk the old ways, to be counted. I walked in a circle in the open space in the pub broadcasting with my mind the following incantation:

B: *Round and round we move in time,*
In and out the barley mow,
Up and down round and round,
Grinding out the barley:
Round the Rowan wends.

You are me and I am you,
In and out the barley mow,
This is how it mends,
You are all the Yew Tree grown:
Round the Rowan wends.

We call all men from here eternal,
To stand and say this is our day,
This my day brings,
In and out the barley mow:
Round the Rowan wends.

Rise and call you men of law,
Rise and do your worth,
For this is law in all our land,
And you are chosen at birth:
Round the Rowan wends.

The rhyming went on in this manner as I walked in a large circle in the pub.

Sian: *Kevin, what the hell was that?*

W/Boys: *Is this the lovely Sian, Kev. Is she coming to live with us?*

B: *Yes that's her; watch out though she's got a bit of a bite.*

Sian: *Hey, what do you mean?*

W/Boys: *We're just going to go off in a corner and chat to Sian.*

B: *(laughing) Ok she can take care of herself, but watch out she's vicious.*

Sian's voice came back to me telling me about what she was up to. It had changed though, she was not brash and harsh anymore, she was absolutely sexy and she was relishing her new contact and the position she was in.

The next morning I went into town and bought a complete new set of bed linen. Quilt, covers, pillowcases, pillows. I stripped the bed and started a spring clean. The flat had to be perfect for when Sian arrived. After cleaning the bedroom, I started to look at the rest of the flat. What I needed was a bachelor pad. I needed a clear out, I needed to start afresh.

The second bedroom was full of children's toys, books and a functioning but four or five year old computer that had been replaced. I opened the front door, went down the 4 flights of stairs to the entrance hall and jammed the main door open. I carried all the toys, books CD ROMs and the computer down the stairs and lined them up against the outside wall. Also any bric-a-brac I had lying around was taken out. The car was loaded and I headed for the waste disposal site in West Kirkby. At this point I had decided that everybody was aware of my activities, so I didn't feel the need to close my front door, I just left it open. On arrival at the waste centre I didn't go all the way in. I stopped at the oil recycling area; at that point there was usually the odd refrigerator or cooker around. I laid the computer out on the floor as if it had been set up for connection, leaving all the leads and plugs and stacked all the CD ROMs next to it. My son had a football table he was given the previous Christmas. I set it up next to the computer and added the rest of the toys and books. Quite an expensive little ensemble.

On returning to the flat I began cleaning and polishing. When I had finished I turned my eyes to the walls. There were numerous photographs of the children hanging up. I took them all down and put them in a bin bag which was to be thrown out. For some reason, I wrapped them tightly in the bin bag and placed them at the bottom of a cupboard. I was so glad later when I found I had done this instead of throwing them out.

The fish tank caught my eye next. My time sitting in the flat with the spirits had played on my mind and I thought having living things in the confines of the flat was bad from a spiritual perspective. 'If they die here their spirit never leaves'. The tank itself was encased in a polished wooden box. I had spent many hours making the 'frame' or box which I stained dark oak. The idea was from the pet shop which had a 'living picture' fish tank which was about two or three inches thick and had enough room to keep a few guppies or neon's in it. I thought this was a bit restrictive so I bought a tank 3ft by 1ft and set about making a wooden box to display it in. It worked very well and I used patterned beading to create the picture frame effect on the front. The box was plugged to the wall and contained goldfish.

I caught the goldfish one at a time, there were five in total. I placed them in plastic food bags. The bags were not the seal able ones, they had handles. I had three bags, one in one hand and two in the other. Closing the door behind me I left the flat and walked for about 25 minutes into Greasby. Just opposite the 12th Man pub Arrowe Brook runs under the road and off in the direction Saughall Massie. I climbed down close to the water and released the goldfish.

After walking back to the flat I began the task emptying the tank and unplugging it from the wall. This was not as easy as you would imagine given I had made it very secure considering it was holding up a substantial amount of water. By the time I had finished it was getting on in time and I loaded it into the car and set off for the waste disposal unit again. If you were buying all the items and wood used new there was about £250 worth of kit. The recycling centre was closed so I took the aquarium out of the car and placed it on the road beside the entrance gates and left.

As I was getting rid of old things, next on the agenda was my flying jacket. I decided I was going to give it to my cousin to see if he could get any use out of it. James is Tommy and Mandy's eldest lad. My father took great delight in pointing out to them that he was my cousin, even though Tommy and Mandy had encouraged him to call me Uncle Kevin. This particularly upset Mandy and on a few occasions she has tried to impress on me, that's just what you do when there is such a big age difference. Anyway according to geniality, James's my cousin even if there is over twenty years between us, so I couldn't see the big deal. This was just typical of petty family one-upmanship and I've never really understood it. Well I suppose I have, there is no great depth of feeling between my father his in-laws (at least he saw them socially, an improvement on his own family I suppose), he had some regard for my Grandmother but the family relationship was one mutual friction. I suppose negative strokes are better than no strokes at all. It doesn't add up in my book. If it's not positive then it falls by the wayside. Any rate, I was about to try and explain this to James.

When I arrived at Tommy and Mandy's, James and I chatted in the living room. I started by saying I was getting rid of old things and moving on in life. I offered him the flying jacket asking if he could get any wear out of it. He said he could and accepted. I went on to talk to him about responsibility and the importance virtue. "As far as I'm concerned, I'm not your cousin, I'm not your Uncle, I'm your mate and I will be here whenever you need me." I was trying to get over the pettiness of family life. James wasn't sure where I was coming from, he knew I was struggling and he tried to hug me. I kept my distance and left shortly after. Later, after I had been discharged from hospital and on the way to recovery, I found the intention had spectacularly misfired. Tommy thought the 'old thing' I was getting rid of was not the jacket but him because I was talking to James like a father. Whilst in hospital Tricia had visited Tommy and Mandy and taken the flying jacket back from James saying I didn't know what I was doing. After leaving hospital, I took the jacket straight back to James and there it stayed, mostly just hanging in his wardrobe until a subsequent episode. For some reason I always lose my jackets and coats when I have an episode. After a future episode, the jacket came home to me again.

On this occasion, back at the flat, I continued to communicate with Sian and the locality. I put some music on the hi-fi and stood with my back to the wall, one foot raised with it flat against the wall behind me. I was pumping out the music in my broadcast. I had no lights on, just the filtered light coming through the serving hatch from the kitchen. I had admired Paul Weller's work since I was a teenager although I listened mainly to the Jam. My thoughts had been about people enslaved by the power of the mind and it turned to rock musicians and pop stars that had broken through from obscurity to become rich and famous. 'Burning Sky' was playing. It struck me the song was about the conflict between Weller's idealism and the lure of success.

B: *That's the way they get you, build you up with talent and following, then they tie you down with a need to perform and keep your fan base happy. It never ends. Your vanity and the thrill of performance keep you busy. On paper you are wealthy; in reality you chase your tail for the good of the people controlling your mind. Your Burning Sky is forever.*

Weller: *You think I don't know, you think I've come this far not realising, my words told the story long before you ever came to understand.*

B: *Your words may not be your own, they are repetition of old stories, you are just the current participant in a long line of examples manufactured to keep the masses happy. You are bound in your lifestyle, do you ever find fulfillment?*

Weller: *its crap Rowan and you know it is.*

I played 'When you're young'.

B: *That's the essence isn't it? That's what we all try and capture and that's what we lose.*

Weller: *Fuck you dickhead*

I had moved as I was talking to the other side of the room and was leaning on my windowsill. I looked up to where I had been standing previously and there was an image of Paul Weller standing in the position I had been. He was strumming away at his guitar. His head was bowed and for some reason he had long hair, about shoulder length, which fell across his face. He was tapping his heel on the wall the way I had been doing and played along to the music. The image faded and I sat motionless, it was not a happy image, it was drudgery and I felt empty.

As the night drew on, I continued listening to the Jam, I continued communicating with a host of people and my confidence grew in the fact I was becoming more and more knowledgeable and that more and more doors were being opened for me, as long as I took people with me and maintained the momentum.

In the early hours I decided to go to Tesco's. The store at Bidston was open 24 hours and I was about to test my abilities. My car was now a tidy Volkswagen Polo 1.0 litre. The drive to Tesco's was free of traffic; there was nobody on the road at all. Having driven through Moreton I came to the Bidston Road and I used the small engine to its maximum, building up speed to high revs at each gear change. It was surprisingly quick. I don't tend to drive quickly as a rule always there or about around the speed limit. This particular road is national speed limit and I pushed the car beyond the speed limit. Its dual carriageway and I used both lanes to power glide from side to side. A slight turn of the wheel and the car skewed one way and then the other. I had the police in my head. They were telling me to get used to the feel of the car.

Police: This is how you get the most out of a small car in acceleration. Feel the glide, always remain in control, and let the car do the work. Your one of us, we have uses for you.

B: I'm just going shopping, you have me on automatic, I don't know how to do this but it feels natural and easy.

Police: Wait till you get to the roundabout.

This particular roundabout I usually take it at about 15 to 20 miles per hour. I approached at about 50mph. As I entered the roundabout, I braked to about 45mph, lifted my foot from the brake and cut straight across the two lanes, straightening the curve of the roundabout, instead of going around the lanes as usual. Halfway across the roundabout I braked again to about 35mph and entered the Tesco exit lane. There was no traffic present and I followed the slip road.

B: how the hell did I do that.
Police: Experience Rowan, experience.

On parking up I entered the store. I was wearing a t-shirt, shorts and training shoes. Walking up and down the aisles, there was nothing of great interest. I was here to stake my claim for the store. There were people behind me and more and more people were sick of the exploitation of big business.

In the middle of the central aisle I took my keys and money from my pocket and placed them on the floor and walked away.

The floor manager was aware of my activity, he picked up the items I had placed on the floor and followed me towards the tills. I sat on the end of one of the tills in the bag packing area. The floor manager handed me the items he had retrieved and started questioning me. I was animated and fielded his questions while ignoring his requests for me to leave. A group of male staff gathered at the end of the checkout and I engaged them with answers and put downs to their questions, still refusing to leave the store. There were five or six of them now attempting to persuade me to leave. When it became apparent that I was not going to do as I was asked, they moved forward and grabbed hold of me, manhandling me towards the door. I resisted and the progress was very slow. Within about 15 metres of the door they tried to change tack and attempted to wrestle me to the floor. I stood against them for a minute or so, then lost my balance and fell. Immediately they were upon me trying to stop me from retaliating. One pressed his forearm against my windpipe and for a moment I was in real trouble. I don't know how or why, my right arm was free and I grabbed his arm and lifted it clear allowing me to breathe again. They carried me out of the front door and placed me on the floor about ten metres away. I got to my feet and began shouting back at them. I singled out one of the staff who had helped eject me and said loudly "You will remember this day, you will remember your actions and you will think again about your life and what it means to you" There was still an audience watching my every move in case I tried to re-enter the store. I stood before them raised my arms to the sky and wiggled my fingers slowly bringing my arms down to my sides exclaiming "Come piggies come!"

The police arrived and I was just hanging around a good distance from the entrance. They came across and spoke to me briefly and I answered their questions. They didn't try and detain me and went off to speak to the store manager. I walked across to my car and made the short drive home. The floor manager still works at Tesco. Initially he used to be wary of my presence, but he has seen me many times, shopping on my own and with my children and now I don't even warrant a second glance. I am sure the activity that night was captured on the in-store security cameras, but unless you know the full story it just looks like somebody being provocative.

The range of people I was communicating with was growing all the time. I had a view and an opinion on everything and so it was no surprise to me when I began talking to Tony Blair. It began because I was making a stand against people who were threatening me to keep quiet and maintain the status quo. It was put to me that I would not speak out if it was the IRA. I launched into a tirade about British Imperialism being the root cause of unrest and dissatisfaction in many parts of the world and Northern Ireland was no different. I owed no allegiance to these people that bled the wealth of nations over hundreds of years to fill their pockets and sustain and fortify their unholy position of privilege. Nobody in their right mind could condone acts of mindless violence and murder to achieve a political point, but the root of the problem should be addressed, not the symptoms.

PM: So you would face the men of violence.
B: I have nothing to lose
PM: You have your life

B: My life is insignificant, I have become aware of the power and control of vested interests and I am not prepared to tread the path of servitude.

PM: What of the Loyalist faction.

B: What are they loyal to, a free democratic society, or the thought of a romantic ideal that seeps blood at its very corners. Should not royalists not be compensated for their loss and repatriated to the land they so love. Is that not the case of the Falkland Isles which is undoubtedly not British soil, is it not the case in Gibraltar, is it not the case in Northern Ireland. Repatriation or harmonious acceptance of the country they live in. Our history stinks and we are reaping the rewards.

PM: So would you represent your country in Northern Ireland?

B: Yes I would, no security, no protection just walk down the street and meet people. Would you do that?

PM: I already have.

The conversations with Tony Blair continued and I became his eyes and ears on the street. He listened with interest to the people in my network and wanted to learn about their drives, hopes and aspirations. In return I became his presence wherever it was required. My face morphed and his prominent smile appeared in front of people to prove his presence. I was now going about my business and grinning inanely at people when the moment demanded.

On my return to work, I only had one thing on my mind. I had to speak to Sian. My desk was fairly clear. I had left some work to be progressed but there had been no movement. Sian came into the office and sat at her desk in a pod diagonal to mine. I walked around the outside of the section and came up behind her. "Sian, can you meet me for a drink after work?" "Kevin, what are you talking about" I had frightened her a little and she disappeared away from her desk. Sheila had noticed that I wasn't acting normally and told me I needed to get a sick note from my doctor. I paced around the office. In my head I was going to get a promotion, I was going to be in charge here very soon. The floor was about half the size of a football pitch. I paced around it, surveying the room. Robert was one of Sian's friends, it's possible she had spoken to him, or it's possible he had seen what was happening to me and was aware I had a problem. Either way he was in fits of laughter at his desk. I just looked his way and caught his eye. He paused nervously but continued to laugh. It was easier to comply with Sheila's request than to continue walking about. I couldn't concentrate on work so I left the office. At the doctors later in the afternoon I explained I wasn't feeling up to work and needed more rest and was given a sick note for two weeks.

The next morning I arrived for work at about 8 am. Peter, the manager of the department was sitting at Sheila's desk. Peter had been a good friend to me, I had known him for about 12 years and we played in the same 5 a side football team. "Have you got your sick note Kevin" "Yes, but I don't want to give it in" "You need to give me the sick note Kev and go and get some help" I took the sick note from my pocket and started eating it. Peter sat and watched as I chewed the sick note and swallowed it. I went back to my desk and attempted to work.

When Sheila came in she quickly arranged for a meeting with personnel and a Union Representative. I was escorted down to a meeting room and once inside I was asked to sign a medical evidence form, a request to approach my doctor for medical information. I refused to sign the form. Sheila began losing her temper, "Just sign it Kevin", I said no. Again Sheila said "Sign the form" "Ok I'll sign" I was passed the form and I signed it Brian Boru. When I was a child my grandfather had told my sister and I stories about being related to Brian Boru, the first King of Ireland. Given the thoughts I had been having about ancestry, I thought it was relevant. Sheila was incensed and another form was produced. I signed this one M Mouse. I was told to go home and that I wasn't to return to work.

That night I played my music until about 11pm. I was not tired and my energy levels were high. I wanted some alcohol but the pubs were closed so I set out walking to Birkenhead to go to one of the clubs. It was a cold night and I wore my black puffa jacket and a pair of leather ski-gloves I had had since going on a school ski trip aged 15. Under my jacket I wore a Celtic football shirt and I communicated with John Barnes and other footballers along the same lines as my conversation with Paul Weller about having ambition and being trapped in the celebrity lifestyle. Gianluca Vialli interrupted.

Vialli: Mr Rowan, you are a considerate human being and I hope your search for enlightenment and justice come to fruition.

B: Mr Vialli, thank you for taking the time to speak to me it is appreciated.

My mind was set on the short strip of bars and clubs opposite the multi-storey car park in Birkenhead Town Centre, I entered the Ice Bar, I think, now called the Cool Room. When I arrived I walked through the door taking my coat and ski gloves at the same time. The coat and gloves were thrown on a seat close to the entrance. The place was buzzing, the women were gorgeous and I ordered a beer. Taking position on a raised area in the middle of the floor I watched the proceedings. Tony Blair was in my head and as the music played and people moved about I grinned inanely. Tony Blair was in the room. For about two hours I kept my position. At closing time, the lights came on and I could see faces looking nervously at me. Out on the street people lingered a while saying their goodbyes. A beautiful young girl came up to me, put her arms around me and gave me a real caring hug. It was the best hug I have ever felt in all my life. So tender yet so much feeling. There was a sudden realisation that I no longer had my coat and gloves. They had long gone and I set out to walk home in just my jeans and football shirt and it was near freezing.

PM: Thank you for representing me tonight
B: I didn't think I had much choice.
PM: You are probably right. You have strong views and unconventional solutions to the problems of Northern Ireland. Is

this your only area of vitriol towards the Government or are there others?

B: *There are others.*

PM: *So how would you tackle the problem of exhaust emissions?*

B: *Well progressive taxation fills the coffers but what you really end up doing is taxing out those least likely to be able to afford the benefits of being mobile. The benefits gained by the working population in terms of freedom of movement will be eroded and we will move backwards in terms of equality. Those wealthy enough to be able to afford the higher taxes will not be too outfaced at the charges, especially since the 'rabble' will be removed from the roads making it easier for them to get about in whatever form of transport they choose.*

It'll be 'prepare my carriage' all over again. What the country needs are people that think differently, alternative solutions, not those that are constrained by the status quo. Some of them may be uncomfortable for some people, but they have to be measured by the overall benefit. The best solutions are those that work within the overall existing framework, but question the seemingly set parameters.

For example, progressive taxation on cars is a logical step. But what if we decide taxation stays the same so that it's not pre-emptive to those less well off. We declare that each household can only have one four wheel vehicle registered for road use at any one time. There would be an option for scooters and motorcycles to be used. Modern scooters can be very light and fuel efficient. Some designs such as the covered BMW are ideal for commuting. Siblings would be mobile, partners could commute to work, mothers could still do the school run, and people living in rural communities would not be isolated.

Yes, it's different, and yes it would need a change in perception of how we travel. Some problems are serious and need drastic solutions but not always in the way it's always been approached. If you changed the haulage system to minimise empty vehicles being driven you could improve efficiency. Interlinking haulage firms to optimise local pick up points and ensure HGV's were fully loaded when travelling. You would need a national bank of HGV vehicles. Driver's could even carry two wheeled transport on the back of their wagon to get to the next pick up point or to ride home after a shift. It needs application and thought, I just generate ideas.

Cars could be looked at in terms of fitness for purpose, so a large family could be entitled to a people carrier of their choosing, a young couple starting out something smaller. People would be more inclined to travel as a family and possibly in shared journeys with other people as a more comfortable and convenient alternative to riding. I don't have any idea how many cars this would take off the road. I'm sure there would be a substantial difference to where we are now.

PM: You know the people are listening to you Kevin, you know they are seeing at first hand the benefit of talking straight, an open society that shares idea's. Things are changing more quickly than you know. What would you do with the welfare state?

B: The welfare state is an important part of our fabric because it protects those that do not have the ability to protect themselves while offering a standard of care to everybody in the country. There has to be a way in which this can be effectively funded and developed.

I am very aware Government decisions are taken based on available finance, vested interest of lobby groups, the ability to deliver and the perceived consequences of the decision making process. There are constraints of centuries of precedent and the acknowledged way of how to go about things. As with the global emissions theme, drastic problems require drastic solutions.

My personal belief is that much of the acquired wealth in this country is the result of Centuries of extortion and malpractice. So the lands and wealth of respected institutions like the Church and the Crown were as a result of oppression and acquisition. The landed gentry who supported these activities benefited in kind. I am not saying that the people living and working in those privileged positions today are morally corrupt; they are where they are as an accident of birth. Much of this Wealth is sustained by the ownership of land. Income in the form of rent from individuals and businesses.

The Church of England for example is one of the largest land owner in the country. Property companies for example, buy land, develop it and earn money on letting it out. Land is a natural resource, if it is to be owned by anybody, it should be owned by the state, for the benefit of the country not for the benefit of a minority. This is not a Communist philosophy, land is land, and it's not to be owned. The businesses running on it need to remain competitive and innovative so no change is required in the way they run.

Ownership all land should be transferred to Government management that includes the Church, the Crown, Property Companies, Landed Gentry, Farmers etc anybody that owns land. The businesses that are run on those lands should be maintained and allowed to prosper. The workforce, given a salary, that is fit for purpose. The owners should be given enough land to live on if it is their home, again, fit for purpose. If they run the company then given a salary fit for purpose too, but not extortionate.

Private houses would also be included, in effect you would be buying a building, and it's what most people imagine they are doing anyway. There would be an average ground rent. This would be calculate by taking out of the sample the skewing factors of properties including land of over an acre and flats and apartments at the other end. Anything over the average would pay more ground rent in bands. All ground rent would be paid direct to the Government. Property ownership in a free market is detrimental to the welfare of the nation. Prices are forced upwards by people with the ability to pay leaving those that cannot afford them at their mercy. So for example you have the growth of second and third homes in resorts and country villages forcing locals out of the market. The proliferation of buy to let, making rich people out of those that can afford and push the market price, but creating a dependant class. It's immoral and will cause more problems in the future. And all for what, an ability to own land and property based on financial standing.

I know that 'fit for purpose' is open to interpretation, if somebody looked at the Queens residence, they could easily asses it and say it's fit for purpose. From my point of view, at the top end, I cannot *imagine an amount of land more than a quarter of mile square not to be adequate for anybody. Wasn't it Prince Charles that set up a village in Cornwall on the same principles, it's only taking it to the nth degree. It's not my position to quantify 'fit for purpose' Tony, that's one for you. Maybe somebody's polo games, or somebody's hunting activities might be affected, the few can be educated to the point of understanding the greater need of society. We don't have to forget our heritage, record it, and let people understand the lifestyles and why they had the position of privilege in the first place.*

Liverpool for example had great swathes of the City built on the proceeds of the slave trade, is it not, even now, more civilised to regenerate this stored up wealth into something more useful, something more respectful than just leave it in the hands of a few individuals. The accident of birth that allows privilege should also be the accident of birth that allows re-distribution in a fair society. Nobody is saying I hate you, I want you dead, and I want you ruined. I am saying you have had your benefit I wish you well; you will be compensated for your loss so that you are comfortable but you will no longer be obscene.

What of new wealth; the likes of pop-stars, footballers and businessmen. Exactly the same rules, nobody is taking ability to earn away from skills and talent. Only from the un-earned activity of controlling the use of land for financial gain.

Society will benefit too, churches would be kept in a state of safe repair, even those closed through falling numbers and opened with a caretaker from 9am to 5pm, given back to the community. I my youth when I walked into the local churches, there was always a handful of people there, lighting candles, reflecting, praying. They were places of peace and sanctuary. They can be that again, people don't need to attend a service to show their respect to god or just to find their own peace.

Royal building should all be opened to the public, exactly as they were in use. The biggest tragedy of the Royal Yacht Britannia was that it was stripped of its treasure's when it was sold on. It should have been a public monument saying this is how your Royal Family lived and this is part of your heritage.

Art treasure and artifacts should be put on display so that we remember, but it's a step change we need to catch up with the modern world, not an evolution that will take far too long.

The profit's would then not go to private hands, but to help fund the welfare state and pension provision.

What a huge responsibility for any Government. It would be charged with the effective management of land and estates for the benefit of the nation. Safeguarding heritage and the Welfare State.

PM: Do you think our archaic system of Government will be able to be flexible enough to cope with your suggestions and then manage the resource as well continue with our day to day job of Government as it is.

B: Do you think the industrial revolution was about evolution or dramatic change. When Britannia was ruling the waves with a navy twice the size of any other nation plus a third, did the launch of the Dreadnought mean evolution in navy strategy or was it obsolete overnight.

Our system of Government is tried and tested, developed over centuries, but the world is facing problems that are serious in their ability to escalate daily. The Government process lumbers on reacting, but slowly and sometimes adequately and sometimes not so.

I dream of real progress in redressing the balance wealth and privilege. To say "To make the rich significantly less rich, would not make the poor significantly less poor" (Anthony Crossland), is a kop out of responsibility. What is required is equity to allow people to live in harmony, equal chances, and equal opportunities. It is not as simple as saying everybody gets an equal slice of the cake, but self actualisation builds respect for self and others and should be achievable through application. In a privileged society Hertzberg's self actualisation comes easy for some and less so for others. Where it is absent, there is scope for achieving objectives surreptitiously and where it comes too easy, greater desires can be achieved through exploitation. Both extremes are the root cause of undesirable behaviour. The point being, change *only happens with a willingness to change. Our archaic system and institutions have served us well, but like with the issues of the planet, if we really want to change, we have to make the effort. I believe in time, not in my lifetime, land and property will become the domain of the state. It will implode on itself. Its ownership is exacerbating the gap between rich and poor and skewing the distribution of wealth creating an ever increasing group of people that are destined to live under privileged in relative terms to their landlords. Who do what? Collect the rent and amass equity with no effort. All you need to buy into the property game is money. Doesn't that say everything about it? An altruistic society where people are motivated in life by self worth is an inevitability, but everybody needs to have the ability to achieve it in a positive way, it's just a question of when. If we keep believing its impossible then it surely will be.*

If you isolate that one variable in the model, wouldn't life be fairer? Wouldn't the Exchequer have additional funds for running the economy from a welfare point of view? Wouldn't everything else be a reason to achieve? It's not a proposition that says "hang on we'll change everything because it's not working. Its one variable in the model, where people and businesses could be compensated at agreed levels worked out by experts appointed by the Government and set a precedent for the future. It's the billionaire businessmen and institutions that would lose most. I couldn't conceive their loss of actualisation, so maybe its best left to someone who can.

I think one of the most obvious omissions from the Government process is the use of technology to gather public opinion to help with the decision making process. Over 90% of homes have access to technology that would allow surveys to be completed by remote control, or individuals by mobile phone. Simple questions asking views on Government policies. Imagine knowing in an instant that 90% of the population agreed or disagreed with a proposed policy decision.

It would increase public awareness of the Government policies, probably reduce apathy as there would be a greater feeling of involvement and give a feeling for the will of the nation. The Job of Government would be more difficult because not only would the decisions be based on Party politics, interest groups, financial considerations, partners and overseas associates etc. The Government would have to decide if they were going to be influenced by the will of the people or go the other way because of the benefit of doing so. Come election time the public would then be able to see when the Government had gone against public opinion, when it hadn't and measure the benefits of its actions, scary hey Tony.

PM: *Just a bit*

B: *the technology is there, how closely and how usefully it is integrated into the political process is for Government itself. I have little confidence of a result.*

PM: *Goodnight Kevin*

I was now nearing home after the long walk from Birkenhead to Woodchurch and needed to catch some sleep. My feet were blistered and my thighs were chapped with rubbing against my jeans.

Common symptoms of Bipolar are increased notions of self importance, feelings of invincibility and cerebral brilliance. I think the preceding text has demonstrated the occurrence of these symptoms in my thought process. Here is another example of how the mind can become pre-occupied with thoughts and ideas. In this case I was in communication with Luke the local Rector. I had been lucky enough to accompany members of the congregation to Iona (Luke had arranged a bursary for me as I was not able to afford the trip at the time, but I paid the money back to the retreat, as soon as I had the money available on my return to work) on a religious retreat and had been exploring spirituality with Luke. I had also recently been to the Cherry Orchard Pub with Wayne, a friend and his girlfriend Alison and Luke. The conversation had been jovial with Wayne enjoying Luke's company. I contributed some and then launched into a tirade at Luke about the hypocrisy of the Church of England earning moneys from rent and storing art treasures. Having been involved historically in unchristian activities and striving to control the masses and demanding support in the form of financial subscriptions for the upkeep of its buildings and institution that was purposely built to impose and impress. Going back to Victorian days and beyond, Ministers were ensconced in large houses with servants looking after their every need. It was establishment through and through and supported and reflected a society that was corrupt in its treatment of the disadvantaged. Is it any wonder that all the largest gravestones and monuments are closest to the church in all the churchyards? It's all about privilege and maintaining the order of things. No one will shed a tear now it's been found out and is falling into decay, but the legacy of financial gain lives on. How does the church maintain itself with such inadequate numbers of followers? Because it is obscenely rich from generations of exploitation. I observed that Luke was a caring and educated man and suggested he would be better suited in a career that made positive changes in people's lives like council work or politics. That night after we had left the pub and Luke had given everybody a lift home I continued the conversation.

Rector: So you believe in God then Kevin?

B: I believe in the unexplained, and in order to describe it to other people you have to try and explain it.

Rector: Isn't that what being a Christian is all about?

B: Partly, but not everybody is a Christian and the Christian explanation is no better or worse than any other explanation. Indeed, every person has their own beliefs and because they believe them to be true, they are as valid to them as yours is to you.

Rector: so what is your belief then Kevin?

B: God, or the creator, is my term for the unexplained. The Universe may well be round like the earth, like the early sailors, if we explore far enough and long enough, we may come back to the point of origin. It may be an infinite plain stretching out in all directions. It may me beyond our understanding to imagine the creation of infinity, because where do you begin. It's unexplained. The most logical thing I can think of is that God is the unexplained.

Something is responsible for everything witnessed by man. Why not call it God.

Rector: Does God have a purpose?

B: God is. Its man that has a purpose, not just man, but everything in creation has a purpose.

Rector: Why do you say that?

B: It's logical. If God created the universe, then there must have been a purpose. God existed before time and will exist after time. God just is. I can't comprehend any other answer because nothing else makes sense to me. There is only an understanding of time because of God. No matter how you unravel it back, no matter how you explain creation, something existed before and is responsible for creation, so I assume it will exist after. There can be no who created the creator, it's not logical.

That is my faith that God exists.

It's my faith because I can't prove it, but I believe it to be true.

I also believe there is a purpose for everything in creation. There is a lesson for each of us in everything we experience. The problem for us is that we don't know what the lesson is. We have been given freedom of thought and it is our charge to use it wisely and do the right thing in all circumstances. Obviously this is an impossible task, because we are faced with a multitude of stimuli from the universe as we know it. Some good, some bad, some marginal in their effect. We do not have an action plan of what is right and wrong, we have primary socialisation were we pick up early values and beliefs, we have secondary socialisation of peer groups and education and we have tertiary socialisation where we start to make our own sense of things. Always coloured by our own individual past.

So what is right and what is wrong? If you are reared and socialised with thoughts of murder and retribution, it may be for a seemingly just cause, or it may be from pure evil, you may think this is right. Who am I to say it is wrong. I can only do what I believe to be right. Maybe the world is meant to be inhabited by people who control and manipulate through fear and oppression. Maybe people in intolerable circumstances are designed to be that way, maybe their sphere of cognisance changes so what would be important to me and you, is no longer important to them. Only God knows because it is not only my belief he is the creator, but also all knowledgeable, why not, if God is the unexplained, then anything is possible. It's not logical, but it's a possibility. So each person has a destiny. Nobody is aware of their own destiny but it is as inevitable as the passing of time that is the way of design. All we can do is what we consider to be right. Even when we do wrong, it is meant to happen, because it is part of the lesson.

Rector: *How do we know if we have learned from our lesson of life?*

B: *In death you reach understanding and become one with God.*

Rector: *What is that understanding?*

B: *The unexplained*

PM: *Thank you Luke your help is invaluable*

B: *Luke, what was that?*

Rector: *Tony has recruited me as his adviser on the role of the church.*

The voices were not always intense or malevolent. I had a good giggle around this period with one particular contact. Dave owned the local video store. I'd known him since 1986, a good deal of time before I was ill, when Trish and I began to use the shop. He made an immediate impact on me because of his way with women. I first thought he fancied Trish, he may well have done, but soon realised that was his way with all women, indeed he was friendly and sociable with men too. I don't mean myself. We are at opposite ends of the social skills table. Where he is outgoing and friendly, I am reserved and suspicious, but we have always been on friendly nodding terms. Over the years I watched how he interacted with people, firstly because of my suspicions and then because it was amusing. Everybody wanted to be his best mate, he is very likeable. A bohemian character is the best description I can think of, not outwardly in dress, but there are hints of that too. He works hard, I knew he ran a mobile disco and managed the shop. As the demand for video and DVD rental waned he explored various ways of diversifying and it is obvious there was effort going into his business.

From almost the first instance I began talking to famous people, I would get acquaintances and businesses and fading stars filling my mind wanting to be associated with the things that were happening around me. Their motives were always publicity and putting themselves in the public eye. There would always be those voices that chided and mocked telling me that it was never going to happen and it was all in my mind. When I began talking to Tony Blair this kind of thought escalated. Dave's conversations on the other hand were funny and amusing. In the end, he didn't even talk at all (which is probably apt because we mostly didn't), he took to placing an image of his face, with one of those glints highlighting his smile on a coloured background similar to what you'd expect to see on a Disney image. I'd be walking or driving around getting some oiks trying to product place themselves, or further their career and this image of Dave would appear in my mind winking and smiling, you really had to be there, but it was very amusing at the time.

The following day I returned to work. I arrived early, about 7.30am. The reception desk was unmanned; the security guard had gone to water some plants. I vaulted the security gates that had been installed after an intruder had entered the building and set fire to the telephone system control panel. The only intention I had was to return to my desk and progress my work. At 9.00am when Sheila arrived, she was surprised to see me at my desk. She called security and with other staff followed me down in the lift. I got out of the lift on level 2 and took the escalator to the ground floor where I jumped the security gate once again and took a seat in the reception area. It was about 20 minutes before the police arrived. They escorted me from the building before taking me into custody and transferring me to Clatterbridge Hospital.

I had been exploring the ideas that not only were people able to talk telepathically, but also people could be manipulated with the mind to do things they wouldn't normally do if the network they were influenced by was strong enough. From my own experience, being guided walking, driving on automatic and dispensing Tony Blair's smile, I knew it was true. During the week spent in Iona with members of the church congregation, we had spent a wonderful evening at a Ceilidh in a local hall were I was introduced to too many traditional dances. On admission to the ward, I was place in Windsor Ward this time, apparently not needing to be on the secure ward, or maybe it was full. My feet were blistered from all the walking but I was running and dancing around the corridors of the ward stamping my feet at moments of impact that forced people to follow my actions and the images I was transmitting. I was entertaining my friends with the dances I had learned on Iona and they were joining in. My enemies were also joining in because they couldn't help it, but they were doing the inverse. So, if all my friends raised their right arm, the enemies would raise the left and those in groups could see who supported me and who didn't. I would get messages;

Peter's doing the inverse and so on.

I had images in my head of groups of people doing the Gay Gordon's and do-si-do ing while having to raise arms or legs or turnaround out of sync with the dance routine, while all the time my enemies were doing the inverse. There was much laughter and excitement on the airwaves and lots of embarrassment too. I stepped and stamped run and jumped up and down the corridors. I soon found a bed in Kensington.

Episode 8

THE LAST OCCASION I suffered a re-lapse was unique in the build up as it included almost two years of mood swings. Being very aware of my condition at this point made me over cautious I suppose, but certainly my recovery from the previous episode was long and drawn out. Mentally I was not able to pick myself up and move on as I had been in earlier experiences.

The return to work was difficult. Not from the Company perspective, they were very fair and accommodating. It was impossible for me to return to the section I had worked on previously. Members of the section had decided they could not work with me given my previous behaviour. Unfortunate but absolutely understandable from their perspective. I was found a role in 'e-transformation' a department put together to encourage everything 'e' in the business. To maximise the use and benefit of computer and communication technology in all its forms. It was an odd period to arrive. The Company was looking at outsourcing the administrative parts of the business, so 'e' projects were put on hold. There was very little throughput of work in the department and even less for me. This had its advantages, when I first returned to work I was still taking a higher dose of medication and was a little 'spaced out' to say the least. By this I mean distant and slow to co-ordinate my mind with problem solving if that makes sense.

Getting up for work was difficult. When I say this, everybody says "I know how you feel." I can assure you they don't. I know the difference only too well. I struggled against the medication regime for too long trying to attain their feeling of not wanting to get out of bed. The work then, was in short supply and when it came it was sufficiently out of my comfort zone to be a challenge, but it was never impossible. The managers there, along the staff were very helpful and I slowly regained a feeling of normality. I was quite surprised, I made number of friends I never really expected and it was a good time considering the situation.

As the Company moved towards reaching a decision on outsourcing, everybody's job came under review and another round of redundancies were announced. There was no longer a requirement for marketing type work so I had to try and find a suitable alternative to apply for. There was nothing I had the relevant experience for. Although I had over 15 years with the company, my experience was quite narrow. I decided to apply for compliance as I had worked on the other side of the approval process so I had a little bit of knowledge in that respect. The role was based on the Financial Services Handbook and its interpretation for the business.

I was duly appointed in time to the compliance team, initially with the Company and then outsourced to the new company. As with every new job, there was an initial bedding in period which was manageable and I gave it my best effort. I knew however that my best effort wasn't what I had been capable of before being diagnosed. As the demands of the job increased, so I became less effective. The FSA Handbook is a complex document with a number of different books covering differing aspects of regulation. It is written by legal experts with a view to making water-tight rules governing financial services businesses and their employees. It is pure legalese. On psychometric tests I score in the top quartile for managers on verbal reasoning. I score in the bottom quartile for mathematical reasoning because I take too much time to work out the answer. The FSA handbook is the nearest example I have come across of language, written in a mathematical format and I struggled with it from day one. The joy of language is its versatility, the imputed meaning of context and expression. This was precise and methodical referenced by indices and addendums. Not only did I have to refer to it, I had to interpret it for the business.

The daily interaction with other departments didn't help. As previously stated, I have never been one for networking and my new role was less of a progressing role and more of an influencing and guiding role. I did not have the confidence in my knowledge, nor the negotiation skills required to effectively carry out the job. As time went by I would review every meeting, conversation, e-mail in my head trying to work out why things were not progressing the way I would like. I was paranoid, nervous and unsettled the whole of the time. It was having an effect on my work, I was so busy reviewing everything, I was not progressing anything effectively. I couldn't focus on the work in front of me, couldn't apply my mind to the problem or issue I was dealing with, just engulfed in why I couldn't move things in the past and why people were being so unhelpful. I knew I was having difficulties and I was also experiencing involuntary thoughts. I asked my consultant to increase my risperidone; there was no problem because I should have been on double the amount I was taking anyway according to my prescription. I did this a couple of times in this period, doubling up my risperidone until the involuntary thoughts stopped, then reducing them again because I felt better on less. I even talked openly to people on my section, admitting that I 'heard voices'. In the main the people on my section were friendly and I enjoyed their company. On a few occasions, I blew and blasted off memo's basically just saying my piece. I didn't like it when somebody took advantage and when backed into a corner I always stand my ground, even then. It didn't have a positive effect though, it never does.

I knew I was not well liked on the whole, but was quite used to that and just carried on thinking I can't change the way people think. Then one day I was waiting for the lift on level G and as it opened Terry was already standing in it. Terry was one of our 5 a side team, we had played together for years. He was now a middle manager, fairly senior. I had been swapping memos with one of his team that had had a go at belittling me. I walked into the lift and said "Alright Terry" he never answered openly just said "cunt" under his breath. It was totally unexpected, here was a bloke I'd shared loads of recreation time with, laughed and joked with and regarded him as a friend and he had just called me a cunt. It was something he would never have done a few years earlier when I was fit and healthy, he was weary of me then, but now I was out of condition and bloated on the medication and he knew I wasn't going to react in a work context. I was shocked and said nothing just rode the lift to my floor and got out.

This was a real turning point for me. I knew I was struggling trying to hold it together and I knew the job was not good for my health. When somebody turns on you as nastily as that, when you consider them your friend, and also you can't fathom why they did, is hard to take.

I couldn't get my head around it, couldn't think straight, couldn't get on with my work. All this time, the days were going by, I was functioning to the best of my ability and no-body had any idea what was going on inside my head.

I asked for a one to one with my manager. Ron was an easy person to get along with and he was quite measured and reliable, as I thought. I had kept him informed as best I could about the way I felt and the impact the work was having on me. We had discussed seeking a less demanding role through personnel and it was a possibility. I told Ron of my experience and said "I know I am not well liked in the Company but I've just had an experience of somebody abusing me under their breath as I entered the lift. Ron asked who it was and I said it doesn't matter. I thought it just confirms that if a senior manager can do that then I have no chance of getting along in this Company. Ron was sympathetic and we left it at that.

The next day I was entering the lift on level 7 and Dick was standing at the back talking to somebody "I said hi to Dick" He said "lying shit" under his breath. I couldn't believe it. Ron was Dick's best friend on the department, and he must have related the story to him. Dick was another middle manager, similar to Terry. That was it; I was leaving the Company from that point on. I wasn't prepared to put up with endangering my health, not being able to relax in my recreational time and taking insults from people I had considered friends. It was obvious I could never get on in the Company where I was disliked in general and in my areas of influence there where senior staff who had absolutely no intention of working with me. I approached Dick at his desk "What was that you said in the lift yesterday?" I wanted a reaction from him, I wanted an excuse. "I don't know what you mean?" I sat and quizzed him angrily. He didn't rise to it and he wasn't flustered.

I was going to leave work, I didn't care about the financial implications, it was a well paid job, but on balance I didn't want to go through life feeling the way I did at that point.

When the opportunity for redundancies came up, I had no doubt about putting my name down to volunteer. I would get just over a year's salary in redundancy monies. The arrangements take a good deal of time to work themselves through from the initial announcement to receiving the payment. I used this time to decide what I was going to do with my life. I wanted to find work that entailed the minimum amount of interaction with other people. I was convinced I was entirely hopeless at moving projects or work in conjunction with other people and the subsequent failure of progress caused me stress. I therefore looked for the kind of work that was reliant on my own endeavour. If I didn't have to rely on anybody, there were no relationships to get stressed about. Regardless of all the good advice I received, I saw a sales franchise as the ideal opportunity for me. The one I chose was selling and distributing pet foods door to door. The franchise was ideally suited to a couple or partnership splitting the work load of sales, deliveries, stock control and administration. I believed I could do that on my own. There were one or two examples of individuals being successful in the business already. In practice I failed. Not only did I fall behind plan, the startup period saw a gradual change in my mood and six months in, I was struggling with a period of depression. It was really difficult motivating myself for canvassing new business and when I was out on the doorstep, I was not exactly building rapport and providing a positive image. I was flat and morose and there wasn't a chance in the world that I was going to build the business.

I knew my business was failing. I had put most of my redundancy money into it and the rest went keeping the business going. I decided I needed energy and vitality to get the business moving and I knew I could achieve this coming off the risperidone. My Consultant was still telling me it was neither here nor there, as I was not taking a therapeutic dose, so I thought, it's worth the risk and I came off the risperidone.

It took a few weeks to come out of my system, but it certainly had the desired effect. I had a two week period when I was just bouncing on the doorstep. More people were inviting me in and more were ordering supplies from me. I recognised my old self and enjoyed buzz of feeling good again. It was very short lived though. Before long the involuntary thoughts were back and I was not being very cautious at all.

The usual pattern emerged and I dismissed thoughts of conversations in my head as just the way my mind worked and was able to disregard them for some time. There were two occasions I should really have been picked up on that spring immediately to mind.

The first was when Liverpool won the Champions League in Istanbul, not the game itself, but the procession through Liverpool. The game had been brilliant and inspiring. I remember thinking of it as a metaphor for never giving up. I was six months into a year's business plan and three nil down. When the team paraded around Liverpool I was sat at home watching on the television on my own. I was seeing Rebecca, it was never anything serious, but she was good company even though I was down most of the time and just dull I suppose. As the cameras followed the open top bus I was communicating with the players. The focus was on the foreign contingent and we were talking about Liverpool and the feeling of the city. I was fairly compos mentis at this point and I can't imagine why I didn't pick up the warning signs.

The second occasion, I had gone around to Rebecca's for the evening. Her son had planned to go out with friends. They all let him down and didn't turn up. I said I would go with him. The last time I had been to a club was the night I dispensed Tony Blair's smile. We ended up in a bar a few doors down, Sherlocks in Birkenhead. I paced myself and just watched the evening unfold. A little later on after a couple of beers I completely lost it for a couple of minutes, I was walking around the bar looking at people as if searching for something. I was on automatic and was moving around checking people out. Rebecca's lad caught up to me with one of his friends and said Kev, where are you going? I snapped out of it and settled down. That was a big warning sign. I had had similar before. One day, during a previous episode, I had already moved out of the home I shared with Tricia, I had a thought of 'I'm going to get into my house' going through my head and I had taken the key to my flat out of my pocket and tried to use it to open Tricia's front door. She opened the front door and said "what are you doing?" and I snapped out of it and thought 'what am I doing?' This was exactly the same.

I usually played music in the van. My son would always play his CD's when I ferried him about so there was some of my music and lots of his. He had taken to playing the Canadian Band, Simple Plan 'Still not getting any' occasionally. I couldn't believe it, it was a good album, but there were four songs on there that could have been written about my life. When I was in the van on my own I began playing these four tracks at full volume and broadcasting them, as I had done in previous episodes. 'Welcome to my Life' reflected the isolation I felt, 'Perfect World' was uncannily close to the way I felt about Tricia. 'Me against the World' told of the struggle between the 'networkers' and 'Untitled' questioned why all this had happened to me. Later it would have an even more poignant meaning to me.

The previous thoughts of sentinels and gents came back; it was always the same theme. Long lost ways of endeavour and valour backed up by ability to calm situations before they got out of hand. Ultimately there was an air of invincibility and protection that had never been tested. This time the theme took a more alarming turn. I was not only the first born runt and unpredictable, I was the rat arsed cunt, bent on finding my destiny in the face of evil. My role was to search it down and confront it, knowing I faced certain death. If I survived there was more evil to find but one way or another and I would reach fulfilment. I spoke with the Kirkby voice and the Woodchurch and Birkenhead voices almost constantly. The Kirkby voice knowingly saying just come and go and do your thing you'll find no trouble here, we know you, we'll laugh and joke, we know you're not a threat to anybody, the Woodchurch and Birkenhead voices disbelievingly questioning the things I said.

I took a drive to Kirkby; I was talking to the Kirkby voice on the way.

Kirkby voice: You've been away a long time you are a forgotten man

B: I just come and go.

Kirkby Voice: Then why do you keep coming back?

B: You know I have family here.

Kirkby voice: You know the 'rat arsed cunt' is a joke?

B: You know the joke is on the person who tests it?

Kirkby voice: Nobody tests it here, or anywhere in Liverpool, the 'rat arsed cunt' is the joke.

B: Well the joke is coming home.

I came into Kirkby via Fazakerley which was unusual for me. I almost always take the Lancs and turn up Moorgate Road. I headed towards the station. It was dark and the sky was black. Co-incidence played a part in my thoughts again, a thunderstorm raged as I drove around Kirkby. Coming up to the station I was playing 'Untitled' by Simple Plan. I was home and I was broadcasting how I felt to everybody. The white light was the realisation of my destiny. The fading away was the loss of myself preservation in steering clear of trouble, I was heading towards death. I'd turned into Mill Lane on the way towards Tower Hill. The lightening lit up the sky and a few seconds later the thunder boomed out across the night. I was driving around Kirkby lamenting my life and exclaiming the coming of the rat arsed cunt and I was bringing the lightning down at the same time.

Kirkby voice: What the fuck are you doing Rowan?
B: Just driving and singing.
Kirkby Voice: What about the fucking lightning?
B: Just driving and singing.

On reaching the traffic lights at the junction of Bank Lane, directly opposite, coming out of Headbolt were two police vans and a car.

Police: We are watching you Rowan.

I sat nervously thinking they were going to stop me. The lights changed and they turned left into County Road. I turned left also and headed in the opposite direction. I spent the rest of the thunderstorm driving around Kirkby, visiting all the places of significance from my youth, listening to the response of people in my head. I broadcast 'Perfect World' and remembered the places we met, it was not just my home, it was our home and it made no sense that we had parted. I was in control of the lightning and it struck all around. I was affirming my dedication to Tricia, she was one of us, I loved her then and now, not in the romantic intransient way, but deeply in a non affectioned way. It was something she never understood, she had a chocolate box view of love and I couldn't match up to it. "Me against the world" was augmented with great passion and matching volume over the airwaves and was an open invitation to anybody listening. This was my stand and it was as uncompromising as my life. When the storm finished I drove home.

That night I lay in bed thinking about the regeneration theme, I had passed the age when it was possible. I was fat and gone to seed; the ability to recover had passed me by too. I had not moved on to another woman in a significant time and my future was sealed. I would decay further and eventually become a target for the people I entertained, taking great joy in my fall and discomfort. My only saving grace would be an honourable end and death. As I lay there, the presumed strength I had always felt in manic situations, the reality was obviously very different, drained away. I felt armour plating under my skin, on my shins, thighs, torso and arms being stripped away one piece at a time. I was now on a final mission, defenceless and accepting my fate.

In the end I couldn't sleep and I headed off to Liverpool city centre to walk the streets, try out the bars, feel the atmosphere. I wasn't intent on finding trouble; I was going to see if trouble found me. I parked in one of the roads off Duke Street. Years earlier after I had finished polytechnic I started my first job there, an insurance brokers in an office in the NCP multi storey car park so I was vaguely familiar with the area. I was in a stone's throw of Concert Square and headed towards the nightlife. All the time my head was filled with thoughts of keeping the atmosphere flowing, fulfilling my role as the runt and entertaining the people I met with my mind. If I met trouble, then I would be put to the test.

My clothes were casual and one or two premises I approached turned me away.

B: Make sure it's clean next time I visit!

Doorman: Ok, there's nothing here for you, go on your way.

There was no problem with the rest of the bars I just walked in, walked around looking and watching, searching for any signs of resistance to my presence. There were none, I relaxed and stopped and had a drink, in one of the bars. I was broadcasting my beat, the atmosphere was lively and the people were brilliant.

Scouse: There's no need for a runt here, we learned years ago how to enjoy ourselves, relax have fun.

B: No need at all.

Scouse: Liverpool learned from the lessons of the past, everybody here is just the same, come and enjoy, come back again.

I very infrequently visited the city centre bars and clubs, only with people from work in the past, never with true friends and I had never been here on my own before. It was really comfortable, a woman was dancing in front of me and she came up to me and started chatting and laughing and touching my arm. I found a seat sat down and stayed a while. After a little while I moved on to another bar and it was the same, I stayed for another shandy and I enjoyed the atmosphere.

Scouse: See Kev, you're not required in this city, we know your type, we've seen it all before, relax have fun, come back for more. Fuck off home you rat arsed cunt (laughing)

B: *(Laughing) what else can I do?*

With that I left the bar and found my way back to my van and headed home. Following my usual route I took the Kingsway Tunnel (the new tunnel to us) onto the M53. Instead of coming off at the Moreton spur I carried on following the Motorway to its junction with the M56. The CD was playing 'Hunky Dory' by David Bowie. It's funny how when you listen to music you can derive a meaning that is relevant to your own situation from almost any lyric. Well at least that was my experience in a manic state.

Everything that is written by recording artists is pre-ordained; it fulfils the prophecy of life. Each individual is guided and recorded by their interpretation of what they are allowed to understand. The chosen few are given credence for writing their proclamations, but they are neither stars nor pawns in the game of life. They fulfil their purpose the same as each and every one who has been born or is yet to live. It is destiny and each will understand the lesson of life as they were meant.

B: *And what is my destiny?*

You will understand in time the same as everybody else.

My driving had been on automatic for some time, I was heading towards Warrington and Bowie was still blasting out of the CD player. I was tired, I needed to get off the road and turn around and go home to bed. I have no idea where I was, exiting the next slip road I looked for a way of turning around. It wasn't a straight roundabout and I found myself on some sort of industrial park/heavy industry. By this time I was getting really confused, it was dark and there were no obvious sign posts. Approaching a road junction, the surroundings became familiar; it was the Tesco and B&Q roundabouts on the way into Southport. I recognised the road and the surrounding buildings, then it was gone, I was back on the lonely industrial estate.

You are trapped; see how easily it is for you to be misled! You will drive off the end of the earth if we want you to.

B: But for some reason you don't want me to.

Following the road in the direction I thought would take me home I somehow ended up back on the motorway, travelling in the direction I had been going originally.

I couldn't break the journey, I was just locked in and outward path.

Your coming to Manchester, see if it's as cosy as Liverpool

B: I just need to go home

The road stretched before me and I just kept on driving, passing Wilmslow heading for the outskirts of Manchester where I exited a slip road, no idea which one or where I was. 'Hunky Dory' had been playing over and over. I was communicating with people but it was confused, tired and I needing sleep. It was a built up area and I looked for somewhere to park. I found a Travelodge or similar and entered an enclosed car park with a security booth on it. The Security staff waved to me as I entered. Parking up, I went to investigate if the motel was open. It was about 3.00am and everything was locked up. Climbing back into the van I fell asleep across the three cab seats. I awoke at about 7.30am and was less confused. Leaving the car park, I found the nearest petrol station and filled up, headed for the M62 and made my way home.

At home I slept until mid-day. The urge to get out and about was overpowering. Driving my van, I had the music on a full volume, 'A town called malice' pumped from the music system and I broadcast it on to anybody that was listening. I remembered seeing the Jam live on the ice rink at Whittley Bay; a fan had climbed on the stage and approached Paul Weller. Weller lost his composure a little and backed off while Bruce Foxton picked up the vocals. I remembered thinking Foxton could carry the tune better than Weller live but the perfectly packaged youth, drive, venom and passion was the reason I found their music exciting and for me Weller had no peers. 'Beat Surrender' vibrated and boomed around the van. I knew I had travelled so far down a path there was no going back. My mind was full of ideas of bribery and corruption. Nobody legitimately owned any of the businesses you could see on the high street. The days of protection monies and coercion were not over. Criminals openly took their choice of businesses on the high street and the police allowed them to do it for the sake of knowledge and control. I was driving around Birkenhead and I was taking mental notes of businesses that had fallen and those which were struggling to maintain integrity.

Parking up in one of the car parks behind Grange Road, I started visiting the shops, a little like the bars in Liverpool previously. I walked in and surveyed the room. Looking and listening for indications of malpractice. I assessed their product range and evaluated their target market and their raison d'être. Visiting a whole range of shops and outlets, I carried on my mission.

You won't find anything here; you're not going to unearth anything that is not beneficial to the people who use our services.

B: *Then you won't mind me taking my time and exploring.*

I had visited almost every outlet on Grange Road and crossed into Grange Road North. I was feeling thirsty so entered one of the pubs. I entered the Dickie Lewis Bar and ordered a pint of lager. On the left hand side of the door as I entered there was a man setting up some sound equipment for some form of live music. I collected my pint from the bar and went and sat in the area he was setting up.

"Do you mind moving I'm setting up here?" "I'll just have my pint and I will be off" "You need to move on now, can't you see I'm busy" he was a big bloke and he was getting persistent. I was totally unmoved, "Just having my pint and I will move on when I am ready" "Look mate you are in the way, you need to move now" "I will when I have finished" Although the bloke was getting rattled, he remained in control and did not attempt to move me any further. After about five or ten minutes I picked myself up and walked further into the bar and found a seat on the left hand side. I sat down and set about relaxing and broadcasting my music. It was then that the owner's wife, owner, manageress or whatever she was came out. Only in her late twenties and quite good looking, she was screaming at me across the table, in my face as far as she could get. She was telling me to leave and that I had no right to do as I did. She ranted and raved, pointing and waving her hands in front of my face, for what seemed like ages. I sat there impassively watching thinking oh god, it's a mad woman. When a female kicks off on you, there is nothing much you can do, so I just sat and watched her waving her arms about getting more and more irate. I wasn't really concentrating on what she was saying, thoughts of the sisterhood were in my head and this one had the bit between her teeth. I didn't answer her; I just calmly got up and left the building.

That evening I took a drive out to Southport. All the time I was broadcasting my music. I felt as if there were more and more people listening to me, people that had been 'woken up' by my broadcast and people that were changing networks. I now had celebrities and pop stars, even the Prime Minister in my network, but it was too late for me, I could never return to normality, the secrecy of networking and the insanity of public display of its powers didn't add up to a positive position. I was acknowledged yet alone, facing the world stripped of my protection with nothing left to lose. It was a quiet night in Southport; I can't even remember what day it was. I parked the van and set off on foot. As in Liverpool previously, I was searching for the bars and clubs. Not far away from the tourist streets of small shops and fast food places that run off Lord Street towards the Marine Lake, I came across two bars facing each other at the point where traffic bollards closed off the end of the road. Entering the bar on the right, I walked in and surveyed the room. There were a good few people in and against the left hand wall; there was a small group of men sitting talking that looked quite shady. The end of the room was filled with a group of girls who appeared to be underage.

    B: Check those I.D.'s and make sure they are all legal.
    Barman: We'll get around to it in time.

There was an empty chair in the group of men, I walked over and sat down in their company. I was thinking about criminals walking into bars and taking over, my thoughts turned to celebrities that had fallen on hard times.

This is where we kick celebrities that have had the good times and have to earn their corn again.

Apparently ex football stars were the favourite in the past, before they earned enough money to set themselves up for life. One day they would be adulated by thousands, the next called from pillar to post to serve their criminal masters, used as a drawing card, to pack out the bars they worked in, but supposedly owned.

The men I had been sat with were talking with their minds about John Barnes and how he was having financial trouble and would soon be fronting this bar. I sat amongst them and they didn't speak. Soon after they got up and left the bar. I got up and followed. When I reached the door I was taken by the bright lights of the bar across the street and headed straight for it. This was a totally different feel, it was relaxed and buzzing. I bought a pint of lager and sat and watched. Thought about broadcasting my music and realised it wasn't needed.

The bar across the road needs you.

Finishing my drink I returned across the road and sat where I had been previously. The music was loud and there was a man standing at the door. A tall black man approached me and started talking to me. I had in my head this was John Barnes, but it wasn't. He was very friendly and he was asking me for my telephone number, he took out his mobile phone to exchange numbers. The music was very loud, so I couldn't hear him and my head was not entirely straight, so I wasn't communicating with him very well. I was communicating with him with my mind, but the reality of the situation was that we were not understanding each other. He shook my hand and I got up and left the bar. Wandering around, not quite sure where I was going to go next, just following the voices in my head I came across the Irish Bar, it was almost empty, just a couple of people here and there quietly drinking. Ordering a pint of Guinness I settled down in one of the corners and enjoyed my drink. Didn't stay long, nothing untoward happened and I left ready to go home. Out on the street I started to get my bearings, where had I left the van? I couldn't remember, I had no idea. It wasn't that I wasn't familiar with Southport, I know it very well and visit quite often, well two or three times a year at least if you can call that often, had done since I was a child, even riding there on pushbike with my friends when we were teenagers. No, as with my experience in Ormskirk previously, I'd completely forgotten where I had parked.

I walked around for about an hour and a half, expecting to see the van as I turned every corner.

What are you going to do now? Think you are smart don't you, think the world is turning your way, can't even find your van, what do you think the police will have to say?

B: It's probably the police who are blocking my mind.

At last I found it and headed for home broadcasting all the usual tunes, playing out the rhythms, with images of me and animal, sending fireworks and projected images of rock stars sitting in the cab. I was entertaining and turning people's minds to the evils of the network.

The next day I started quite early, my business was in my mind. There had been difficulties in making progress and now

I was assessing my decision to take it on in the first place. The franchisees were glorified maids in their pretty uniforms fetching and carrying for people and I was renouncing my decision to pay to become subservient in time and effort to the franchise company. I had given away my resource and labour far too cheaply to become a servant. I was on the road and it was going to end today. Broadcasting to the world I called down my fate. On the one side I was going to be a hero, returning to a high profile position in business, on the other I was going to meet the personification of evil and I was about to find out about my destiny, would I really react and take it out, or would I stand and fall in the attempt. There were alternatives but I knew there was only one way to find out, I had to confront the odds, I had to find my destiny, I had to be there and I had to make the right decision. Where I had to be, I had no idea, all I knew was that I had to look. Evil was at work everywhere, the biggest example on my mind was the war in Iraq. I had always been anti-war, the only time I discussed it was with my father on a Saturday morning. We talked of football, politics, family, television, all the usual things. Right from the start I was against the war in Iraq. "It would build resentment and problems for years to come" I could not have foretold the incessant murder of Iraqi's and allied forces that was to be the reality. Broadcasting "Little Boys Soldiers" by the Jam, the words had never been more true than they were now and dispensing Blair's smile was a long gone memory.

Inevitably I had driven to Kirkby, all the time broadcasting to all and sundry searching for the way forward, searching for a way to make sense of my life, whether it was acceptance by the establishment or an act of total obliteration for the greater good.

Kirkby voice: You're not going to do anything, you're just going to continue going back and forth as usual.

B: I'm here aren't I? Isn't that enough?

Kirkby voice: You know it's not enough, you know its actions that speak volumes not words.

B: You'll have your actions soon enough.
Kirkby voice: When?
B: Very soon.

The journey to Kirkby had passed by almost unnoticed as I had been pre-occupied with the thoughts going round in my head. Passing through Tower Hill I was approaching Melling Mount when I veered across the road and mounted the grass verge on the right hand side of the road and stopped. Climbing out of the van, I left the door open; windows wound down, took the keys from the ignition, including the key to my flat and threw them over the fence in the direction of a new development of residential flats. The keys fell on open grassland between the fence and the new buildings. I pulled my t-shirt over my head and threw it to the floor. I was now wearing training shoes and white ankle socks and a pair of shorts. It was a hot sunny day; I turned my back on the van and began to walk in the direction of Tower Hill.

B: How's that for action then?
Kirkby voice: You're mad.
B: I probably am!

Walking the full length of County Road recounting my youth, the familiar places, passing the estate I grew up on and the site of my now demolished secondary school thoughts and images from my past were being broadcast to the locality.

Kirkby voice: We're bored of all this, it's our lives too, we know, you know, why don't you just get on by?

B: It's not me I don't know where it's coming from.

Kirkby voice: We heard you when you were young, the rise like lion's speech.

B: I know what you mean although I didn't know 'Rise Like Lions' until I saw it on the back of a record sleeve and had no idea it was 'The Mask of Anarchy', not long gone in our history. Can you imagine if they treated their own in this way, how they treated the Empire? Glorious isn't it.

Kirkby voice: We know, we heard that too, everybody did. You're trying to change something that everybody understands but you. It's no big deal, its life that's the way it is.

B: There has got to be more to life than this. Where's the control, who keeps the status quo, shouldn't it be challenged, shouldn't it be changed.

Kirkby voice: You know as well as us, we like it the way it is, it's our own backyard and we like it that way.

B: There is so much more to do.

Kirkby voice: Not by us.

B: By whom then.

Kirkby voice: Try the plastic scousers like yourself.

B: Do you know the kids queue for the bus at the bus-stops after school, something I couldn't believe when I first moved over there.

Kirkby voice: You don't know what the kids do here now.

B: I know, but it's all the same, Middlesbrough, Hartlepool, neither was far removed from my experience, and I would lay good money on it that working class areas are similar throughout the land. It's not about where you live; it's about expectation from life, education, application and wanting to change. But as you say, you like your own backyard.

Kirkby voice: What about your backyard?

B: Yes, I'm comfortable as a plastic scousers in my backyard, I've given up too. Apart from this journey.

Kirkby voice: What is this journey?

B: It's a search for the truth.

Kirkby voice: What truth?

B: My truth, I'm narrowing the alternatives.

Kirkby voice: Forcing the issue more like.

B: I will find my path and I will stand on my own.

Walking as I talked I had reached Moorgate Road and followed it to its junction with the East Lancs. Standing on the corner I leant on the low railings looking out onto Southdene.

B: I no longer have any idea of who is listening or what are the consequences. I am standing leaving my home town probably for the last time and whether I have learned anything or not, I open my mind to be mixed with whoever cares to join me.

Standing gazing blankly as I had done previously in the hospital while looking out of the window I relaxed and as I thought opened my mind. After about fifteen minutes I began walking again in the direction of Liverpool.

Govt voice: Not many takers in Kirkby, but many people tuned in to your mind. Your network is growing faster than you can imagine, you need to take great care in what you say and do.

B: Who am I talking to?

Govt voice: Just somebody who knows better than you, your views on the government will not be tolerated.

B: But isn't that just confirming my pre-conceptions.

Govt voice: You mean your mis-conceptions!

B: If the government wasn't so interested in maintaining the status quo of vested interests and more interested in encouraging a true natural order, then there would be less to be misconceived about.

Govt voice: You don't understand the problems of the world, of running this country and the best way to approach them.

B: I understand when something is wrong. I understand when dynasties are created from the misery and exploitation of people and nations; they should not be allowed to prosper in perpetuity. Compensate these people for the unfortunate position of them being born into a position of wealth and power, but level the playing field, make their resources equal to others. Look at the dynamics of the way we live, the way we amass wealth, the way relate to each other. Sometimes evolution is not the best way, sometimes human intellect could make a difference.

Govt voice: You are seeking the impossible

B: I am just questioning things taken as a right or for granted. We have the lessons of communism, we know that is not the answer, but so too I can see much suffering and hardship balanced by opulence and decadence. Evolution of our society suit's the stronger, the better off, isn't evolution about survival of the fittest or most able. Able in this case referring to those with the resource to live as they please, nobody really cares about the people who can't.

Govt voice: And do you not think the Government tries to do this.

B: Yes, but the pace is slow, if powered flight had relied on the internal combustion engine for its future, the age of the jet engine would never have arrived. Why is it that in politics new ideas are frowned upon. The answer is vested interests of the strong and mighty. Individuals, businesses, countries. Do you think the war in Iraq is not about vested interests.

We are supporting the veiled imperialism of the U.S.A. coveting natural resources the way the British Empire did over hundreds of years. It's the natural course of events, strong nation exhorting control over weaker nations and we are supporting it. It's everything about what we do to our people.

Govt voice: You need to be very careful Rowan, you will not be allowed to continue with your misinformation, it only needs a car to veer of course, or a push from the right person and you will be history.

B: Do you think I care, do you think I'm worried about my thoughts when you have people like George Bush walking the earth with the blood that is on his hands. I could rub him out today.

Skipping I clapped my hands above my head and said the word 'dead'.

Govt voice: We're getting news through that George Bush has just dropped dead, the power of your network has grown beyond what we are used to seeing in an individual, the President is no more.

B: I can only continue my walk, there has to be an explanation, if it is true then I am bewildered but it does not stop my purpose, I have to confront my demons and I have to continue on my way.

Walking down Everton Valley I switched my attention to my place of work before redundancy. I thought of colleagues, some helpful some not, but all were serving the cause of American ideals. Their business expansion around the world was the new imperialism, funding and fuelling exponential growth of the

American ideal, admirable in its successes as it is grotesque in its failings. I was to return, a role had been identified and I would be answerable only to the Company.

B: *I can't do this, I can't begin to imagine how to put things right. My role is nothing to do with establishment. It is to wander and confront life wherever I find myself. There is one person who can take on this task. Angela, with the help of the network will do the right thing.*

Peter: *It's not for you to decide the rights and wrongs of business.*

B: *the rights and wrongs of life have no decisions, they just are. I still say Angela is the person to go forward with.*

Peter: *You need to touch base and make sure you are capable of rational thought. I remember well your trick with the sick note, is this not just the same?*

B: *I will touch base with you in about thirty minutes I am not far away now.*

Peter: *I meant you to touch base with your doctor, make sure you are well.*

B: *I will see you in about thirty minutes, hope you have the kettle on.*

Peter: *Do you want biscuits too.*

B: *It's up to you, but I will walk in the office and look for your desk.*

Peter: *Take your time, I'm here all day.*

My feet were blistered by now and the sun had started to colour my skin. I walked down Scotland Road and up Leeds Street towards where I had worked less than 12 months earlier. Communicating with ex-colleagues, friends and foes alike I made my way to the building. I walked into reception in shorts, trainers and little else, burned by the sun and asked for Peter, giving his full name. The man on reception said "He's not in today" and I turned and walked out of the building heading for the centre of town.

On reaching the City Centre, I began to think about how I was going to get home. Passing the massed taxi rank, I jumped in the first available taxi. The driver took one look at me and said "Out, I'm not having you in my cab, out" so I got out of the cab and climbed in the one in front of it. The second driver reacted in the same and ordered me out of the cab.

Climbing out of the cab I thought it must be because I had no shirt on and set about buying a shirt. I walked into Next. A shop I never used for my clothes and took the escalator up to the men's department. A t-shirt jumped out at me and I bought an xtra-large. It was a size too big at the time, but very soon I was to fill it out. I put the t-shirt on in the shop. It was emblazoned with Seattle Hawks, Slivertown Stallions. I was wearing an American uniform, the way I'd learned to think of the British flag, it would be really good if you cut out the cancers. I caught the train through to Hamilton Square in Birkenhead. Again I set off walking, heading for home.

By the time I reached home I had walked from Melling Mount in Kirkby to Woodchurch, only taking the train for the trip beneath the Mersey. I was desperate to relax in my flat and shut the world out. Of course, when I arrived I realised I had thrown my keys away when I left the van. On the landing in the communal stairway looked at my front door. Jacob always had junk and bric a brac cluttering the landing, there had never been an occasion in all the years I had lived there when he didn't have some form of junk outside his flat. Leant against the banister at the top of the stairs was a double aluminium ladder. Picking it up halfway down its length, and gripping it under my right arm with my left arm steadying it two runs down, I charged my front door. The door was on a latch and also locked with a mortise so it was solid in the frame. The legs of the ladder penetrated the first skin of the door leaving two holes two thirds of the way up on the locking side of the door. I tried to break down the door four or five more times using the ladder without success.

The realisation that the door was not going to open dawned and I began to think of alternatives for getting rest and refreshment. I walked back into Upton and entered the Horse and Jockey Pub, this was the first time I had ever been in there and I ordered a pint of lager and found a table out of the way. It was still early afternoon so it was quiet. The pub shared its name with a pub we used to use as sixth formers, our crowd used to meet regularly there so I began thinking about the people I used to know and communicating with them in my mind. They were all going to come and have a party in the Horse and Jockey like the old days. I could hear their progress as they came nearer and nearer and I looked out of the windows and got up and walked out of the door in expectation of seeing them arrive.

Friends: We'll be there soon, we are on our way.
B: I'm not going anywhere it will be good to see you.

I stayed in the pub as the evening moved on, drinking lager. My friends had advised they were not coming after all; it was too dangerous to be seen with me. There was a female singer on in the pub, the atmosphere was good and I didn't care. I just sat back and enjoyed the evening. About 9.30pm I realised I was hungry and crossed the road to the Chinese takeaway. I used this chippy frequently and I chatted as usual with the owner. Ordering special fried rice as more than as often I did, I took the meal, crossed back towards the pub and sat on a bench.

Chinese Owner: There is always a job here for you Kevin.
B: Thank you my friend

A conversation continued in my mind with the owner of the Chinese takeaway discussing business and how I could be of value. After only one mouthful, I could not eat any more and I dropped the meal onto the floor emptying it out of the carton. Standing up I returned to the warm atmosphere in the pub. Staying until closing time I watched the barmaids, rushed of their feet and their relationship with the pub manager. I looked at the characters around the bar and I felt entirely comfortable.

It was a great night and I felt refreshed and unconcerned about anything.

At closing time, the bar emptied and it took me twenty minutes to walk back home. I couldn't get in so I waited on the landing hoping somebody would come and give me some help. No-body arrived; I needed the toilet and relieved myself in the large pot plant on the landing. I can't remember when, but I passed out banging my head on the floor as I fell. When I woke it was still pitch dark outside. I could feel a swelling and cut above my right eye. My mind was re-tracing the thoughts of being alone and penniless and walking. Descending the stairs I left the building and walked back towards Upton along Arrowe Park Road. Past the fire station I turned right and right again into the Woodchurch Estate.

You can't find your way out can you.

B: *I don't know where I'm going, so I'm not looking for a way out.*

You are bound to stay; there is nothing you can do.

B: *I'm not trying to leave, I'm not trying to stay.*

I was confused and tired and couldn't get my bearings, walking from street to street, stumbling, half asleep, half awake standing in the middle of the road, trying to move but asleep on my feet. The dawn came and I was still within 200 yards of the fire station. Finding my way to the petrol station across the road I noticed three taxi's waiting for fares. Approaching them I asked if one of them could take me to Kirkby. The driver said he wanted £50 upfront. Looking in my wallet it was empty and I had to visit the cash point.

Sandra: Where have you been, I've been waiting for you.

B: *I've been walking, looking for somewhere to go.*

Sandra: You know I've been expecting you.

Sandra worked as a supervisor on the night shift at the local Asda. I visited Asda almost daily to pick up supplies, never buying enough provisions for more than a couple of days at a time. As my mania took more and more hold I used to notice the attractive females more and more. I would also think that my presence in the shop calmed the atmosphere, it would be 'cut' when I was in the store and the quicker I moved around the aisles, the more relaxed and more pleasant it would become. I would do a few circuits of the store to take away bad feeling and malcontent. I chatted with a few of the checkout girls, on the day Sandra caught my eye, she was looking at me. I started to approach her each time I entered the store and to speak to her. Nothing sinister, but I made it clear I was attracted to her. All the time in my head, she was talking to me saying it would be good when we could be together and she looked forward to holding me close. On the way home, we began to chat with our minds.

B: *It's ok Sandra, I've been busy I'm on my way to see you.*

Sandra: *Be quick then I finish my shift soon and it would be good to have breakfast.*

Asda was about thirty minutes walk away from the petrol station, I chatted to Sandra on the way, just about where I had been and where I was going. She'd been listening all night and she was worried. When I walked into the store she wasn't at her usual position in the store, so I walked around the aisles 'cutting' the atmosphere. After a circuit of the store I saw her talking to a colleague in one of the aisles. She saw me coming towards her. The fact that I had approached her previously had worried her and she turned on her heel and fled. I can't remember ever saying anything untoward to Sandra, but I can appreciate it is not pleasant to have the attention of somebody you do not want. I had spoken to a handful of girls in the shop but she was the only one to re-act the way she did. I must have scared her by my presence. I stayed in the store and the police were called. There were some minor discussions with the store detectives who were asking me to leave and I was refusing, but the police duly arrived. After my admission to hospital and treatment I continued to use Asda. The store detective and his assistant who had challenged me when I approached Sandra noticed me using the store. I was with my son and his friend buying groceries. He accosted me in the store and told me I had to leave saying quite loudly in front of people "I know what you were up to". I tried to explain to him that I had been ill, but he wasn't interested, only in taking my shopping from me and ejecting me from the store, to the amusement of the staff I had spoken to, who smirked and grinned as the store detectives had spoken to them before approaching me. He informed me that I was barred from the store. A few weeks later I had a visit from a couple of police officers, one male, and one female at home. They had come to advise me that they had had a complaint from a member of Asda staff of harassment. The female officer proceeded to caution me from approaching her. I interrupted and told her that I was unwell and had just spent a month in Clatterbridge Hospital being treated and if the same circumstances arose again, I would do exactly the same again as I was not in control of my actions. I couldn't understand why they didn't know the detail as the police had taken me to hospital on that day. The male officer took over and listened while I asked him to pass the message on to Sandra that I had been unwell. I don't to this day know whether my protests were taken into consideration or, if indeed I was cautioned, but I suppose if there was ever a point of law I'd be locked away, like being found menacing people with a table knife and a cheese sandwich.

On the day, outside Asda, I was taken into custody by the police who were very considerate and helpful. Somehow, I don't know how, Rebecca found out the police were holding me at Arrowe Park Hospital. While at the reception desk I was trying to walk away and go home as it was only a matter of metres away from the hospital. The police let me walk into the car park and followed me. In the car park I was approached by a drug user who had been beaten up the previous night. He was trying to explain to me not to get on the wrong side of the police, his head was saying something completely different. He had a strong chemical smell of class A drugs coming from him.

Drugee: I'll see your son ends up this way. I used to be successful and in control until my mind was turned.

B: You don't frighten me, you just annoy me.
Drugee: I'll frighten you when you see yourself in me.

The police led me back to the reception desk, Rebecca was there talking to them, trying to talk to me. The drugee was still with me, annoying me; I was getting irritated by him. The police came across and put handcuffs on me. (Rebecca later said she had asked them to do this, I can't imagine why) They left this individual spouting bile and smelling of drugs sitting next to me. I started swinging my arms back and forward whilst cuffed in line with his head. He asked me what I was doing and I just said experimenting. After about forty minutes I was taken to a waiting room in the hospital. A doctor came to see me and I was held there for a few hours. The policemen I came in with were replaced at the end of their shift and I was eventually moved to Clatterbridge Hospital. Rebecca had experienced at first hand my unusual behaviour in the short time since I had met her. She was concerned and contacted my father to inform him of developments and to suggest I needed help. My father's response was "Rebecca, he will just have to deal with it."

At Clatterbridge I was admitted to Buckingham Ward on the ground floor. I did the usual thing of circling the ward to assess my situation. The charge nurse was in her late fifties and I noticed her being offhand with a helper. I assumed the person helping was an ex-patient for some reason. I took umbrage with the treatment of the helper and whilst trying to find a toilet, I had noticed that it was difficult to open the toilet doors. The handles were round and your hand slipped off them easily.

Staff: You can only use the toilets when we say you can.
B: You can't stop me with your mind games, I will open the doors regardless.
Staff: We are in control here not you and you will only use them when we say you can.

I opened the door to the toilet.
B: Say's who?

I started walking around the ward at an increasing pace; I was breaking the mind control of the staff and setting up my own. The doors would only unlock when I said they would and the charge nurse would have to wet herself before she could go. I walked into her office as she looked at the PC screen. "So now what are you going to do when you wet yourself?"

She looked at me quizzically and told me to leave the office.

I continued to walk vigorously around the ward breaking the hold of the staff network on access to the rooms and toilets; my network was allowing the patients to move freely. Male nurses started to appear on the ward and they stood watching my activity. I walked straight up to one of and pivoted three times like you do when playing basketball.

B: they called me Kev the pivot

The lads in the school team thought it was funny, but in reality I was small in comparison to most basketball players so I had to make room. On the third pivot, I faced the male nurse and passed him an imaginary basketball. Four other male nurses descended on me from behind. I was frog marched up the stairs to one of the other wards and taken into an empty room with a mattress on the floor. The five nurses wrestled me to the floor. At first I gave and went into a crouched position, and then I tried to stand up. We wrestled for a few moments, at the time I thought five of them took time to get me down, but in reality they were taking care in what they were doing. I was held down while my trousers and boxers were pulled down and injected. The five nurses left the room and held it shut from the outside. I don't know whether it was meant to knock me out or not, but it didn't, I sat on the window ledge until they eventually opened the door and came in again. I was transferred to Kensington Ward.

I spent a week or so on the secure ward. While I was there an Irish Occupational Therapist lady attended to give OT in the mornings. She was about 25 and very pretty. I was transfixed by her. Chatting and attending her sessions. In my mind I was discussing with her the pros and cons of the issues concerning

Northern Ireland, in reality I was sourcing Celtic designs from a range of books she had brought with her. In the period leading up to this episode I had been exploring the idea of getting a tattoo. Tattoos were something I had always rejected out of hand but I had come to the opinion that I wanted to illustrate my mania in some form or other and was playing around with complicated designs of wolves howling at the moon they were standing on. I discussed it briefly with the OT lady and she said there was a Celtic sign for a wild animal. I looked it up; it was used on shields to show the attributes of a fierce animal. I thought this was perfect, I had been looking for something to illustrate wildness with understanding, but this was even better, if I was to mark my body it would be the ironic symbol of a fierce animal on a bloated body, forever carrying the shame of what I was and what I had turned into. If my mania had been allowed to run its course I would have no doubt of found that glorious end, now I was to live with the memory.

The design was A4 size, so I followed the directions of the OT lady re-sizing it in stages by drawing it onto paper, firstly top to bottom, then again, left to right. I was pleased with my artwork and placed it in my glasses case for safe keeping. A couple of weeks after being discharged from hospital, I took my design to the local tattoo parlour and had it tattooed onto my right arm. The tattooist merely rounded the rough edges and replicated my design.

Back on the ward, the OT lady was avoiding me, she had seen the signs that I was becoming infatuated, the staff at the hospital see this kind of activity often so they are not shocked, they just handle it. With not seeing her, I became engrossed in other activities. Singing was one of them and pacing up and down.

After being transferred to Sandringham Ward I found a female patient to spend time with, we played snooker and table tennis and chatted. She was in her twenties and we amused ourselves by pushing the table tennis table up to the wall so that one person could play rebounding the ball off the wall, while the other played pool, we then mixed it up so we took turns, singing at the same time. We probably spent about two days messing about. I was still walking into the common room and the smoking room and singing on occasions. I walked into the smoking room one time and Michael was there talking with his mother and his sister. Michael was about 28, 5'9' and stocky build; he had let it be known that he was ex-army. He had been intimidating one or two of the young lads on the ward and had also been quite forward with some of the women.

Michael took offence at my singing as I came into the room and we exchanged words. I carried on singing and ignored him. He then said I had insulted his mother, but I smiled and carried on. The three of them got up and walked into the day room. I stayed for a while singing, then got up to go to the games room, I was taking a short cut through the day room. I met Michael five yards inside the day room. He walked towards me and placed his forehead on the top of mine saying, can't we just be friends. I walked towards him pushing him back with my head against his. Michael head butted me in a downward direction on the top of my forehead. I momentarily lost consciousness as I slumped to the floor. Through a blur I could see him aiming kicks at my head. Blood started pouring from a wound on my forehead and I managed to grab hold of the kicking foot. Staff must have been pulling him off at this point, or he decided to stop, I don't know which. My head cleared in about half a minute, I had a two inch gash in my forehead and it was open and bleeding profusely. The blood ran down the sides of my face and covered my t-shirt. I stood up and looked at Michael and began singing Beatles songs at the top of my voice. I felt no pain, no fear and chatted with the staff when they asked if I was ok. I was taken back to my bedroom and sat on the bed waiting for arrangements to be made to be taken to Arrowe Park Hospital. Two male nurses accompanied me to the hospital and we chatted and waited for about an hour and a half. I was seen by a specialist and she inserted 32 micro stitches into my head. On my return I was transferred to Buckingham Ward to keep Michael and I apart.

Amongst other patients, Buckingham had three lads on the ward, probably early twenties all of them. They never caused any real fuss but used to congregate and smoke dope when it wasn't discovered and confiscated from them. One of them, Terry, used to talk about mind games and getting into peoples' minds and scaring them with his thoughts. I heard his voice in my mind but then I heard everybody's I spoke to at some stage or other. One day after the staff had confiscated his block of cannabis resin, he was busy throwing his thoughts around. Carrie was on the door and started wafting her hands at imaginary flies and cobwebs. Whenever I felt anything like this was happening I used to sing and 'cut' the atmosphere and make it calm again. Carrie stopped waving her arms around and I spoke to her saying "I know you can see these things too" she just laughed and said "they won't get to me."

Another one of the lads was Karl. He was often worried by events going on around him and would ask for support in terms of verbal encouragement at times. When he got really worried he would pace around the perimeter of the ward. Once when he was doing this Terry piped up "Who are you stalking Karl, I hope it's not me?" This rang true with me because when I was annoyed with somebody I would pace around trying to find their thought wave, trying to work out where they were and how I could get to them. It continued in the same vein with Terry and Karl seemingly corroborating my personal experiences. At this stage the medication had begun to take effect and I was wary about the implications of mind control. Not the normal conversational ones, but here I was touching on the inclusion of the spiritual world and how it could be used to control and influence people. Terry in particular had a black side verbally, but in fact he seemed one of the most harmless people you could meet. There is no doubt that he was mixed up and I have seen him since on the outside world and he doesn't appear to me to have the faculties to cope with everyday life, but then a high percentage of the people I came into contact with at Clatterbridge are in the same position. I am very lucky that the same cannot be said for myself.

Conclusion

For the first twenty nine years of my life, there was no indication of the health issues I would face for the rest of my life. I have never indulged in recreational drugs nor had a family history of mental illness. My experience can happen to absolutely anybody, it's an illness and it doesn't discriminate. The fact that you can't see or measure its effects makes it difficult to understand. How can somebody effectively describe their symptoms if they believe nothing is wrong? How can somebody understand, if all their experience of thought proves otherwise? It's not physical, even if the cause is a chemical imbalance in the brain; it's the thought process that goes astray. You can't isolate a thought and thoughts cannot be shared as they happen, to provide proof. They can be described by speech and documented in writing. Speech and the written word are accepted or not based on how they fit the cognitive process of the person receiving them. Essentially it can't be proven, only understood.

If I had read anything, or been party to any discussions about the kind of experiences I have detailed in this account, I would have not believed it could be possible and looked for a more rational explanation. Given my previous disposition, I have to accept that the majority of people will not believe my account of events. There is no mileage in me trying to prove otherwise, there will either be acceptance or not, but I hope it's been engaging in its own way.

The recollections of involuntary thoughts or 'voices' are only the most memorable instances of my thoughts, there were many more. In a psychotic episode, this kind of thought is a constant.

As I have mentioned before, probably the nearest I can get to an explanation of frequency, is if you try and quantify how often you have normal thoughts on a given day. Only mine were not thoughts, they were conversations that affected me, the same way as the conversations you have every day.

I have tried to understand why these thoughts occur to me over the years and the best description I can come up with is subliminal cognitive resonance. In effect, I have a thought and somehow, almost immediately, I get a response from a relevant person in my mind. The response is drawn from my personal experience and knowledge of people, so it fulfills my stereotype of them. The brain returns the response with virtually no processing time. I believe it is true that manic responses, both physically and mentally are only possible to the degree that you would carry them through in reality given the same situations. So for example I would never be capable of gratuitous violence because firstly my thoughts wouldn't lead me in that direction, but I believe I could be violent for self protection or unreasonable behaviour. I use violence because it is the most graphic description to make the point, not because it has ever been a serious consideration.

It's important too, to remember that mania also affects the reasoning part of the thought process. Whilst I am a socialist and republican by nature, in reality my outpourings would be restrained by common sense and practicality. I have knowledge of historically unscrupulous acts of institutions such as the Church, the Government and the Monarchy, but I am not a raving revolutionary with any great passion to turn the world upside down. So for example, I do not wish George Bush dead and I understand that the armed forces carry out a valuable and dangerous job, after all, it's politicians who make war, once the decision is made, there is no turning back and we rely upon the people who have chosen to be trained for such circumstances. It's a disgrace many of the ranks injured, disabled or suffering health problems as a result of conflict are not cared for the extent they cared about their country, but then compensation, like in other walks of life, is always about loss of previous lifestyle or potential earnings, isn't it?

I do not believe that the people running and belonging to our institutions have any more or less evil intent than anybody else. I can appreciate the civic duties of the Monarch and some of her immediate family and that they wholly believe they are serving their country to the best of their ability. Indeed the Queen is an exemplary example and there are not many people who could devote the time and effort that she does to accomplishing her duty. (Strangely, I have stood within two feet of her as a child visiting the Isle of Man in about 1972, for two or three minutes, standing next to the man she was talking to in the crowd. She seemed a very nice lady). I just believe the whole concept is morally flawed (excess wealth and privilege, supported by people who benefit and enjoy the trappings of the regime, whilst many of the people they serve are disadvantaged, just by life circumstances. I can't really get my head around the fact that logically there must be another way that maintains the wealth of the nation, but distributes, educates and develops society (not just sending a few deserving youths on self awareness and development courses that teaches them how do well in this context, that will perpetuate inequality, instead of a changed environment - really getting to the root of things and making positive changes for the long term). I try not to single out institutions and inherited wealth in my thoughts. There are plenty of examples of business and sporting and celebrity lifestyles that appear inappropriate given the general well-being. However, you cannot try and live by Christian values and believe in absolute destiny without accepting the order of life as it has been created.

I will happily take my dreams and voices to the grave. My thoughts and experience may well be at odds with the vast majority of the population, but in context, they are as meaningless as the next man, be he of royal birth or otherwise.

I do not, in reality, bear any ill feeling to the police force, they provide an invaluable service to the nation and life would be very different if they were not present. Nor do I have any particular yearning or need to be associated with life in my home town of Kirkby (nor any need to distance myself from it). I have fond memories of a great childhood but love life on the Wirral.

Whilst I enjoy the work of The Jam, they are not usually my first choice of listening material having moved on in taste like everybody else, 'Beat Surrender' the Jam. The teenage angst of Simple Plan is not something I would normally associate with today, but it wasn't the presentation, it was what they were saying. Their relevance fitted my manic persona perfectly and they are good tunes regardless.

Additionally I do not pine over my ex wife. She had come to the view that life is too short not to enjoy it and my condition was preventing that, as I would not accept her way of dealing with my illness. She was tired, quite understandably, of my refusal to take prescribed medication and scared by the subsequent lapses into mania, although I have never harmed her or been violent to her in any situation, well or unwell. I get annoyed when Tricia tells the children we split up because we were always arguing, she will argue with whoever she is with, that is her way. I think that when Tricia gets annoyed and her temper gets the better of her and she is unable to reason logically, she shouts, screams and curses and is likely to say anything that is derogatory about me in front of the children. I am not concerned of how that may impact on them. I am a patient man where my children are concerned. As they grow older I am happy for them to make their own way in the world and their own mistakes. I have never been demanding of them in any respect and my door is always open, but firmly my door. If they decide they would rather not visit, I respect that, it is their choice, in that respect I am the same as my father.

Apart from the occasional irresistible comment of her being a control freak, as she undoubtedly is in my opinion, to explain her illogical actions, I do not say negative things about their mother to them, because I do not think it is productive in any way. This does not mean I do not have strong opinions about where her parenting skills fall short of a desirable level of competence.

Where she has shouted and screamed at me in the past about how I should do this and how I should do that were the children are concerned, I obviously have an opposite view. Trish has custody of the children and in the main she does a good job, so I can hold my tongue, after all, speaking my mind wouldn't change anything, I haven't been in a position to practice effective parenting skills since she asked me to leave. To achieve that, you need the cooperation of the other party. Trish's outlook is, 'do it my way, or not at all.' I chose not at all, as she was in a position to do as she pleased regardless and she did. When I have verbally disciplined the children, Trish's reaction is to effectively call me a nasty man and collect the children from my home immediately so there is no continuity, no benefit, and no point in me doing anything other than enjoying their company when they are here. Now as teenagers when they scream and shout at her and use aggressive behaviour as a first line of defense, they are only copying the way they have been taught to react by her in a conflict situation. I only hope that in time they learn, as in all other areas of life, the loudest voice is not necessarily the wisest. When they think about what they know about their dad, through experience, not through what is said about him, they will understand the difference. My belief though, is simple, if I hadn't have become ill, we wouldn't have split up. Tricia couldn't cope with my illness and I accept that, she had to take counseling at one point because she could not handle the situation. Although I continued to love her for some years after we split, I moved on quite quickly in terms of logistics and life, my lingering disappointment is that all I have is a sense of agape, lost eros and phileo.

I have never mixed in circles were I needed to be afraid, so in that respect too, I have been very lucky. The closest I came to such an experience was on holiday in the Canaries about six months before I had my first psychotic episode. We had been on chatting terms with one of the apartment's entertainers (He was actually playing up to Tricia and she was having none of it). One night after leaving the bar, we noticed he was getting grief from somebody. I asked him if he was ok and this Scot turned on me with the foulest expletives I've ever had the fortune to be on the receiving end of. I grinned at him thinking, "He's talking my language". He stood about six feet away from me by the pool and he said "If you don't get yourself on, I going to throw you over the railings into the pool" only a bit more colourful. I grinned again and said "You can try". The entertainer intervened and said "He's just enjoying a holiday with his wife". The Scot said, "No, there's something about him". At that point the security team made their presence known and after staring at each other for a few moments we walked in opposite directions. I'd like to think we 'danced the jig that night.' The entertainer later informed us that he was the son of the owner of the apartments. I realised then that I was far away from home and had just squared up to a bloke who had a security team and god knows how many other contacts in close vicinity. For the rest of the holiday I didn't settle. I was very aware of everything around me. I didn't drink too much and I watched for signs of people watching me. I even saw him in the in the departure lounge at the airport and when he saw me enter, he moved on to another area. My paranoia however had grown over the last days of the holiday and didn't ease until after we left Manchester airport on the way home. The nervousness and preoccupation was very similar to what I was soon going to experience. It could then have been any stressful situation that triggered the condition in reality. The work issues could easily have been replaced by some other circumstance; I think the fact is this was always going to happen to me.

Even with the limited information I have given in this account, it is understandable from my experience, values and background that I should have such a non-conformist point of view. I admit my manic thoughts are not entirely original and must be some sort of subconscious reasoning process based on the extremities of my tolerance band for thought. The unnerving part for me, in a manic episode, is that there seems to be no middle ground, both in interpersonal contact and in thought, it is all black and white, with decision making on the black side.

I realise I will never progress in a work environment again unless I find one that doesn't have a stressful affect on me and my reasoning process, given my mind is delicately balanced on just enough medication to keep me well without stress, but not sufficient to be too debilitating in other ways (some seemingly stressful jobs are not stressful to everybody. Whilst I was a useless salesman (a positive factor, I can assure you, given the tricks of the trade), i.e. willing to take no for an answer from a prospect, there was no need to build relationships further than the immediate sale, you saw people for ten or twenty minutes then moved on. The application of effort was not a problem, only the mindset, there's another book in me somewhere about sales positions, but then most people are wise to such companies these days. If there is a match in comfort zones, then even a job considered stressful can be enjoyable. It's as individual as the person.

I do still occasionally experience involuntary thoughts in the same manner as when in a psychotic episode, but I believe I am 99.99% in control and that I have enough insight to request an increase in my medication if required. I can however become preoccupied with a prominent thought if it concerns me in any way, to the exclusion of the activity I am supposed to be carrying out and make basic errors in judgment and application. Having said that, I have the benefit of functioning to an acceptable level when stable. I just have to find the right job to support myself, not easy with the resultant credit rating (financial service jobs nearly always credit search an applicant) and medical history of my experience. I have been lucky enough to have been employed, or had sufficient realisable assets to see me through the majority of this time, so life could have been very much worse.

I have now had a full eighteen months where the balance of my mind and the impact of the side effects from my medication are extremely acceptable. I have started to enjoy life again, I strum my guitar, read the papers, exercise lightly (still can't face a proper workout, "Everybody is like that "I hear you say. I wasn't). On the negative side, I am out of work, had notice of court proceedings for the repossession of my home, my finances are exhausted and my prospects look bleak.

Would I change anything? Not in the slightest. I have regained my health, I believe I, like everybody else, have a destiny and you have to fulfill it to the best of your ability. I have given it my best shot, so I have no regrets. I hope I can maintain this outlook in the years to come.

If I can achieve two things from putting my experience on paper I will be content:

Firstly, I hope it helps people to understand that mental health issues are complex and require greater understanding. The old adage of "just because you can't see a physical sign, doesn't mean there is nothing seriously wrong" is very true. I would go further and talk about the medication regimes. They are uncomfortable and debilitating in themselves at times. I have witnessed many psychiatric patients, both in hospital and occasionally when I have come into contact with them on the street or in outpatients. You can see people who are struggling in their demeanour, in their face and body language, when the medication doesn't particularly suit. I suppose I see this because I remember how I felt and can relate to their situation. I acknowledge, this is not the case for every patient, but when it is, the quality of life can be very poor.

Secondly, I hope that I have given my children an understanding of why their father slipped from being a confident, fit and well founded person into somebody obviously struggling with the demands of life at various stages of their childhood, not always capable of being the father I would have liked to have been.

Some years ago a friend said to me. "Kev, some people spend large amounts of money trying to experience the kind of things that happen to you, you do it naturally." He was absolutely right of course, apart from the total devastation of my personal life, it's been one hell of a fun trip.

There are many examples of people in the public eye, generally footballers and entertainers who have had their story to hell and back splashed across the media, when in fact they may have had it a little rough, but no more or less than anybody else. I've ran the gambit of thinking what are these people complaining about? To realising I have shared hospital wards and recreational time with people who far worse off than myself and that is before you even comprehend physical disabilities and illnesses that I would never change places with.

"As a dream comes when there are many cares ....."

Postscript

My property was not re-possessed. I sold it at less than 80% of value to avoid repossession, leaving no funds available from the sale. I now rent the property back for over £100 pm more than the original mortgage. On the positive side I am now working again and can afford to pay my way.

In August 2007 I found temporary employment at a call centre based in Kirkby. My role was Customer Services Assistant for a well known retail outlet. In January 2008, as a result of the call centre being relocated to Manchester, I transferred within the same temporary organisation to work as a Postal Clerk in a major organisation in Liverpool City Centre.

I haven't enjoyed my work so much since I worked in a marketing environment. There appears to be no adverse effect on my health as a result of work commitments, my colleagues are easy going, good company, supportive without ever trying to be, it's just the way they are. So life is good.

In addition, prior to starting work at the call centre, I joined Tescos EDiet website and followed their recommendations for healthy eating. I have managed to lose 56lbs in weight; it's been over three years since my last episode and have not felt as fit and healthy for over ten years.

Every now and then in life, a person of the opposite sex comes along that you get along with and enjoy their company. If you have the same affect on them, the feeling can be quite sensational. I was lucky enough to have had such an experience and quite foolishly allowed my drunken fantasy world into the equation. The response was non judgemental and understanding in a caring way that made me realise I can no longer afford 'home alone binge drinking'. There was never any chance of there being a relationship, other than friendship, with this woman, as she was already in a long term relationship and just enjoyed the attention I was giving her. However, my depth of feeling and desire to change as a result of realising I could not continue to do this to myself or to other people, confirmed to me there is indeed a time and a purpose for everything. I now drink socially and infrequently. I have noticed the difference in my thought process. I am significantly more stable and not as unpredictable. Something I would not have appreciated if I had carried on drinking the way I had been, two or three times a week, not realising the effect it was having on the balance of my medication. I believed I was perfectly fine; I can appreciate the difference in general, but specifically because I no longer want to indulge in the destructive fantasy world I had created. I can indeed, for the first time since leaving "My Home Town", see myself when I look in "The Mirror".[3]

By July 2008 I had sourced alternatives for publishing this work and was sufficiently near final draft to show copies of the manuscript to my immediate family. I left a copy with my father who, on reading the title, asked "What does Bipolar mean?" Quite incredible really, considering I was diagnosed in 1991, but it made me smile rather than get annoyed; I just thought:' that's my dad!' He would say quietly when there was a need, "keep trying, it'll come" and I believe it has.

I also started a relationship with a local woman about this time. Whenever I met a prospective partner in the period after my marriage broke down, I would always inform them of my medical history on the first or second date. I strongly believe this was the right thing for me to do, because one day I felt sure I would meet somebody who would understand and look beyond what I was saying and see the man. On this particular occasion, I

---

[3] Reference to poems from "Biographical Paradox, Avon Books 1997"

also had the full manuscript of this publication which she read. It is such early days in our relationship that I have no idea how long it may or may not last. However, from day one I felt this woman understood me and given the lessons I have learned in life about people, feelings, emotions and how to give and receive love, I can honestly say I have never felt this way about a woman before and my life is highly enjoyable and fulfilling.

".... There is nothing better for men than to be happy and do good while they live. That everyone may eat and drink, and find satisfaction in all his toil."

"........For the living know that they will die,
But the dead know nothing;
They have no further reward........"

Ecclesiastes

I wish my children everlasting life (I don't think I'm capable) through following the two basic requirements of this neighbourhood we call earth, but for goodness sake kids, don't go to church unless you really want to: Mark:12.30-31.

Poetic Hospitalisation - 2005

A collection of poems written while receiving treatment in hospital during Episode eight and still experiencing involuntary thoughts.

Revolved[4]

It used to fall, it used to bend,

It used to feel at times on the mend.

Feeling nothing, nothing new,

No bends no breaks no filling you.

With pity, sorrow or even worse,

This time the bend is nothing worse.

Than a good night out, stretched for weeks,

Or even partying over peaks.

Something's changed, made days amend.

Altogether all around, instant you, instant me,

What do you suppose I want to be.

Not yet known, no choice involved,

But one more or less day the world revolved.

---

4   The bend is putting your mind back into shape through medication.

Over the Rails[5]

Over the rails the mind was lost,

Over the rails the train was pushed,

Over the rails never a turn,

And over the rails the train returns.

Training, working moving time,

In and out,

The crying line.

Found unyielding, found too true,

This is for me, for you, for who,

Over the rails once again,

Over the rails,

How many dead men ?

---

5   Out of your mind, how many suicides?

Stitches[6]

In the crowd, bowed down to the corpse,

Gone today, listing back to the dawn,

Safety will not avail and eyes vamp to the decibel cry,

Every crying game put to shame.

None shall say fairness entered the game,

None shall weep for just rewards.

Was just a day well told,

Never to the boiling point,

Never to explode, yet !

---

6   The day I had 32 stitches in a wound made in full view of everyone in the hospital common room. He was the corpse, a dead man. The decibel cry was my constant singing. Apart from the initial seconds of lost consciousness, I felt no ill effects or pain and sang. I never reached boiling point, my adrenalin subdued by medication.

Warmer Nature[7]

Opposing nature, creeds not bent,

Male and female money spent.

Future ruin or heaven sent,

Not quite sure of the amount of rent.

Opened up and standing true,

What on earth happened to you.

Literal style, piss taking days.

Curl up with your stink and let your mind decay.

Rotten through and apple me,

What's the due to pay to you?

Forever, earth mother bound,

Until the filth is swallowed into the ground.

So play by me I'm in the game,

But rest ye not for the fame,

Turn and twist at every corner,

My road is straight,

For you no warmer !

---

7   A disgusting view of family life I attributed to a female patient who spat in my face.

Feline Thoughts

Talking, talking, every case,

Just the words to move apace.

Covering holes in ethereal space,

Not really knowing place.

Place is found by womankind,

Found in ground and male entwined,

The price paid matches the heroine true.

For every life is born anew,

Settlement, grievement, every day,

Torn and wasted price paid high.

What's your name, what's the game,

Is this man your saving grace?

Or is the female stalking true and

Has she put her name on you?

Butch Kitchen[8]

Kitchen drama, polishing drink,

Made for Martyrs made for life,

Showing sides of feminine life.

Who's on show, who's in tails,

Never knowing the truth in days.

What's the source, memories grind,

Who pulls the cord who makes the strides.

Breaking atmosphere kitchen trails.

Singing anything it's trail tail brings.

Who is your father? What is his name?

Did he teach you this from beyond his mane?

Like him, like you, too hot to touch,

What is a Kitchen if it can't be butch?

---

8   Male patients taking it in turns to clean the communal kitchen

Females

See it in their eyes, catch it in their hue, see

it in their clothes, be by next to you.

Feel it in their hair, smell them on the wind, caught

in all their ways, spoilt with looks and chained.

Never roaming free, always following time,

Never reaching home, never needing crime.

Always on the path, always loving true,

what does every female mean to you?

Bend it back to basics,

Leave it out to dry,

One and every aspect,

Can be seen to be a cry.

What does every female mean to you?

And how do you cut the spare? I bet it's very

different, to the way I do and dare.

Garden Grove[9]

Garden Grove,

Is looking fine,

Is working hard,

Places thought and worried minds.

Outdoor space, cool and tight,

Never leaving, giving light,

And all the grove,

Who's apple sent,

Can't deny the giving rent,

So turn away and enjoy it not,

It's meant for minds and people spent,

But goodness still radiates above,

And Gods own sun delivers good.

---

9 The square enclosed brick garden in the centre of Buckingham ward allowing access to air and sky.

Another Game[10]

Calling dawn, not yesterday's base,

Thanking god's heat, not in haste,

Making room for another day,

Wander this and every way.

Building fortune, leaning proud,

Walking in and around.

Lost in every call that's made,

Yet the sloth like days presume,

Another day for me and you.

Standing sides experience the same,

Who will put an end to this game?

---

10   Abject moroseness of medicated sloth.

Initiation[11]

Heat turned high, newcomers face,

Fear of the unknown, fear of the known.

Wrapped and frapped in a concluding bibe,

Settled on stomachs, lining veils made.

This is not talked about,

This is not made.

Fear insipid, fear through and through,

Can't be helped, but not quite true.

Holding out from fears last stand,

Knowing the last throw is at hand.

Push too hard and on your back to land,

Fear of me? Or fear of you?

Tell me now, who are you?

---

11   Fearful first time patients.

Walking[12]

Walking round in circles, walking round in squares,

Walking just walking,

Wherever the paces spare you, from

feeling repressed and sodden,

In the mauling trap, and from the

creatures soften, the wailing tap.

This is not the first, or last tool in the box,

But spending time pacing, walking, leaves the time lost.

Without scars, without pain, discomfort hearty true,

But walking, walking, walking, works for me and you.

---

12   Walking and pacing around wards

One Day

Television, newspapers, games, books

And cd-rom.

Left to take the mind off,

When the switch is not on.

Blank and filling blanker, searching body

and soul, feeling actions thoughts aloud,

Rubbing nerves together.

How they rub, how they feel,

As individual as never.

We play, we read and watch the news, but

time is measured here, some joy, some grief, some

shared relief, but time still has its say.

I will be home one day.

Nourishment

Three times a day, maybe four,

Food comes our way, maybe more,

Not nutritionally balanced,

Or what, Chips twice a day,

Exact nature know not how,

But still the day is run,

By nourishment through the time,

Living on the line.

Expecting far too much,

Eating just as such,

Fullness already found,

Weigh the cost pound for pound,

Nourished not bled,

This is my dread.

Dig In[13]

Century's old, pagan life living,

In too many minds, control the man, usurp the wife,

By crawling, searching love,

Of earth and mother and family view,

that shrieks out this is wrong.

And wrong may be and wrong is said but look at my family.

Strong and resolute covered in hazy love, that stinks

and stenches pathways made and drags us all below.

What can be done, what existing aspects

frivol around the edges, and pulls and drags us

all back to the times beyond the trenches.

---

13   A view of obnoxious family life.

Sanctuary[14]

Green room, green home,

Spaced amongst the space,

Sparsely crushed into the frame,

Relaxing truth is just.

Tidy, unkempt, dirty, clean,

A sanctuary is seen.

Time away makes it all so real,

To relax and drift away,

Sleep, wake, listening joy,

Even other world, cannot break the security of my file.

And I will open sanctuary, to whoever is by my side.

---

14   Reflection on my home.

Different Days

Two minds is what they say, split between two minds.

Never, knowledge of true life made,

Ground down and bailed,

Not for giving in,

Strong and very true,

The antithesis of you.

Revelling in madness haze,

Seeing through the malaise,

Clarity of thought through sleepless nights,

Not what I thought,

No better, no worse,

Just different days.

Slept[15]

Sleep may come and does on an hourly basis,

Striving thriving from minute to minute,

Then deadbeat days are here.

Sleep fast, sleep tight, too much sleep to

heal blue, this is the way to you.

It could be wrong, it could be right,

But institution called,

So sleep well, sleep tight,

Around the clock so true.

12 hours here, 6 hours there

And be found to be,

Slept well, slept fine,

Slept in open view.

---

15   The medication regime. When the initial dose starts to work, you are in fact over medicated and sleep comes easily and often until the balance is restored.

Spent Time[16]

Time is wasted on everyone,

Time is spent,

Not just done.

Spent is how you organise time,

Many ways, mealtime mine,

Makes such sense to see me through,

Feed a stomach settled true,

And when it's finished bloated gut,

Sleep gets through until the next rush.

Stages of the day, breakfast, early start, lunch half apart, dinner days done good, supper time, the toast, the toast.

And some media make their spend, what time by the programme they pretend, and others medication bend, but my favourite in the incomplete end, no cares no fuss, just us.

---

16   The ways in which patients measure time and help it pass.

Pipers Weft[17]

Ring the waves and waft the weft,

Lazy days, spinning draft.

Draw the line, cross the debt,

Land the prize cause the weft.

This is all the piper plays, loud and soft true

and blue, punishing me and punishing you.

Gentle humour wafting wave,

Embarrassing egocentric days, wind the weft and let it go,

If no change then shrug and say, it was

not my weft that ruined the day!

Talk me true and talk me down, but it is

not right, you know, it's not right.

---

17   One of the patients liked to play mind games. The weft was his flotation of a thought, an idea, he was the piper because he was, or he thought he was, influencing people. When he was reprimanded by staff he would say "You know it's not right."

Strictly True

Strictly true, the hue on you,

Sailing past turn to view,

Fragrant days of stern approval,

Quality sight burnt into eyes,

Never touched too far away,

Never couched from this day,

Beautiful grace in other space, what does she do to me?

Stirs and quiets the long low days,

Brings and bias to each dawn day,

Not far from thoughts,

In absent time.

Stirring yielding, if only mine.

Sail on by, watch my switch,

Just a dream reality tiff,

What may be, this is not,

But on this fountain I would quaff.

Paranoia[18]

Broken minds will not mend,

As easily as broken glass,

When treated for the first time,

The paranoia built is far too deep to respond.

The only way I know to work, is the regime forced

on me, medicated, institute born, but burnt true.

Would there be a way to idealistically try, to cut

off contact sit alone and let the voices pass, emerging

like a butterfly from a gorging life that's past.

Or would it just be a death, not re-born at all,

What would be the wastage rate,

Best no waste at all.

---

18   I would jump at the chance of a controlled, non-medicated attempt to see the illness through, a fitting end.

Waves[19]

When all the dreary days fall to ground,

No life, no lift,

Ideas black fall and drown.

The cleaning cycle makes its way,

To clean the filth right away.

Some don't want to touch its mind,

Just mop and mop,

And clean and find,

Clean it here, clean away,

But the artists have their day.

No spot mopping in this chair,

Half and half if you dare,

Can't get clean another day,

But watch Tracie's waves,

Maybe today.

Spotless, pointless not to find,

Walking on the renewed half ground.

---

19   Cleaners mop the floor in different ways, Tracy made waves and smiled as she worked.

Devil's Bell[20]

Every room is tainted tonight,

Blighted by the children's evil play,

Every day is dated now,

Even adults play,

Not a dual, not a game,

A deadly play of minds,

That will grow and decay,

The players open kinds.

If I fall and if I play,

It's not because of want,

Drawn to side, the other half,

And live beneath its font.

Too little, too much,

Who can ever tell,

But I will not be drawn,

To serve under the Devil's bell.

---

20   The ringing tones of spiritual malpractice played in the minds of patients with intent. My interpretation of other patients mind activity directed at subversion and my thoughts on entering the fray.

True Waves[21]

It was never the end intend,

It was never the fail to see,

It never did the unseen,

It wasn't yet for me,

Creeping up from behind,

Lined and drawn from above,

Truth stained waves that could never be,

Now the truth for you and me,

It's started now and can't be stopped,

Momentum guiding through,

But who were you and where was I

the day the waves became true.

---

21   Sound waves or voices.

The Eye[22]

Slow down the firing line,

Cause the pool to flow,

Let the pattern disconnect,

See the plough unfold,

Break the given party field,

And make it new with gold,

And never let the seed grow cold.

All the space is crowded out and

All the land is new,

So call the afterlife from me, and grow it inside you.

Spirit blown is lost forever,

None to fade away,

And in the air the fortune cover,

Is never made to pay.

So call on down and make your stand,

And live until you die,

For all the thoughts I have tonight

can be seen within the eye.

---

22   Windows to the soul.

Unconventional Rhyme

Mind the time that bedside rule,

Is meant to be by right.

All the moves that make the day are carried out at night.

See the dawn and watch it rise,

And live refreshed and bright.

Not yielding to the sun and remembering the night.

Remember deep inside your wounds,

Remember the relief it brings,

And walk tall and proud in other days

as long as you have proved.

Recuperation, death born sleep will re-invent your time,

And in that time your life may bring

an unconventional rhyme

Community Care[23]

How are you,

How are we,

Are we not listening fine,

Head nods, eye contact,

Aren't you just sublime.

Empathetic without the em,

Since all you really do,

Is nod and say the words,

And pick the pay for you.

Even when it's made quite clear, a subject is falling down,

the measures made, the measured paved are not for this clown.

Because you do not know,

Or really understand,

The depth of what you see,

Just pass the medication mate,

And what will be will be.

---

23   Jobs worth Community Psychiatric Nurses. I've had one or two exceptional CPN's, and one or two that were not. One from the past was on duty in hospital.

Out to Play[24]

Out of the basket the little toys run,

Out of the casket the blue boys' fun,

Into the parlour, with games going on,

Play, play, play with nothing to say.

Out in the courtyard playing anon,

Out in the garden pulling the wool,

Who has seen, or heard or felt this,

What is the card, or the game or the twist.

Nothing to say to the world all alone,

No one to turn to as you grow old,

Nothing to do, to be or to whom,

Play in your room,

You have built and your ruin,

Nothing to say, nothing to say, Never be told it was today.

---

24   Unruly patients smoking dope and being a nuisance.

Printed in the United Kingdom
by Lightning Source UK Ltd.
135822UK00001B/89/P